"This book is a real gem. It's deep, yet accessible, readable and helpful. I recommend *How to Make Friends With Your Feelings* to you if you're serious about gaining true insight into your emotions and your relationships. Jay Uhler brings his considerable knowledge and keen insight together in this wonderful book."

> Gregory J.P. Godek,
> Author of *1001 Ways To Be Romantic*

"I have been fortunate to receive the friendly counsel and wisdom of Jay Uhler at first hand, and to read this book. My advice is that if you can not meet the man—then his book is the next best thing. They are of one piece with each other—and both are well worth getting to know."

> John Hutchinson,
> *Managing Director, Organizational Dynamics Inc.,*
> *United Kingdom*

"Written in everyday language and without the jargon so often associated with works of this kind, author Jay Uhler provides a sense of direction as an antidote for an almost chronic sense of helplessness among people everywhere. It's a good read."

> K.H.D. Cohen,
> *Psychiatrist*

"Few people have the wonderful capacity for caring that Jay Uhler has. Through *How to Make Friends With Your Feelings* he has shown us all how to accept ourselves and make peace with each other. Your life will be richer for having read this book."

> Jim Cathcart,
> Author of *Third Thoug   lationship Selling*

D1418182

"Jay Uhler's insights are as relevant for the office as they are for the home. He asks you to listen, and most importantly, to ponder and embrace the power of love and compassion to help facilitate change. As an executive, and as an individual, this book has been invaluable."

> Dr. Robert Gough
> *President & CEO of ODI*

"I applaud and agree with 98% of your book! I especially like the phrase 'family of Learning' which is more true than family of origin. I like your use of 'super-imposing' which gives a different angle to understand what is called transference. It's a very beneficial book."

> Rev. Earl Custer,
> *Pastor*

"Thank you very much for writing this fabulous book. I always thought Americans don't have problems like I have; however, I know now, we do and they do. I was born in Tokyo. I understand that America is made by people like me. I have learned a lot about myself and others through reading your book. I feel closer to people around here now."

> Reyka Kulihala

"It's a friendly inquiry woven around captivating stories and intellectual vitality. Useful for everyone who wants insights into the patterns of human relationships."

> D. J. Lee, M.D.

"Fortunately, it's not too late for mankind to face feelings. Jay Uhler leads the way. He expresses his feelings and helps us all to understand ours better. Read this book."

> Dr. Gloria Spitalny,
> *Psychologist*

"What makes this book a must for everyone to read is the fact that it will help in the most important journey of life—discovering oneself. The journey of life, as any other journey, needs a companion. This book will be their best companion in that journey of exploration of one's life. The value of this companionship is that it is coming from an experienced therapist who is unique himself. This is well reflected in the way he describes his own techniques of helping people to better understand themselves.

I have known Jay for more than six years. I am always highly impressed by the personable and professional approaches he brings to resolve problems and also to any topics we discuss—a rare combination that is a great contribution to his profession and the field of psychotherapy.

This book is going to be of tremendous value to those who will have it in their personal library for this is the reference they will always turn to in explaining any present situation they are facing, as well as future ones. I highly recommend this book for everyone. It will help them to share in this imperfect world with greater understanding. It will lead them to a harmonious life that has peace of mind. It will help them to coexist in a meaningful way in their own lives and the lives of others."

Camelia Anwar Sadat,
Professor of Peace Education at Harvard University and Middle East History at Bentley College, active member in the peace movement in the world, a book reviewer to the *Los Angeles Times* and *The Washington Post,* and author of *My Father and I*

"Excellent...A truly up lifting and positive read."
Jane Frosdick
Twickenham, England, UK

"I enjoyed your book. I was especially interested in the chapter on Conflict. I found some ideas that I hadn't seen anywhere else. Especially helpful was the reminder that sometimes the best thing to do is 'punt.'"

>Stephen Broydrick,
>Author of *How May I Help You? Providing Personal Service in an Impersonal World*

"I am grateful to you for putting me in touch more deeply with my own feelings and for helping me to be better able to help others interpret their feelings."

>Dwight S. Haynes,
>*Pastor*

"Jay Uhler is the pot of gold at the end of the rainbow."

>John McPherson,
>*Host, Booktalk, WSJS, Winston-Salem, NC*

"Textbook English goes 'out the window' as Jay Uhler speaks to the reader in a conversational way about getting in touch with the directors of our lives: our feelings. Unless we become understanding friends with them and learn how to control them, they will control us. Jay tells us how to befriend and direct our feelings—something that can complement our growth as spiritual beings."

>Rev. Christina Gummere Laurie
>*United Methodist Church Pastor,*
>former newspaper writer and editor

"Fresh approaches to solving today's problems. Every page is filled with new opportunities for enlightenment."

>P.S. Boleen, Ph.D.
>*Family Counselor*

How to Make Friends With Your Feelings

*Best wishes to you
as we share the journey.*

Jay Uhler

Caring is contagious!

How to Make Friends With Your Feelings

Jay Uhler

Ambassador Press International
Boston

© Copyright 1993 by J. Robert Uhler II.
All rights reserved.

Second Printing

Published by:

Ambassador Press International
P. O. Box 1661
Andover, MA, USA 01810

Printed in the United States of America

Cataloging Data:
Uhler, Jay
How to Make Friends With Your Feelings

1. Self-help
2. Psychology
3. Relationships
4. Family
5. How to

Includes Index

Library of Congress Catalog Card Number: 93-90497

International Standard Book Number: 0-9637188-8-6

*D*edication

This book is dedicated to all the people past, present, and future, who have the *courage* to look at themselves and their families of learning and "fix it."

And...

To my family of learning:

To my parents who had their problems, and kept a sense of humor about life.

To my Father who, when I was young, said, "When there is a problem, you fix it." He is my greatest cheerleader.

To my Mother who says: "This too shall pass" and who I call when I need information about cooking, getting stains out of clothes, and the proper English when I'm writing.

To my sister, Tina, who was my playmate. Doing the evening dishes was even fun. One time though, she gave me Vigero water (plant fertilizer) and said it was peach juice. Maybe that's why my hair is thick and wavy.

To my sons, Jeph and Matt, who are best friends and teachers and laugh with me and keep me young.

Jeph, when he was eight years old, sat with me to read and give me moral support as I typed the weekly "Jay's Jottings" newspaper column.

Matt, in his teens, a few seconds before I was to give a motivational speech, put his hand on my shoulder and said, "Go get 'em, Dad."

And...

To my clients who have trusted me with their growth.

Appreciation

I prefer people to paper. That is why twenty years ago, when colleagues put signs in my office at various angles with the word "write" on them, I would simply smile.

At the National Speakers Association, Jeff Davidson, author of many books, spoke at a concurrent session. He convinced me that *information in books benefits people.*

I decided I would get the book out of my head onto paper. Janice Foster asked a friend of hers, Natalie Fortin, to help and Jan's husband, Ted, a computer expert joined in. After it was printed, Natalie practically held my hand as we edited *How to Make Friends With Your Feelings.* Her husband, John, joined in with moral support.

Thanks, also, to Michele Kenna for all her help.

My Mother and Father both read it and often provided encouragement for me to get it in print. My Dad insisted that he wanted to buy one.

Raymond Krise is a master motivator and book building technician. He and Jonathan Kardell have been wonderful through the publishing process. Their suggestions, enthusiasm, and technical skill were invaluable.

Bishop F. Herbert Skeete has been very supportive of me and my ministry. He encouraged the publication of this book and set a deadline by having a book signing at the Annual Conference of the United Methodist Church. Without his efforts, *How to Make Friends With Your Feelings* might now be only a manuscript.

Many other people have edited, encouraged, cajoled, held me accountable, pressured with friendly persuasion, and supported me to be uniquely human. Clients wished me to hurry up and get it done! I thank them all.

Each of them is worthy of at least a chapter to describe their individual contributions to me as a person and to *How to Make Friends With Your Feelings.*

Lists of this kind are risky, because they always omit names of people who deserve to be included. I have taken risks throughout the book, so why stop now.

Bobby Albre
Dr. Lillian Arleque
Father Paul Baily
Dr. Harrell Beck
Bill Bethel
Sheila Murray Bethel
Catherine Carney-Feldman
Bert "Pap-Pap" Confer
Laura "Grammy" Confer
Dr. Alan Knight Chalmers
Margo Chevers
Charles Colburn
Peri Eaton
David Feldman
Tom Fulton
Ramona Garcia
Craig Halliwill
Rev. Dr. Richard Harding
Shirley Harding
Jonellen Heckler
Lou Heckler
Bruce Holloway

Dr. Homer Jernigan
Linda Marcous
David Marcus
Father Bill McLaughlin
Richard Moreno
Dr. Melvin Rosenthal
Dr. Andrew Rubman
Naomi Rhode, CSP, CPAE
Jim Rhode, CSP
Cavett Robert, CSP, CPAE
Dr. Linda Doran Stern
Robert G. Stern
Dr. Danutia Stakievitz
Dick Syatt
Joan Tuney
Rev. James G. Todd
Mary Todd
Dr. Horace Weaver
Dr. Patricia Wiklund
Professor Irene Williams
Terry Wilson
Bill Windt

Author's note on gender words

In an attempt to be gender conscious, early drafts of this book were written with s/he, her/him, himself/herself. As I edited, I found it very awkward and it disrupted the flow of my thoughts.

Since my intent is to clarify life's issues, such confusion is unacceptable. I pushed on. My research discovered that the most used and most acceptable usage is they, their, them, themselves.

I hope my selection makes your reading easy for you and that you enjoy learning *How to Make Friends With Your Feelings*.

Contents

If I were physically present with you,
I would shout, whisper, sing,
dance, or do anything I could
to encourage you to receive your
feelings as gifts.
They are your friends;
cooperate with them.
Love yourself when you experience
them.

This is one of the ways to peace.

GREETINGS TO YOU

I am writing this book to emphasize to you the **beauty of your humanness**. You, as a human being, have your own individualized, personal life experiences that make **YOU Unique**. You are **Uniquely HUMAN! Uniquely YOU!** You are **wonder-ful!**

Did the thought cross your mind, "If you knew me the way I know myself, you wouldn't think I'm so wonderful"?

My rebuttal on your behalf is, "I don't see you the way you see yourself. There is a strong possibility that I know more about the real you than you do." I hope you'll give me the chance to explain such an outrageous statement.

The perceptions you have about yourself often are not the real you, not you at the core. Most people are beautiful at their core. It is not a matter of **discovering** your beauty. It's a matter of **recovering** it. Much of what you know about yourself comes from what you have been told about yourself by others. You lost yourself in a maze of labels.

The problem is this. At an early age, when these messages *to* you *about* you made such a potent impression, you had no capacity to assess their truth.

Let me illustrate from my own experience the way we internalize what we hear. I had many ideas that I learned from my family about how a person should talk. My Mother emphasized that English, as defined by the textbooks, was the only way to speak. Slang was terrible. Swearing was worse. I had my mind filled with many good words, all quality English.

I worked in a steel mill during my graduate school summers. In the steel mills they don't talk the way I learned. The language used was "cursing and swearing," with a word of English thrown in here and there. I would walk home from work thinking about a conversation I had with any of my fellow workers. Most of the words they used, which I had been taught were unacceptable, would flow freely through my brain. I was remembering the conversation as it had occurred. I had internalized their way of speaking.

I could have blamed myself and felt guilty for thinking those words. Fortunately, I did not. I liked the men I worked with. They were nice and friendly to me. We all talked to each other with the vocabulary we had learned, and respected each other.

This example is to show how you absorb the words around you. What you hear makes an impact on you, especially when those words are addressed *to* you *about* you. Depending on whether the meaning is negative or positive, judgmental or supportive, their impact can influence you to like yourself or dislike yourself.

Someone says to you: "You are stupid." "You are rotten." "You are a troublemaker." "All you do is create problems." "Shut up." "You klutz." "Children should be seen and not heard." "No one will love you if you act like that." "Can't you do anything right?" "I hate you." As you hear these labels you begin to believe you are bad, inept, unacceptable, unlovable.

Children want to please and be loved. I have spent hours with people who turn themselves inside out trying to be loved, and with others who have given up believing it is possible. Those who haven't given up in bitterness want to be different, would like to change the way they act, and wish to improve their lives—but they don't know how. They need to be taught the skills of positive relating, and shown the loveliness of their beautiful being.

You may be told: "You are great!" "You are so smart." "I love you." "You are really handsome/beautiful." "You are so kind." "You have so much talent." "You are very thoughtful." "I love your hugs." "You are a lot of fun." You will believe you are an intelligent, capable, lovable person.

I hope it is clear that the words we hear about ourselves from other people, especially from our parents, become a significant influence on how we see ourselves and become a large part of our internal conversations about ourselves. These messages, our innate attributes and our life experiences create each of us as a unique person.

My intent is to show you how terrific YOUR uniqueness is!

In my years of contact with people as a therapist and in a variety of corporate, religious, and social settings, I have developed the conviction that there is always a reason why each of us has any specific thought or feeling. It all makes sense if we understand our past. Our past has a powerful impact on our present.

The information that each of us receives about ourselves, the montage of our personal experiences, our inherited physical attributes and talents, the emotions and sensations that are natural to each human being, when blended together, combines to make us Uniquely Human!

My Challenge to You

I challenge you to peek through the layers of labels and the walls that surround you, to discover what is underneath. I want to give you new lenses with which to see yourself. I want to provide different glasses to see others. I want to show you creative options that will help you to connect with, act toward, and treat yourself and other people more kindly.

You may be looking for supporting evidence from research for the views I'm presenting. Look elsewhere. This is **not** a textbook. It **is** a book about **living**. A friend told her parents,

"It is a book about the basic truths of life, put in a folksy way."

Occasionally a client attempts to entice me to use technical psychological terms or to present formal theories, and we joke about it when I concede. I prefer to use everyday language and to focus on each client—on his or her needs. General theories or research results often miss the subtleties of a particular person's uniqueness.

I encourage you to look inside to see if the ideas I'm presenting about human nature apply to you. If a particular thought isn't relevant to your life, then it is not relevant. Do not try to force round you into a square hole. If it seems to fit, try it on. If you know that it is true about you, great. Use the insight to improve your life.

Various Ways to read this book

I have written this book so that the whole book is an integrated, systematic overview of the inner life of any one person. Each chapter is self-contained, standing on its own, yet connected to each of the other chapters, just as a particular part of a person's life can be separated for clarity of examination, yet is an integral part of the person's total being.

"Fear" may be the first or the fifth or the seventh chapter that you read. Just like every other chapter, it is a separate entity, yet gathers greater meaning from the other chapters and from being a part of the whole. Each chapter intertwines with the others, just as the heart, mind, and body intertwine. That is the way life is—an ebb and flow of feelings and thoughts and actions.

This is not a book to read and give away. I encourage you to reread these chapters again and again as they apply to each new experience. I worked hard on the index to help you quickly find what you need in each chapter. My hunch is that if you read a chapter two months after your first reading, it will have a different meaning as it applies to your life at that moment. Just as the incidents that provoke your anger change, so will the meaning that you draw from the chapter on "Anger" be refreshingly different as it applies to each new situation. As new people cross the path of your life, the chapter on "Affection" or the one on "Fear" can give you delightful insight about yourself and your actions, or sometimes knowledge that helps you protect yourself from others. Segments of the chapter, "Sexuality," can be reread as affirmations or to add creativity to your sexual sharing.

Some of you may read through the book very quickly and find pleasure and relief from what you learn. Others of you may struggle from paragraph to paragraph. Whatever your need, I hope it will be met.

Do not blame

There are four truths for us to acknowledge before we move on. These have become clear to me as a psychologist hearing people's life events.

1. The first truth is: Most parents are not to blame for their mistakes as parents. Most parents try to do their best. Some parents are just vicious, but most parents are attempting to be the best parents of which they are capable.

They do their best to cope with: a) the inadequate parenting education they received from their parents, b) their own personal deficiencies, c) the idiosyncrasies of the child they have received, d) the stresses of living in an imperfect world, and e) the changing social circumstances. This is an overwhelming task. Even if their parents had taught them everything they needed to know about life and raising children perfectly, the culture of the next generation is different, and their "perfection" is out-dated.

For all these reasons, being a parent is difficult and a most blamed endeavor. Psychologists blame them, teachers blame them, friends blame them, their own kids blame them and they blame themselves. Oy-vey!

Blaming parents benefits nobody.
Blaming ourselves as parents is pointless.

2. The second truth is: Children are not born bad. They are born unsocialized. They are found offensive because they do not act the way adults want them to act. They need to be taught by kind, caring adults what is expected of them in a "civilized" world.

One of the problems that infants have is that they only know how to "squawk," not how to talk. If they have problem-free parents (which no one does), they are indeed unbelievably fortunate. Because parents are human, having learned from their own imperfect parents, they are ill-prepared to educate "squawkers" in ways that give the child a good image of themselves.

There is no point in blaming children.

3. The third truth: No matter how strange, bizarre, outrageous, or unreasonable your thoughts or feelings appear, they all make total sense and are completely natural for you when you see them in the context of your previous experiences. Thoughts and feelings are not a moral or an ethical issue. Actions are. Thoughts and feelings are not. Any thought or any feeling that you have is a part of you. It is present now because of your previous experiences or because of the experience you are having right now. Your unique experiences, which lead to your thoughts and feelings, all contribute to your being **Uniquely Human—Uniquely You.**

It makes absolutely no sense and is totally unfair for you to harshly judge yourself about your thoughts or feelings. They are all naturally a part of you.

4. The fourth truth is: By accepting your thoughts and feelings in a kind-to-yourself manner, you can evaluate them, get information from them and then decide what you want to do with them. If you block your feelings and thoughts from your awareness, either because you have been previously punished for expressing them or for fear of guilt (self-punishment) associated with them, the feelings and thoughts

are still there. They haven't gone anywhere. You just don't want to know they are there; therefore, they are out of your control, and are controlling you.

By allowing yourself to experience your feelings and thoughts, you can consciously, purposefully decide what to do with them; therefore, you can control your actions.

It makes great sense to accept your feelings and thoughts, gently evaluate them, decide what to do with them and take control of your life.

I would like to encourage you. Do not blame your parents. Do NOT blame YOURSELF. When you get into blaming someone you go back and forth in your own mind, pointlessly trying to decide who is to blame.

If you have been blamed as a child, you become self-blaming and full of guilt. That is so painful that you learn a way to protect yourself from the pain of self-blame, which is to blame someone else.

The result is that this pattern seldom protects you from pain. When you blame somebody else, it creates hostility and upset between you and your family, friends, or in work relationships. The blaming leads to causing yourself to be attacked, which hurts, or to being rejected, with the resulting pain of isolation.

It takes a lot of energy to go back and forth in your mind, trying to decide who is to blame, and it can drive you "crazy." If you can reduce or eliminate your need to blame, you conserve your energy.

When you are not in a blaming mode, you can look at yourself much more realistically. This allows you to make changes in yourself that you would value, and allows you to value those things in yourself that you do not want to change. If you don't blame others, it provides you with the possibility of resolving misunderstandings.

If you eliminate blame from your thinking, there can be much contentment with yourself and others, much peace.

So, my precious reader, go easy on yourself, whether you are a parent, an adult, or a child. This book is not to judge you or to give you new information with which to accuse or abuse yourself. This book is to assist you to make peace with all that is within you. My interest is not to make you "perfect," but to encourage you to accept that you are **perfectly human**.

A Kindness Pact

I would like to invite you to make a pact with me. I will be as open and honest about myself and the stuff of life as I possibly can be throughout this book. I would ask you to be open and honest about yourself as you read it. In order to do this you must be kind to yourself.

In the process of revealing my humanness, I will be mentioning my life experiences. The stories that show me in a positive light you can use as a model for yourself, and those which are negative can show you what to avoid.

Graduate school emphasized to me the importance of being an understanding listener.

I also learned that you build trust by sharing yourself. I have experienced other people trusting me as I trusted them with my own vulnerability. I hope you will respond to my openness by taking the risk of being vulnerable yourself—by looking at yourself with painful honesty.

I know I am leaving myself open to misunderstanding and criticism. If you benefit by my risk-taking, it is worth it. **YOU are worth it.**

When clients works with me as their therapist, they often have various perceptions of me. One client may think I surely am hung up on anger. Another thinks I must have a lot of pain. Another thinks the foremost thought on my mind is sex. Another perceives that my life must be filled with feelings of fear or helplessness. Because I keep coming back to a subject constantly, the client believes I must be consumed by it.

Then the person becomes aware that it's the issue they want to avoid that is my focus. They find it is their issue which they need to resolve and find comfort with!

When I use illustrations about myself, I would encourage you **not** to focus on **me**, but to **focus on yourself** and learn about yourself through me. Look at yourself clearly and realistically, accepting the thoughts and feelings within you. Understanding yourself is the payoff. The resulting power of inner strength and peace is the ultimate pay-off.

When you focus on a particular feeling, it may appear as though you are consumed by it. To focus on a particular feeling gives it a disproportionate perspective. One of my supervisors and mentors, Father Paul Bailey, C.S.W., used to say, "When you focus on your anger in therapy, it seems as though you are ninety-five percent anger and five percent of whatever else is you. The reality is, the anger is only five percent; it just seems like ninety-five percent." Whatever feeling or issue you explore as you read these chapters, remember, "It is only five percent of you."

It may also be useful for you to know that, as you read, your mind may wander. Do not immediately jump to the conclusion that the reason is my authorial ineptitude. If that is true, I apologize. Let me suggest two other possibilities.

One is that the material has triggered your memories of a previous experience relevant to the information that you are reading, and you are relating the two. Terrific! Then we are synchronized.

Another reason your thoughts may wander is that your mind is escaping from the ideas or situations about which you are reading because they are stirring up feelings that are uncomfortable for you. If you experience a numbness, especially in your head, there is a high probability that the underlying feelings are frightening to you and you are blocking them with numbness. When this occurs, it will be worth the time and effort to discover what those feelings are and why they are not acceptable to you.

My wish is that you enjoy the adventure of self-disclosure and hug yourself or get hugs from others often as you pursue self-**revel**-ation with me.

Nothing I write is intended to judge you. It is all intended to state the reality as I see it. It is a positive and affirming reality about you.

I ask you to give me the benefit of the doubt that I care about you, dear reader, as a person. Please trust me that these words come from a desire for you to have the best life possible.

I ask you to give yourself the benefit of the doubt that you are beautiful at your core. What you dislike about yourself either comes from what you have been taught, or has been learned as a defense against being hurt.

Sound believable? I hope so, because it is yourself in whom I want you to believe. It is your inner beauty and self-worth that I want you to see. I want to help you believe that your unique humanness is beautiful!

I hope you will be rewarded by a better life for yourself and your family. I know it is not easy to look at either yourself or your parents in an objectively critical way. In fact, it takes a great deal of courage, because challenging family patterns has often been forbidden.

As one who has walked that painful, frightening, risky road of self-revelation and family evaluation, I can fully understand your struggles and joy as you apply the guidelines of this book to your life.

My hope is that this journal of my inner journey, my insight gleaned from my deep involvement in other people's lives, my search for the universal truth, and my conclusions about reality may be a guide for you.

My ultimate hope for you is that these words inspire you to love yourself, to give yourself affection often, and praise yourself for the person you are. Your Unique Humanness is beautiful!

May this belief support a commitment to be more kind and caring with other people, especially members of the family you create. Your family is the foundation for the world family.

People sometimes refer to me as a "shrink." I laugh, unoffended, but respond, "No, I am an **exp-a-a-a-nder!**"

I am so expansive that I believe these ideas, applied to everyday life, can make the world and the universe a better place in which to **thrive.**

*To be "perfect" is to act as someone
else has defined you.*

*To be perfectly human is to be
exactly who you are.*

WIN THE WAR WITHIN

The battleground is our own mind. It is fertile soil for feuding. We joust with the differences between what we hear and what we experience, between what we are taught and what we feel. How bludgeoned our brain becomes from the constant violent confrontations depends on the rigidity of our teachers and how much we have absorbed the criticisms imposed on us.

Many people win the social, scholastic, marital, and vocational battle, but lose the "War" of life because of their internal conflicts—sometimes referred to as stress. Whatever its name, it is the opposite of peace, happiness, and tranquillity. Most people who read this book have, to a large extent, been taught to master the forces of the outside world and want to fight the battle on that front.

Few people have been taught, therefore often do not know, what to do with the forces within—such as feelings, uncomfortable thoughts, pressures from within to act out in self-destructive or antisocial ways.

I want to explain the battles, reduce the conflicts, and show you how to live successfully, and I hope comfortably, with your insides. This makes for better quality of life and greater ease in living with what's outside.

My intent is to help you develop a realistic self-awareness, build an armor against the pricks of external criticism, enjoy the marvelously unique person you are, and calm the inner struggle.

It is helpful to simply think of feelings as energy. Each feeling—affection, pleasure, pain, anger, fear, or helplessness—exists within us as a form of energy. That energy is a positive, constantly moving/shifting force within us. Our only choice is whether to let that energy flow, or to block that flow. What we choose to do with our emotions is strongly influenced by what we have been taught about them.

What we have been taught about emotional energy influences most of our actions, and influences how we perceive ourselves. These influences affect our emotional well-being, our physical well-being, our vocational well-being, and our social well-being.

If you get the impression that I think it is important to understand your feelings, you are correct!

Many of your internal battles are with your emotional energy, with your feelings. If you are *unaware* of the messages you received about feelings from past teachers, then you are struggling with an invisible foe. If you have blocked yourself from being aware of your feelings, you may even miss the battle. In either case, you lose the war.

The internal war is only won by peaceful co-existence between who we are and what we have been taught to be. Let us together look at the battles which make up the war within, and the strategies for creating peace.

A major battle is the struggle between being "perfect" and being *perfectly human.* Some people get caught up in the idea that they need to be perfect. What does that mean? Who decides what is perfection ?

To be "perfect" means to live as someone else has defined us.

To be *perfectly human* is to be exactly who we are, which is a composite of our past and present experiences, our thoughts and feelings and our own individual self which we brought into this world when we were born. To be *perfectly human* often means to embrace feelings and thoughts that are very different from those we have been taught are acceptable.

We are taught exaggerated expectations about ourselves, both negative and positive. Some people are taught to have exceptional integrity and others are taught to be exceptional liars or thieves. Imposed teachings from others are often in conflict with our personal wishes and abilities as human beings.

We also get taught about feelings. We are taught that some are positive and others are negative, that some feelings are acceptable and others are not. We are told that some feelings are appropriate at one moment and not at another. We may be punished for expressing our feelings.

I want to state emphatically that to be human is to have feelings. Every feeling is acceptable at every moment. We may be unaware of them because we have blocked them from our awareness by defense mechanisms or drugs, but that does not mean they are not present. When we treat every emotion as totally acceptable, we can choose how to manage it. We are in control of it.

I use six words to categorize feelings: pleasure, pain, anger, affection, fear, and helplessness. There are many other words that describe our feelings, but they are subfeelings under these six.

So why is there such confusion about feelings? The confusion stems from what we have been taught, primarily in our family, but also in school, at work, and in social settings.

We get taught that some feelings are "good" and others are not.

In some families sexual sensations are "good" and in others they're "not so hot."

Our friends get different messages in their families from those we are taught.

All this leaves us with a horribly confusing plot!

We are often on our own to solve the mystery. Thus there is a constant struggle within us between "right" and "wrong," between what we have been taught and what we experience.

Feelings are not an ethical issue. Feelings are a part of being human. Everybody has feelings. There are two kinds of people: those who have feelings and know it, and those who have feelings and don't know it.

What are some of the teachings that lead to conflicts about being "perfect" and *perfectly human?*

You may have been taught that you should not express your feelings. When, as a child, you express anger (as all children do), and repeatedly get hurt by physical punishment or rejection, you quickly learn that anger is not acceptable.

You may have been told that you should not cry. One of the fear-filled phrases often used is "break down" and cry!

I want to help you understand that **crying is *not* breaking down. Crying is letting go.** Crying is a natural way of washing pain or tension out of yourself. Crying is a way your body frees itself from the stress of blocked energy. Crying is a harmless means of self-expression. Crying is a wonderfully relaxing way of releasing pain.

You may get taught to limit your excitement and enthusiasm or laughter. "Calm down," "Cool it," or "Don't laugh so loudly" are common stifling phrases.

When **joy** is "bustin' out all over" in you or in someone else, it can be one of life's greatest pleasures. To laugh freely from deep inside yourself can be a totally relaxing form of fun.

Feelings are a part of you, a part of being human. Often people try to eliminate feelings. All this does is create a "war" within yourself which is enormously painful.

Let us together attempt to reduce the war of internal conflicts.

Let me emphasize the difference between feelings and thoughts and actions. Often when I ask someone, "What are you feeling?" they tell me a thought or an action, or a thought about an action. Thoughts are ideas, concepts, attitudes. Actions are behavior or activities. Feelings are energy.

I believe the core feelings are **PLEASURE, PAIN, ANGER, AFFECTION, FEAR, HELPLESSNESS.**

There are also combinations of these feelings. For instance, I think of frustration as a combination of anger and helplessness. Guilt is directing your anger toward yourself, the core feeling being anger. Sadness is a form of pain.

It is very important to distinguish feelings from thoughts. Feelings are a form of energy. Thoughts are ideas or concepts about what we believe or perceive. We can use our thoughts to control our emotions. We can use our thoughts to change our upsetting emotions to pleasurable ones.

We all have thoughts about our feelings. No big deal, if the thoughts are positive. When we have feelings about our thoughts, that can be a very big deal, negatively or positively. Feelings give vitality to thoughts. They give agony or enthusiasm, pain or pleasure.

I also perceive a difference between body sensations and feelings. Sensations can help us to know what we are feeling.

For instance, when I am doing therapy with a person whose emotions are so blocked that they don't have any idea what they are feeling, are experiencing no feelings, or have gone numb, I ask them to describe their body sensations.

The type of sensation, and its location within the body, can be a clue to their feelings.

Anger is often stored in the lower back, or it can cause migraine headaches.

Often fear is in the stomach area and can be connected somatically to ulcers, tight muscles, digestive disorders.

Pain related to the loss or death of a loved one, or rejection, is often experienced physically in the heart or chest—a "broken heart." Pain can also be anger, as alluded to by the phrase, "S/he's a pain in the neck."

Affection is experienced as warmth, and may be combined with a tingling sensation flowing through the body. Affection may be mixed with fear and cause "butterflies" in the stomach. That combination can be exciting! (Often people confuse the tingling sensation that occurs when energy flows though the body with the tingling that accompanies numbness. The difference is subtle, but significant.)

Helplessness is not easy to define as a sensation, but is an overall sense of immobility, often combined with a despairing heaviness.

Pleasure can be experienced physically in opposite ways. It can be muscle relaxation, or a surge of excited body activity.

The reason I'm making every attempt to help you know what you are feeling at any given moment is because many of our actions, and much of what happens in our relationships, are dramatically influenced by our feelings. To be unaware of the feelings means they control us. To know our feelings gives us choices, therefore, control.

Sometimes when I explain to a person how the patterns in their family of origin influence their present life, they (especially men) respond, "That happened a long time ago. That doesn't affect me now."

The truth is that much from our past affects us now and we choose not to believe it, because we want to believe that we are in control of our lives. However, we are only in control of our lives to the extent that we are able to be aware of and deal with our emotions.

There are people who, when I show them family influences that have affected their feelings, will say, "What you are telling me makes sense, but the feelings can't be influencing me now, because I don't even know what they are." This is especially true when I am attempting to help a man understand the anxiety that is affecting his life in many ways.

Picture a very intelligent, highly successful, self-contained man, prominent in his vocation, listening to me tell him about his anxiety. I say, "You don't know what you've got, and won't be able to know what it is until you have less of it." Telling him that is like attempting to sell a refrigerator to an Eskimo .

Fortunately he usually trusts me, and later in the therapy will say, "You know, I didn't have the least idea what you were talking about when you mentioned anxiety, but now I understand, because I can experience the difference."

Feelings can be like that. They can hide from our awareness when we don't know what to look for or are afraid to recognize them.

Anxiety is especially "sleazy." When we do recognize it, it wants us to believe we can't accomplish anything if we aren't driven by it.

Very young children know what feelings are. They can't label them, because they can't talk yet, but they know. Their primary connections with others are feelings, energy, vibes.

You have probably seen a child who is afraid to go near a certain adult. Even though the person is speaking kind words, the child will hold back. Or you may have seen a child go comfortably to somebody who looks gruff. The child senses the anger or hostility that lays beneath the kind words, or detects the kindness under the gruff appearance. The child `believes the vibes.

Two problems adults have are: One, they don't trust their own reading of someone else's vibes, and two, they don't think someone else can read their emotional vibrations.

The truth is that there are messages being sent on several levels. First is the emotional. Second is the physical. Third is the verbal.

My chorus director, Dr. James R. Houghton, an internationally known baritone, frequently reminded us, "Music is the universal language. You can sing in English to a non-English speaking audience in Germany, and they will get the meaning of the music."

"Prof. Houghton," as we affectionately referred to him was a perceptive man.

Since then I have learned that **emotions are the *universal* language**. Music is an excellent vehicle for conveying emotion. When a person or group sings with feeling, others can grasp the message, because they receive the emotion.

I have heard people sing in English and have slept through it because there was no emotional expression in the music, or because the emotions were blocked by the musicians. I have slept through talks given in English because the speaker did not connect emotionally with the audience.

It is also obvious that a person can speak a phrase but impart many different meanings to it depending on which emotion accompanies the words.

I can't emphasize enough the importance of understanding our feelings, because they so profoundly affect the messages we send in our family, business and social settings.

If you do not experience your feelings, then you have learned that your feelings are unacceptable, and you have blocked them from your awareness, or numbed them out.

Because you are not aware of your feelings does not mean that others are not aware of your feelings. Other people, if they are sensitive and have not stifled their own feelings, can detect your emotions from the vibrations you emit.

Again, feelings are not an ethical issue. They just **ARE**.

Actions can be an ethical issue. We can act in a particular way that is either positive or negative, kind or hurtful.

Actions are not the same as feelings. Feelings can motivate actions. We can judge actions, but judging feelings only leads to problems.

I encourage you to give yourself permission to experience every feeling that occurs in you.

What happens when you don't? Feelings are like gas. The more you try to repress or stifle them, the more pressure they develop until they burst through the constricting container.

A water bucket illustrates the point. If a bucket is half empty, you can pour water into it. If you have a bucket full of water and you add more water, it overflows. If it can't overflow, the intensifying pressure will damage the bucket.

The same is true of our bodies when it comes to emotions. If our body is full of a feeling, and more of that same feeling is added, it must go someplace. The energy will usually overflow, releasing the emotion in words or actions, often in destructive ways. If we hold it in, the feeling will build up inside and cause some destructive form of physical symptom, such as pain or sickness.

I hope I've made it clear that you do have feelings, because to be human is to have feelings. I want to go further in the following chapters, to show how to express your feelings constructively in ways that will benefit you and will not harm anyone else.

Knowing your feelings and having the skills of positive self-expression lead to self-control. Many people think that, if they never express their feelings, they have more control. The opposite is true.

To be aware of your feelings gives you control. You can choose options for dealing with those feelings. Choosing when to express them gives you control of your life. Selectively releasing your feelings when **you** choose is a way of keeping your bucket of emotions half empty. That helps your body, as well as your relationships.

You may even choose to express your feelings in ways others consider negative. Sometimes in our culture that is a choice which needs to be made.

You may choose not to express a feeling now, but to release it later in a more appropriate setting.

When my Grandmother died, I sang her favorite song (and the song she most liked to hear me sing), "How Great Thou Art," at her funeral. I knew I could sing without crying because I knew I could express the sadness of losing one of my best friends before and after I sang.

It was not simply a matter of blocking out all my feelings. To do my best and to honor my Grandmother meant to release the feelings that fit the words of the song she cherished. To sing at her funeral meant to express the emotions of that powerful, gentle, adorational song and at the same time temporarily block the emotions of grief for my Grandmother's death.

I could choose to be selective about which emotions to express while I was singing because I emptied some of the pain of losing my Grandmother by sobbing in quiet times beside her casket before the funeral.

Another example of choosing not to express my feelings at the moment is illustrated by a tennis match. A first-time partner, not playing as well as I, criticized me every time I missed a shot. I could feel my anger increasing and yet knew he and the other people present would not handle my feelings very well. I didn't express them to my partner, but did release the anger later when I was alone.

You may get the impression from much of what I say that I think you should "let it all hang out." I hope the above two examples of restraining my feelings offset this possible misconception.

Much of the information in the following chapters will explain how each feeling is most constructively expressed. The main point of this chapter is to let you know the value of being aware clearly and distinctly of the presence of each of your emotions. To experience your emotions when they occur is not only not bad, it is eminently wise.

Another battle that can rage within us is the attack of internalized criticism, which is also based on what we were taught. This may be referred to as GUILT.

Guilt is based on a belief that we are bad, and lends itself to the habit of being angry at ourselves, often, of "putting ourselves down." We focus on things we have or haven't done that we believe justify our self-blame and shame. This burden comes from frequent negative criticism that has previously been directed at us. It makes an overwhelming impression on us early in our lives.

One of the messages that can lead to guilt is: "You are responsible for other people's feelings."

An example of this going to the extreme is the idea that, if one of your parents is in a bad mood, it is your fault.

You may have been blamed for another's physical pain. Have you ever heard, or been blamed for, "letting your sister or brother get hurt"?

Some parents "make" children responsible for the feelings the parent has. Have you been told, "Stop doing that, you are upsetting me," or, "You're making me mad"?

We get the message in all these statements that we are responsible for other people's moods.

I want to declare to you emphatically: **You are not responsible for any other person's feelings.**

I once gave an illustration during a talk about a boy and his dog. During the discussion that followed there were five different interpretations and emotional responses to that one story. Each person brought his or her individual experience to the story. Their interpretations and emotional reactions were a result of their own personal history. Each person's feelings were his or her own, not feelings that I put in them.

Each person's feelings are their own, not feelings that you make them have. You can't be responsible for all the past experiences, emotions, and learned responses that other people accumulate throughout their lives. If you are kind or helpful to another, all you can be responsible for is your own intentions.

(Let me quickly add: If you are attempting to provoke somebody or are acting in a hurtful or hostile manner, you *are* responsible for your actions that precipitate the feelings the other person has.)

The point is this: **A person's feelings are their own, not feelings that you caused him/her to have—nor are you responsible for.**

A person can have guilt that has nothing to do with him/her. Sometimes I tell a super-responsible client, "If you saw a man walk under a tree and get hit on the head by bird droppings from a fowl above, you would feel guilty because you hadn't warned the man that there could be birds in the tree."

The client laughs at the lunacy of their guilt education.

One of the things I would like to do in this book is to challenge what you now believe about yourself. Often, a few sessions after clients begins therapy with me, they say, "I am really confused."

I say, "FANTASTIC! What I'm trying to get across to you is getting through. You're confused because you don't know whether to believe what you learned previously, or to believe what I'm telling you about you. HURRAY!"

If you are confused while you are reading, don't be concerned. Your confusion is MARVELOUS, because it means there is a struggle inside between the affirming information I am giving you and the negative information you have received in the past. My hope is that, as you read this book, you will at times be confused. That is TERRIFIC!

I have clients who get upset with themselves because they did not learn things they needed to know at a younger age. Some people blame themselves because they didn't do something earlier.

I tell them, "You have a choice to put yourself down because you didn't learn sooner, or you can praise yourself because you now have the courage to face issues and the opportunity to learn what you need to know."

To young clients I say, "Be glad you're acquiring information and resolving these issues at a younger age than I did. Be thankful you are so quick."

I hope you will stay with me. I want to show you some things I have learned the hard way. Some of these things I have learned by virtue of my bungling, my suffering, my joy, inquisitiveness, enthusiasm and some by the wisdom of my friends and mentors.

I have a client who, as her therapy was ending, said, "It is really exciting. People have been telling me lately how beautiful I am. One friend said,'I knew you were beautiful, but now you are BEAUTIFUL!'" She had made peace with herself, had let the beauty at her core show through, and had become **radiant!**

The more you are open and let your inner self show through, the more you will get messages about how beautiful you are—beautiful from the inside out.

Let me encourage you to appreciate the person you are. There are always reasonable explanations, based on your past or your present, why you think or feel as you do. Negative messages about you have led to many internal battles. The more you value yourself, rejoice in yourself, like yourself, then the more you can give up the layers of protection you have developed around yourself.

This does not mean there will be no struggles within, no difficulties with decisions or relationships, or no difficulties at work. There will always be pressures from the outside which lead to internal upset, but you have far more energy to deal with the stress from the outside when you are not also fighting with yourself on the inside.

It is much easier to win the battles around us if we have won the internal conflicts. The War Within is won by peaceful coexistence between who we are and what we have been taught to be.

My plea is this:
   Stop fighting against yourself.
   Begin making love to yourself.
   End the inner war and live in peace.
   Enjoy the fact that you are Uniquely Human!

YOU are *SO* BEAUTIFUL!

To be taught of your beauty,
  To be valued for the unique person
    you are,
  To be encouraged to be all that
    you can be.

That is the major role of the
  family.

The Hurtful, Frightening Family

In The Hurtful, Frightening Family, just as in The Helpful, Fun Family, the parents set the tone. Members of a Hurtful, Frightening Family see and live with much pain and fear, developing patterns that, if uninterrupted, continue to plague them all their lives.

I want to make one point as clear as possible. In my years and years and years of experience as a therapist, I have come to the conclusion that most parents do not intend in any way to harm their children, or their mates. Husbands and wives would prefer to have a safe relationship. They do not want the hurt and pain they create between themselves. It exists because in the family in which they grew up they learned what seem like self-protective patterns of relating to others. Instead of bringing the security and happiness they seek, these ways of relating cause painful, frightening distance in the family they create.

I will be referring often to a phrase which I believe I have originated: *family of learning*. By this I mean the family in which you were taught attitudes about yourself and about life. You learned what and how to think, whether or not to feel, how to act and how not to act. You learned how friendships operate, what goes on in marriages and families. You developed behavior patterns, coping mechanisms, and beliefs about others. Much of what you know about yourself and about life comes from your family of learning.

Your family of learning can be a bedrock foundation of security. It can be a springboard to success. Or it can be a quagmire that constantly drains you of energy and sucks you into depression. It can be a source of internal and external conflict. Whatever impact it has on your present life, it is *your* family of learning, and it has made a powerful impression on you.

I hope you will contrast the description of The Hurtful, Frightening Family with the chapter on The Helpful, Fun Family. The difference is crucial for us as individuals and for our society.

As a therapist doing consultation, I have gone into a hospital or clinic and been presented with a family whom I had never before seen. Without discussing anything that was occurring in their present situation, but only asking questions about their original families of learning, I could tell them the problems they were having in their present family. They were surprised at the accuracy of the assessment. Some of the family members would occasionally cry with relief, realizing that their difficulties were not just of their own making, that the cause had been beyond their control, and that someone understood their predicament. They could see that there is a reasonable explanation other than that they are bad people. They experience hope of reducing their pain and of learning new skills to improve their life.

A similarly high degree of predictability has occurred with couples who are planning to get married. When I do the premarital evaluation, I have found that, by getting the information about the families of the bride-and-groom-to-be, I can tell them the types of problems they can anticipate in their marriage.

Often they begin to laugh because they have already begun to have difficulties in those areas. Unfortunately, if the problems go unresolved, they will continue to intensify the negative and destructive patterns they have begun experiencing. By knowing what the problems are and resolving them before they are under the pressure of married life, the couples have a jump start on their life together.

This book grew from my desire to assist you to gain the knowledge and skills necessary for you to reduce the pain and fear in your life, and to increase the pleasure and joy. I am offering these illustrations to emphasize that much of what we learn about ourselves, many of our actions, and much of what we do with our feelings comes from what we learned in our family of learning. If we are doing what we learned, how can we blame ourselves when we act like terrible parents or terrible mates? The word "terrible" in this context means: we cause pain for ourselves and for the persons around us.

It seems very unfair to blame yourself for being smart enough to learn well what you have been taught.

There is another complicating factor that gives us reason to stop blaming ourselves. When you create a family, you are bringing together in a marriage two people who come from families with different values, different ways of viewing feelings, and different attitudes about life.

It doesn't only happen with people from different cultures. Both people may be from a German family, or both Italians, or both Jewish, yet what they learned in their respective families with the same national origin can be very different. The mere fact of coming from different families of learning, even within the same culture, can create stress on a new family or upon couples getting together. It takes exceptional relationship skills to resolve differences so each person in the conflict is satisfied with the solution.

Blaming is not helpful. However, it is enormously useful in understanding yourself to look seriously, with a critical eye, both at the negatives and the positives you received from your parents.

I encourage you to read this chapter not in a harsh or blameful way, but with a positive approach, to learn more about yourself so you can improve your friendship with yourself and others.

Having said this, let me also say that the parents in the Hurtful, Frightening Family do not like themselves, because they were criticized and abused by their parents. They have experienced rejection and rebuke in the families they came from—a lot of put-downs, a lot of negative criticisms, even abuse, which have been internalized. Parents who abuse or stifle their children physically or emotionally usually convince the child that they deserve the abuse because they are "bad."

If a parent is upset before his or her child walks through the house singing, and the child is punished for making too much "noise," few children are sophisticated enough to realize that their parent was just looking for an excuse to release tension. The child instead believes they must be a bad child, or they wouldn't get punished.

It is tragic when a mother or father treats a child badly, or tells a child they are bad, when the child is innocent of any wrongdoing, but has become the butt of the parents stored-up anger, pain, fear, or tension.

Parents at times expect children to know things the child has no way of knowing.

One time my sons and I were at a camping and trailer show. My son, Jeph, who was five at the time, walked between two people who were standing a distance apart from each other to pick up a brochure about a trailer. I was embarrassed that he had walked between the two people, and reprimanded him for it.

Fortunately, he spoke up to me, "But we've been picking up pamphlets all day. You never told me I shouldn't pick them up." I then realized that with the two people that far apart, it did not occur to Jeph—because of his size—that he was being impolite to step between them to get the brochure.

I was glad Jeph felt safe with me to give a rebuttal on his behalf. Many children are supposed to simply accept rebukes like this quietly, and internalize their feelings. His comment gave me the opportunity to realize that he was absolutely right. I could not expect him to know the intricacies of social settings from an adult perspective.

When children come home from school, mention a new word they learned from one of the other kids, and get their mouth washed out with soap, they do not reason, "My parent overreacted." They think, "I must have done something terrible! I must be bad."

When parents who have been verbally or physically abused try to create their own family, they bring to the new family a dislike of themselves, believing themselves to be unworthy, unproductive, "bad" persons. They then create a negative tone in their new family.

People who dislike themselves and have experienced a lot of negativity in their families as they grew up communicate very indirectly. For instance, they may see a question as a threat. When you ask this person, "What time did you come in last night?" they become afraid that a direct answer will result in some form of punishment, and therefore dodge the question or answer it indirectly.

The fear stems from years of criticism or punishment in his or her previous family. However, the fear is perceived to exist in the present situation. Therefore, a question becomes a threat, and the best means of protection is to give an indirect answer, or change the subject altogether.

This kind of person also asks questions in a vague way. If you have been hurt and are afraid of a direct question, you may believe the other person will be uncomfortable with a direct question. You therefore don't ask questions directly.

This attitude of indirectness as a form of protection creates suspicion and distrust. Indirect questions are frightening because you don't know what you are being asked. Consequently, a lot of fear is being generated.

Conflicts in such families never get resolved, because nothing is clear.

When beginning therapy with a couple, I always ask, "How did your parents resolve their conflicts?"

The response sometimes is, "They never did. They always fought. They were always screaming and hollering at each other." It is obvious that a person who answers this way did not learn how to resolve conflicts in any productive way in their family of learning.

On the other hand, a lot of people to whom I ask the question, "How did your parents resolve conflicts?" respond by saying, "We had a perfect family. There was never any conflict in our family."

My belief is that they did not learn how to resolve conflicts either, because they couldn't observe how conflicts are positively resolved.

Either the parents in this family were avoiding conflicts, which can be a frightening situation for children, or else one parent was giving in to the other, which is also frightening, because one parent is perceived as the powerful parent, and the other is perceived as the weak, helpless person.

In some families there are verbally or physically violent confrontations. In other families, both parents avoid conflicts. In another type of family, one parent gives in to the other. Any of these families of learning instill fear in the children.

It is also possible the parents were resolving their conflicts or differences away from the children. This is a disadvantage for the children, who need to learn how to resolve conflicts constructively. Unless the children learned how to do so somewhere else, they haven't learned to resolve conflicts constructively, since they didn't learn it from their parents.

When you try to build a relationship with another person it will be a difficult task, because there are always differences between any two or more people, which lead to conflict. You cannot avoid conflicts and be happy. It is essential that you know how to resolve conflicts satisfactorily.

Where are you going to learn? There are places where people can learn, such as classes, couple groups, or therapy, but if they have not been exposed to any of these options and have not developed the skills in their family of learning, they come into any relationship with a tremendous deficit.

This is not only the case with friends, but is also true in business relationships. A person brings into the business world patterns of behavior which they learned in their family. It is enlightening and useful to know that a company can replicate a family. A corporation can be similar to a Hurtful, Frightening Family, or can resemble a Helpful, Fun Family, in both the way the executives set the tone and the way the members of the company treat each other.

(For more information about conflict, see the chapter entitled "Conflict.")

All this is to emphasize that there are going to be conflicts. **Conflicts are part of life. The important question is how to resolve them in a positive way. In the Hurtful, Frightening Family, conflict never ends and no one wins.**

Needs do not get expressed in this kind of family, either. As I said before, things are stated indirectly. When one person attempts to let another person know what they need, the other person will miss the meaning of the request because it is not expressed clearly.

There are also some people who have learned an unfortunate attitude, typified by the following syllogisms: "If I have to ask for something, then I don't want it." "It isn't worth having it if I have to ask." "It becomes tarnished if I have to ask, because the other person should know what I want." "If they really loved me, I wouldn't have to ask."

I once had a friend who was angry at me because I didn't recognize her wishes when she had told me the opposite of what she wanted. I responded, "If omniscience is the criterion by which you assess my love for you, then I flunk. I'm not a mind reader." My response was not kind, but it was true.

You will emotionally or physically starve to death, with your needs unmet, if you don't ask for what you want or need.

People don't ask because their needs were ignored in their family of learning. They stopped asking, and often even stopped "wasting" their time and energy to figure out what they needed, because the need would not be responded to anyway. Why spend time asking yourself what you need, or telling someone what you need, when you won't get what you need?

In the Hurtful, Frightening Family, the mother and father did not get their needs met by their own parents in their respective families of learning. Because they were deprived, they don't know how to respond, or resent responding, to the needs of their own children. Since they as parents did not get their needs met, they expect their children to take care of them. The family their children create, since they met their parents' needs instead of having their own needs met, will expect *their* children to take care of *them*, and on and on it goes.

That is backwards!

What must happen is that the parents must respond to and care for their children, so their children and grandchildren —when they become parents—will care for and respond to the needs of their children. This nurturing passes from generation to generation, with the children's needs being met by their parents.

In a family where the child's needs are not met and the child is inhibited or abused, there is much anger. The Hurtful, Frightening Family manages anger in three ways. Anger is: (1) turned inside on oneself, (2) expressed indirectly or passively, or (3) comes out violently. All this adds to the pain and fear that already prevail in such a family.

When a person never expresses anger, it is because they are afraid of their anger. The person has learned that, if they express anger, they get attacked physically or emotionally, or are isolated. That is painful!

Anger that is not expressed directly, will be expressed indirectly. That leads to more pain and destructiveness within the family. Because the family members do not learn to express anger in constructive ways, their anger eventually disrupts their relationships both inside and outside their family. What they do learn is to fear anger, either their own or others' or usually both.

When you express anger passively, you may harm the person you intended to receive the anger, but you do more short-term—and perhaps long-term—damage to yourself. When you express anger by withholding something, or by withdrawing, you hurt yourself and your relationships.

Some children express anger passively by failing to do school homework. The resulting poor grades may make a dent in the family image, hurting the parents, but the consequences to the youth may be failure to achieve college admission, or lower job earnings.

Passively expressing anger always backfires.

Anger in the Hurtful, Frightening Family may come out in violence.

When I talk to people about anger, I mean anything from mild resentment to rage. When you ask people if they are angry, most say, "No, I'm not angry." That is because they are not violent or in a rage.

Our culture connects anger and violence. What people often learn in the Hurtful, Frightening Family is that anger leads to violence—either their own violence toward someone else, or someone's violence toward them, or toward another member of the family. This connection between anger and violence is obviously very painful and frightening.

In the Hurtful, Frightening Family, anger is either (1) denied and repressed, and comes out indirectly; (2) expressed passively by withholding; (3) stuffed until it can't be contained, and then explodes; or (4) comes out in extreme or violent form, verbally and/or physically.

In the Hurtful, Frightening Family, affection is seldom or never expressed. There is fear of physical or emotional contact. There is an avoidance of emotional connecting, for fear of being hurt. There is the fear of physical contact leading to sex. There is a discomfort because of the fear that sexual sensations will lead to sexual actions. Physical touching is therefore feared as being a preliminary to sexual activity.

There is also the fear of rejection if affection is expressed. If a person has been taught that they are unworthy, unlovable or "bad" in their family of learning, they will find it difficult to accept affection from anybody.

There are two reasons why. One is if you don't like yourself and believe yourself to be unlovable, then, when somebody says, "I love you," you don't trust their words. The fear is that you will be hurt in the long run. The belief is: "If they love me now, it's because they don't really know me. Once they get to know me (the way I know myself), they will find me as unlovable as I believe myself to be."

Did you follow all that?

There is another reason why a person who does not like themselves has a fear of being hurt if somebody expresses affection for them. That is, "If you do know me as well as I know myself, and I don't like myself, then you surely don't like me either. You must want something from me. You are attempting to manipulate me to get what you want. Once you have received it, you will stop being nice to me or will reject me and that will hurt." The fear is: I will be hurt when I find that you didn't like me, but that you seduced me to get what I could give you.

Mates who have been used, manipulated, taken advantage of under the guise of love in their family of learning become afraid to accept affection in the family they create.

Affection is feared in the Hurtful, Frightening Family.

Pain, also, does not get expressed in the Hurtful, Frightening Family. When you see somebody in pain, you tend to blame yourself, because you were blamed by your parents when they were upset. You were told it was your fault. You then internalized the messages you had been given. If somebody is upset or hurt or in pain, you believe you must have caused it. Either you will blame yourself and feel guilty, or you will be afraid you will be blamed. The fear that you are to blame prevents you from comforting anyone who is in pain.

There can also be similar discomfort with feeling helpless. When somebody is in pain, often there is nothing you can do to eliminate it. If you already dislike yourself, the sense of helplessness that occurs when somebody else is in pain can stir up tremendous feelings of inadequacy in you, which only adds to the sense of inadequacy and self-rebuke you carry inside yourself. You, then, end up with a lot of pain because self-disdain is painful. The form of self-protection you employ is to try to inhibit the pained person from expressing their pain so that you can avoid feeling the guilt, helplessness, and pain that are stirred up.

There is another reason why pain is not responded to in a comforting way in the Hurtful, Frightening Family. A parent who, in their family of learning, has experienced the treatment I am describing brings a lot of pain into the family they create. When you see somebody else's pain, it can stir up the pain that already resides in you. If you have been taught not to express pain, not to cry—"big boys don't cry," "crying is weak," "crying means you are crazy"—the pain intensifies because of the fear of crying.

To have pain and release it is a part of life, no big deal. It is a very big deal if you are hurt and have to hold it in.

Parent who have been punished for crying will often prevent their child from expressing pain as a way to avoid intensifying their own pain. The child will not get comforted and may even be punished, which leads to more pain.

There is obviously much pain in the Hurtful, Frightening Family.

Fear is also unacceptable in the Hurtful, Frightening Family. The parents associate fear with weakness and vulnerability. They learned that if they showed fear, weakness, or vulnerability, they would get hurt. Fear was seen as wimpy, which was unacceptable. Showing fear brought judgment or rejection to them. Their child's fear triggers the fear that lurks inside the parents from their family of learning. Since it was unacceptable there, it continues to be unacceptable as they relate themselves to their children. They teach their children not to show fear. This teaching becomes another form of pain.

It is isolating when we must stifle fear, which brings more fear and pain.

Although there is a large amount of fear in the Hurtful, Frightening Family, expressing it is, sadly, unacceptable.

Creativity in the Hurtful, Frightening Family is undermined. It is seen as a threat by one or both parents, who already do not like themselves. Experiencing themselves as worthless, they attempt to feel better about themselves by putting themselves in an elevated position, and putting down what their children or their mate creates. The parent attempts to compensate for their feelings of inadequacy by demeaning the creativity or accomplishments of other family members.

Differences are also denied. Parents who dislike themselves require everyone to agree with them as an ego support. Someone who thinks differently or acts differently raises the fear in the parent that they may be wrong. In order to avoid any attention to "wrongs" or "badness," this kind of parent attempts to have everyone think and act alike.

Creativity and differences are denied or rejected in the Hurtful, Frightening Family.

Leadership is discouraged or confused in the Hurtful, Frightening Family. People are afraid that, if somebody else has the position of leadership, their needs will not be met. What occurs is, when one person makes a decision, someone else undercuts it.

Here is an example: A couple has to decide about going to a restaurant. Shirley says, "Well, where would you like to go?"

Ron responds, "I don't really care. Why don't you decide?"

Shirley says, "Fine, let's go to Bishop's Mid-East."

Ron replies, "Well, I don't really want to go there. Let's go to a Chinese restaurant."

Shirley becomes frustrated because she was originally told to make the decision. An angry Shirley replies, "I'm not going for Chinese food, so you can come with me to Bishop's, or do what you want."

Ron is then convinced that he was right. Shirley doesn't care what he needs.

There is another scenario that could follow the part of the dialogue that introduced the idea of Chinese food. Shirley, in this scenario, says, "Chinese food sounds good to me. Let's go get some."

Ron then becomes frightened, since he cannot conceive that Shirley would want to respond to his needs. He can't believe it is really agreeable to her. He "knows" that even though she seems agreeable, she is really upset underneath, and eventually he will get hurt or rejected by her in retaliation, so he must continue to question and confuse the decision.

There is yet a third possible scenario that could grow out of Ron's recommendation of Chinese food: Shirley, afraid that Ron is just trying to control her, states, "Chinese food is good, but let's get Italian. Wouldn't you like it better?" On and on it goes, through Syrian, Mexican, French, Indian, Vietnamese, and so on. Decisions do not get made, because of the fear that the decision is only based on the need of the decision maker, not on the needs of the other family members who are affected by the decision. Distrust prevents easy decisions and the pleasure of relaxed companionship.

Another possible feature of family leadership, such as it is, in the Hurtful, Frightening Family, is that parents give their rightful power to their children, who don't know how to use it. Parents who have learned that they are bad, worthless, or unlovable are afraid to make a decision for fear of rejection. They are afraid they don't know how to make a positive decision because they were criticized for every decision they made in their family of learning. They fear making a decision, yet distrust allowing anyone else to make it.

As you can see, any decision becomes painfully chaotic in the Hurtful, Frightening Family.

Parent and child roles in the Hurtful, Frightening Family are unclear, and often reversed. The children in this type of family are put in the position of being "parents." The children have the responsibility of taking care of their parents' physical needs and/or of protecting them from becoming emotionally upset. My belief is that the parents should take care of the children, so the children can then grow up and take care of their own children.

The role reversal in this kind of family can also take the form of one of the children being a "mate" to their own parent. The parent has more emotional intimacy with that child than with their husband or wife. The remaining mate may assume a child's role within that constellation, or may seek another child in the family to be their emotional mate.

The children may thus become emotional mates to their parents in households where the parents have weak or negative bonds between them.

The choice of a child as the parent's emotional mate is not based on gender. The mother may pick her son or her daughter, and the father may pick his son or his daughter. Gender is irrelevant. Getting emotional needs met are the major factor.

Parent/child emotional mating creates ambivalence in children. They need attention from the parent who has se-lected them as an emotional mate.

At the same time, the price a child pays is that they are not allowed to *be* a child. Also, they are often resented by the excluded spouse for being in that spouse's rightful position.

In some Hurtful, Frightening Families, one parent will bond all the children to themselves, leaving the remaining parent isolated. This dynamic may be concealed from the children because the parent who is the outsider may abdicate their parental role by burying themselves in work or outside activities as protection from the painful isolation in the family. The impression the children then have is that their parent has abandoned them, and they resent that parent.

In some situations, a parent will abuse one or all of the children because of rage over their spouse's picking a child or children to take that parent's place. The child will then perceive the abusive parent as a bad person who does not love them, instead of as a person who is horribly inept at dealing with the painful family dynamics.

Children need to see their parents express a lot of affection and respect for *each other.* **The bond between parents must be the strongest bond in the family, with each child receiving affection from both parents.** Children need affection from both parents in order to establish a strong sense of their own identity, and they need to observe parents giving and receiving affection in their family of learning, so they can learn how to create a loving family of their own. This does not happen in the Hurtful, Frightening Family.

There are other distortions prevailing in the Hurtful, Frightening Family because of lack of clarity about roles relating to tasks. If the husband is unclear about his role and the wife unclear about her role, confusion reigns.

Such confusion is particularly common in the post-Sixties era. If a man comes into a marriage with a clear-cut traditional expectation that his role is to be the provider for the family, to coach sports, to maintain the cars, and so forth, and that it is his wife's role to take care of the children, the home, the social activities schedule, and so on, it gets confusing if his wife decides she no longer wants to be the caretaker of the children and house. She may also want an out-of-the-home career. If there is not a mutual decision about this, the husband winds up being the breadwinner as well as the person who cleans the house and does the cooking. He becomes tremendously resentful because he is performing tasks that he never thought were his in the first place, and he is now performing the roles of both husband and wife—plus his wife is performing "his" role! If this couple doesn't know how to resolve the conflict, the result for that family is tremendous stress, and an enormous amount of pain, anger, fear, and helplessness.

Role confusion adds to the fear and the pain in the Hurtful, Frightening Family.

Let me refer to gender. In the Hurtful, Frightening Family, attitudes about gender are very biased. There are set patterns that are expected from boys as males and from girls as females. Boys are to be "masculine" or "manly," which means: aggressive, competitive, strong, tough, cool, unemotional, sexually active, not like girls. Girls are to be "feminine" or "womanly," meaning: nice, polite, shy, unassertive, emotional, nonsexual, not like boys. The "feminine" traits that are quite natural for a man are denied them, and the "masculine" qualities that are very appropriate for a woman are discounted.

We do not feel loved for being ourselves when this kind of prejudice is put on us. We believe we have been labeled and put in a box, and are only lovable if we behave, feel, and express ourselves in specifically defined ways. Gender deviation is to be "unlovable." Gender compliance is the only way to be "loved."

We are inclined to reject ourselves if we must avoid or deny a basic part of ourselves, such as a thought, emotion, or action that is different from the gender description assigned us. It hurts to reject yourself, and it is frightening to anticipate the rejection of somebody important to you, such as your parents, siblings, extended family members, school-mates, and friends.

When my son, Jeph, was two or three years old, we were visiting my parents in their home in Kentucky. At that time, Jeph's favorite toy was a clothes iron. People usually consider an iron as something only a girl would like, but that was his favorite toy.

On Sunday we all went to the church. Jeph went to church school carrying his iron. Some of the folks were surprised to see a boy with a clothes iron. Jeph certainly wasn't looking at his toy as anything strange. It was simply fun to play with. He was being himself and taking his favorite toy with him.

Who would believe that Jeph—who, as a boy, enjoyed a toy clothes iron—would become the catcher and slugger on a championship baseball team, a good basketball player, co-captain of his lacrosse team, a member of his high school wrestling team, a construction worker, a very handsome, masculine, assertive, competitive, kind, caring person? I would!

I believe both men and women have qualities that are their own unique blend of "masculine" and "feminine," which makes each person Uniquely Human. Such a belief is scorned in the Hurtful, Frightening Family.

Sex is complicated in the Hurtful, Frightening Family. It can be seen as a form of exploitation, or perhaps as a weapon. Women have been accused of using sex if they want something from a man. If the man doesn't do what she wants, the woman will withhold sex.

I, as a therapist, would like to declare: A woman has no corner on that kind of behavior. There are men who do the same thing.

If either men or women have learned that they can only get their needs met by withholding something the other person wants, or if they are in a relationship in which they feel they must use manipulation to get what they want or need, they will resort to such tactics. This is not an approach to getting one's needs met that is indigenous to only one gender.

Sex may also be avoided because it can be a way of being intimate. If you have experienced the pain that comes from being reared in a Hurtful, Frightening Family, then intimacy can be tremendously frightening. Fear can breed a belief in the need to be constantly in control as a self-protection from getting hurt. There is the fear of vulnerability and closeness. There may be the fear of letting go or the fear of loss of control that accompanies achieving orgasm. For these reasons, *intimate* sex is avoided.

If you have learned in your family of learning that you are worthless, or you are "bad," or incapable of doing things well, you may have the fear that you cannot be a sexually potent person. I am not just talking about men. This fear can exist in either gender. The fear is that you cannot share your sexuality in a way that will please the other person. If you believed that you were displeasing to your parents, it can be difficult for you to believe you can please another person in the artful, tactile, physical contact of sexual activity. You may not have an awareness of the emotional aspects of sex, so it becomes more of a physical activity instead of an emotionally intimate connection. This lack of awareness can lead to making the sexual experience empty.

Incest is much more common than anyone wants to believe, including incest between mothers and their sons. Secrecy in a family and repression among family members can be so strong that only therapy or hypnosis can bring childhood incidents of incest to the conscious awareness of an adult. It is seldom a problem isolated within the family unit; it is most often a disturbance that involves every member of the family in one way or another.

Children are tremendously torn apart inside when there is incest in their family. The child feels guilty. If the incest was the only form of attention the child received from their parents, then the guilt feelings are attached to getting a need met by sexual contact with a parent. Everyone, after all, needs attention.

The child will often take the blame, although the child is always innocent. Shame—a combination of fear and pain—is another feeling in the child who is the object of incest. The repercussions of childhood sexual abuse can manifest themselves in many hidden ways for years into adulthood. It does not only have an effect on the abused child, but other children in the family carry its scars.

In the Hurtful, Frightening Family, sexuality is feared and sexual sharing is empty, unsatisfying, demeaning, abusive, and painful—or not shared.

Children cannot leave families where there is a great deal of fear and pain. They are held in emotional bondage. This bondage is partly the result of the children not knowing how to deal with the feelings of leaving. It is partly because both parent and child perceive leaving as a form of rejection. The major reason why children don't leave is because they do not have a safe springboard from which to propel themselves into a new family or new lifestyle. They cling to the family out of fear. The children may marry and live in separate houses or different towns from their parents, but they do not leave. They are emotionally glued to their Hurtful, Frightening Family.

Separation or grieving never happens. The child as an adult within a Hurtful, Frightening Family may sometimes go thousands of miles away, but the emotional umbilical cord is never severed. The full-grown person remains a child. As you can imagine, the members of this type of family suffer from an overwhelming degree of pain, fear, confusion and distrust.

Adults who never leave their family of learning have great difficulty when they attempt to create a Helpful, Fun Family of their own. Their major alliance remains with their family of learning, which takes a significant portion of their physical and emotional energy. Therefore, the children and spouse in the family that the grownup child/parent creates do not get their needs met.

You may be asking, "Am I destructively involved in my family of learning?"

If you feel more emotionally dependent on one or both parents than on your spouse, the answer is, "Yes!"

If you are more concerned about your parents' needs and are spending more energy taking care of one or both parents than of your spouse and your children, "Yes!" (One or both parents being elderly or ill may be an exception, if you have previously constructively separated. However, these issues can also be used by parents to manipulate their children into never leaving.)

If you talk to your mother or your father about difficulties in your marriage more than you discuss those problems with your mate, "Yes!"

If you are constantly calling one of your parents, or routinely receiving calls from one or both of your parents, or allowing them to disrupt meals and other family times, "Yes!"

If you are often "bailing out" your parents financially, or relying on them to supplement your income without special circumstances, "Yes!"

If either one or both of your parents is addicted to alcohol, the probability is "Yes!" (unless you have made a powerful effort to separate).

Just because you are good friends with your parents does not mean that you have a destructive emotional bond. There are many advantages to multigenerational families sharing various facets of life, such as family gatherings, a couple doing things with their parents without the kids, or activities with one or both parents without having your mate present.

Helping each other financially is not necessarily negative. Affection and mutual respect between parents and their children who have become adults can be wonderfully satisfying to everybody. It is only a problem when the relationship with parents drains energy from the grown child or from the family that the child (as husband or wife) creates and puts stress on the grown child's marriage and on their children.

My parents and I broke off any contact with each other for about six weeks. This may not seem like a long time, but it was a clear separation. I have wonderful parents, but things were not wonderful between us at the time, so I decisively ended the relationship. Fortunately, my Father contacted me to establish a friendship, and shortly thereafter my Mother did the same.

I recently invited them to go with me to my college reunion. We had a great time together. They are very supportive and fun to be with.

There is some natural sadness at reunions. Monday morning after the reunion weekend, my Dad was reading a chapter of this book in progress, and I was reading a devotional message he had mentioned to me. He looked over and saw a couple of tears on my cheeks.

He stood up and came over to where I was sitting. I stood up and he held me while I sobbed on his shoulder. My Father is obviously a wonderfully caring man.

At this point in my life, my parents are two of my best friends. It has been a struggle, and taken a lot of effort on all our parts to get to this place, but it has been worth every bit of it.

As Jackie Gleason used to say, "How sweet it is!"

There must always be some clear separation from parents, no matter how smooth or how disruptive the separation is. Pain and fear and unmet needs prevail in the parents, in the children, and in the children's children when this does not occur. When the separation is clean and the grieving is complete, however, the quality of friendship between parents and children is wonderfully freeing for all.

Let me conclude by emphasizing again: If our parents created a Hurtful, Frightening Family, they don't deserve blame. They deserve understanding because of difficulties in their respective families of learning. That does not mean that we cannot be angry at them. We *will* be angry at them. That's natural.

It does mean that we can express our dislike for negative treatment with kindness. It may mean that we powerfully, verbally confront a parent about negative treatment if it continues. It may also mean that we have nothing to do with a parent who perpetuates the pattern. It may mean that we stop any contact with our family, do the grieving, and go on our way.

Since your parents cannot change what was, the positive option is to tell them what you need from them now. If they respond to your needs, the possibility then exists for building a rewarding relationship. If they respond insensitively and in a hurtful manner, then get away from them and put your energy elsewhere. Do whatever is necessary to have the best life possible for yourself and all the wonderful people in your life—be they family or friends.

If you came from a Hurtful, Frightening Family, it is not in your interest to blame yourself. You don't deserve the self-inflicted pain.

If you have developed a Hurtful, Frightening Family with your mate and children, it certainly is not in your interest to blame yourself, either. You have a choice. You can either put yourself down and hurt yourself because of this situation, and continue to perpetuate the pattern of pain, or you can praise yourself that you now have an opportunity to do something different, to learn new behavior, to learn where all this self-rebuke is coming from, to begin affirming yourself, and to invite other members of your family to learn new ways of being with each other.

I applaud you for reading this chapter. I encourage you to explore new directions that will be better for you and for the people around you. One way is to read the chapter, "The Helpful, Fun Family."

When you appreciate your uniqueness, are kind to yourself, and affirm your self-worth, it will lead to connecting with other people in a caring way, which will inspire other people to respond to your needs, and on and on and on—kindness after kindness after kindness.

And don't forget: You are wonder-full!

The issue is NOT
whether there will be conflict.

It is how to master conflict.

Creative Conflict

I knew a couple who said they never fought in their marriage. Sadly, I believed them. They both had bleeding ulcers.

People find it difficult to imagine it is possible to have a conflict or disagreement in which the persons involved all get their needs met.

I remember a couple who came to a therapy session ready to fight to the death for what each wanted. When they left, they walked out with a solution that had previously occurred to neither, but that was to the advantage of them both. In the process of resolving their differences, they began to think creatively about solutions. By combining their ideas, they came up with a result more satisfying than either of them had previously conceived on his or her own. The result was not a compromise; it was much better.

Why are people unable to come to these conclusions themselves without the help of a therapist? It is because they do not know how to resolve differences or conflicts. They have not learned the skills or the techniques for settling arguments.

Another reason is that when you have not experienced people who are interested in your needs, it is hard to trust someone who wants to respond to your needs, and it is difficult to believe that anyone will ever respond to your needs. The resulting perception you have is: You must fight for what you want, even if it means "dying" in the process.

Some people *do* die emotionally, or at the very least, prevent themselves from attaining what they need and want in the midst of a conflict, because they come to the conflict with fear and distrust. They approach the conflict striving to wield power, or else they give up far too easily.

Creative Conflict occurs when each person involved in the conflict is working with the others to come up with solutions that will benefit everyone. Everybody uses their creativity to find ideas that are mutually beneficial and also devotes their creativity to the resolution process itself so that all involved may get their needs met in the best possible way. A **Creative Conflict** approach can be applied to decision making in family, business, or government settings on behalf of people who are not present to represent themselves.

The meaning of **Creative Conflict** will become more clear as you read on in this chapter.

One of the questions I ask clients during my initial evaluation with them is, "How did your parents handle their conflicts or differences?"

Sometimes the answer I receive is, "They didn't. They fought all the time." Those parents never resolved anything, and the child never learned how to resolve conflicts. Sometimes my client will say, "I had wonderful parents. They never fought." Other clients respond, "My parents went off to another room to work out their disagreements."

The problem in each of these types of families is that if you never saw your parents resolve their arguments, the chances are very slim that you ever learned how to settle conflicts creatively. You had no models to copy. You had no one in your family of learning to teach you the skills necessary to constructively resolve differences. You may have learned conflict resolution some other place. Often, however, other settings instruct how to outmaneuver the other person, instead of teaching how to build solid friendships.

As I use it in this chapter, "friendship" refers to husbands and wives, parents and children, salespeople and clients, employees and employers, competitors—all forms of personal and business interactions. I am using the word to mean any positive experience with another person, ranging from a business telephone conversation to the intimacy between you and your loved ones.

Some people learn how to deal with conflict in business settings. For businesses where the profit motive is primary, and people and friendships are insignificant, employees at all levels operate from the perspective of getting and keeping the advantage by whatever means necessary. They come from a power base that uses a variety of manipulative, destructive, anxiety-inducing, and distrust-inducing approaches. The more intimidation or deceit is used, the more fear, distrust, defense, attack, and tension are in the air.

When this kind of atmosphere prevails, the maneuvers are not only directed at competitors. There is also a lot of maneuvering (a subtle form of manipulation) that exists between departments and project teams, between management and labor, between the sales and service departments.

The result is an insidious, cancerous environment that not only causes physical and emotional stress for the people within such a company; it also disrupts the production process. Some indications of this sort of environment are tardiness, frequent sick days, employee turnover, slowed work, emotional outbursts, and reduced creativity—all which affect production and profits.

I don't mean to insinuate that companies that operate with the kind of tension I've just outlined do not turn profits. They do. Not as much as they could with a different, more enlightened approach, however. Only the most astute chief executive officers, chief financial officers, and members of corporate boards of directors consider the hidden costs that occur as a result of employee preoccupation resulting from company-related stressors. A negative work environment costs companies money due to lost time on the job. It shows up in the cost of reduced quality, and the cost of customer complaints that follow on the heels of employee upset and lack of attention to the business at hand. The physical and emotional symptoms related to job stress add to the companies' health care costs. These all affect the bottom line —and the human toll in physical illness is enormous.

My belief is that a congenial business atmosphere between and within companies generates innumerable benefits for everyone involved, and provides greater productivity and profit.

As consumers, or in business transactions of any kind, we reduce conflict in our lives when we deal with people who have integrity. I extend myself with my time and money to do business with quality people. It is always worth it. There are many wonderful people out there—especially when you treat them openly, fairly, and with respect. Expect and do not tolerate anything other than the same treatment for yourself.

I drive several towns away from my home when I need tires or alignment work, because I have found a service center that makes the trip more than worthwhile. My friend Bill Windt, an engineer and auto "guru," assists my sons and me in purchasing and finding quality places to maintain our cars. Great treatment, service, and advice are so rare in the business world that I will go out of my way to get them.

Our family of learning influences our actions in our work, family, and social relationships. If you experienced lack of attention to your needs in your family of learning, and have come to believe that the only way to get a positive response is through manipulation or power moves, that will become your mode for operating in your vocational and relational settings. What a miserable way to live!

I saw a poster hanging in the office of a friend and colleague which said, "Just because you're paranoid doesn't mean they're not out to get you."

If you are dishonest, you have reason to be paranoid. You bring it on yourself. People will not trust you if you do not have integrity. They will try to "get you."

The point of mentioning business attitudes is that the corporate setting is seldom the place in which to learn conflict resolution skills that lead to friendships where mutually satisfying solutions are the objective. Fortunately, more and more companies are moving away from the competitive posture to a position of cooperation within the company, with their suppliers, and even with other companies making the same products.

Here is another observation about the link connecting an individual, a family of learning, and business: How a person functions in their vocational setting—whether it is in a corporation, small business, government, university or professional organization—is greatly affected by their family of learning. We bring it all with us. **The more we understand our own background, the better we will be able to understand our mode of interaction in our workplace.**

When there are conflicts at work, it is common for a component of the difficulty to be connected to previous experiences you have had with parents, siblings, other relatives, friends, teachers, or former employers. It is easy to superimpose attributes, and sometimes the "looks or expressions," of a person from your past onto a person in your present. When you are not aware of taking something from your past and superimposing it on someone in your present, you will treat a person with whom you are having a conflict as if they were the person from your past. That confuses the person in your present, and renders conflict resolution difficult or impossible.

In one company to which I was a consultant—assisting it to restructure its human system from the top on down—one of the managers and I met privately. He agreed to explore his past, including his family of learning, to discover who his employers represented and who the employees he supervised resembled from his original family. Such an understanding assisted him in his working relationships with others in the firm.

In families of learning where conflict has been avoided, fear of conflict is carried into adulthood by the children. John, who comes from such a family, is in a relationship with Jane.

She is openly expressive about opinions or emotions. She says clearly what she wants or needs. When a disagreement occurs, John becomes frightened and backs off. Jane wants to resolve the issue clearly and directly. When John withdraws, she becomes frightened or hurt, because there is no opportunity to connect constructively with John.

It is frustrating to deal with someone who withdraws. It is difficult to get your needs met, especially if one of your needs is to be close to them. It is painful to watch someone you value, or with whom you want to be friends, give up in needlessly painful resignation.

People who withdraw do so because their experience in their family of learning was that disagreements or conflicts lead to pain.

I am the kind of person who likes to have things out in the open. I like to discuss disagreements and come to some kind of solution to them. In one situation, however, a wonderful friend just walked off in the middle of a conflict. I was frightened, and said, "Come back, and let's finish this."

My friend replied, "I need some distance from you, because I am afraid I will say something I don't mean, and hurt you. I don't want that to happen."

It was tremendously caring for her to walk away from the disagreement, gain perspective on it, and re-enter it in a way that would ensure a safe atmosphere. It certainly reduced my fear. It made space for an affectionate solution.

Some people need to blow up and blast away at each other. They get it out of their system, then settle down and discuss the issues, and have a great time making up.

In contrast to the couple who blast away at each other, there are those who withdraw during the course of a disagreement. If they simply withdraw and ignore the issue, then resentment and fear will build to the point where these feelings eclipse the affection between them.

The reason there are so many different types of conflict is because people come from different families of learning. It is extremely rare for two people to come together from families that functioned in the same way. Even if they did, there is the chance that they do not want to adopt the same patterns their parents had.

There will always be differences. When some people blow up, they appear to be angry, and intimidate others. It can help to realize that, when a person explodes, there is usually a lot of fear and helplessness underneath what appears to be anger. Some people hold in their feelings, and have come to a point where they can't block the feelings any longer. Then their actions indicate that it is time to "clear the air."

It is unfortunate when a person believes that they must always stuff their feelings. It is far better to express yourself when an emotional situation occurs than it is to allow things to build up to the point of explosion.

It is wise for each couple to sort out the best way for them to cope. Some couples need silence for a while, to think things through. Others have to take turns: While one person is shouting, the other remains quiet. At another time, the second partner may need to shout while the first partner keeps still. Then they can bring their antagonism to an acceptable conclusion.

There are no set patterns for conflict resolution that couples must follow. Most important is for a couple to have sufficient caring and sensitivity to put the effort into finding ways to resolve their differences that work for them.

My preference is to discuss the issue; go back and forth with opinions, feelings, and points of view; and arrive at a conclusion with which everyone is comfortable—and, ideally, even ecstatic.

Few things create more safety and compatibility in a date-ship or mateship than to experience the joy of going through a clash in a kind way, and reaching a cozy conclusion. Seldom is there a more serene pleasure than finding a suitable solution to discord with a friend. There are few more cheerful work experiences than to make a sale, conclude a transaction, or resolve a dispute in which all parties benefit.

Conflicts do not need to be handled perfectly. That would be an unreasonable expectation. Sometimes they even remain unresolved.

The point I am trying to make is this: Everybody is different, so each person's needs are different. Successful conflict resolution occurs when you find the style within each relationship or situation that brings a harmonious solution.

Let me suggest some ways to find compatable solutions or to mend the damage caused by unresolved conflicts.

The first is to be objective. It helps a lot if you realize that the outburst or attack directed toward you may have nothing to do with you, but instead comes from issues in the attacker's life. This calls for the capacity to stand back and look at the circumstances compassionately. Was the disruption in the relationship precipitated by something you did, or have you become a focus and outlet for something upsetting to the other person? Are you being blamed for something that has nothing to do with you?

The old adage that "it takes two to make a fight" is not true. It can take only one person to start a fight, and one person can keep a fight going, even if the other person doesn't want to be a part of it.

I have experienced this phenomenon with both clients and friends. It was clear that I had done nothing to deserve the blame or attack. My motives and actions were positive.

You may be thinking, "What makes him think he knows himself that well? He must have done something. It always takes two people to cause a fight."

Please trust me and believe that I contributed nothing to the controversy. If you believe your parents and society about this point, you will suffer needless guilt and you will spin the wheels of your mind trying to discover what you are doing to keep the battle going. If you were criticized and abused as a child, or are from a family of learning with an alcoholic parent, this is especially important for you to know.

A fight can occur without you in any way contributing to it. If you can grasp this, you can then focus on understanding the other person's motives, instead of turning inside yourself, totally confused and feeling guilty, while you try to discover what you did wrong.

Why would someone start a fight when you have done nothing? One reason is because some people are just plain mean and enjoy mistreating other people. A second reason is that they are superimposing—unconsciously perceiving you to be a negative person from their past—and are treating you as though you are that person. A third reason is that they are afraid of intimacy and, when you get close, they must push you away by attempting to start a fight to create distance.

I have experienced all these in relationships with friends and with clients. I have had clients try to pick a fight by attacking me because they were afraid to disclose a personal incident, or afraid to face an unresolved issue. They try to shift the focus from themselves to me by attacking me and making me the issue.

This leads to the second way to master conflicts. If you can understand the other person's agenda—which is often unconscious—you can respond in an appropriate manner. If they are mean, you can protect yourself. If they are superimposing, you can try to help them see the reality of who you are. If they are frightened, you can attempt to assist them to feel safe. You can also face the possibility that none of these tactics will work, and feel sad about the situation; but that is less painful than to blame yourself for the fight.

Third, you and I must also be aware of our own humanity. We must realize that everyone at times makes mistakes, overreacts to situations, and blames others when blaming is unjustified. Cherish the capacity to forgive the other person and to forgive yourself when the conflict has gone too far in a disruptive direction.

Fourth, to keep a sense of humor is also essential. A timely comment that breaks the tension and helps everyone involved to see the ridiculousness of a loggerhead can neutralize many conflicts.

Fifth, I encourage you to try to understand your opponent. Because of their fear, some people are far better fighters than they are lovers. If you are committed to caring for your combatant, try to recognize their fear, pain, or helplessness behind their words and strive to respond to that feeling. Sometimes they only need to hear that you understand their feelings. Sometimes they need you to simply be quiet and listen. Sometimes a kind look, a smile, a gentle touch, a warm hug will provide the safety to reduce the fear, eliminate the harangue, and bring harmony to the friendship.

These suggestions will not always resolve a conflict.

If you discover the fighter wants to fight—for whatever reason—and you cannot summon a peaceful solution, then just leave. **Unless there are good reasons to stay in the fray, get away.**

Sometimes space from each other, and the passing of time, can bring a new perspective on the part of both people in the struggle.

It is also true that not all conflicts or differences can be resolved. **When it becomes clear that the differences are so great as to incite unresolvable conflicts, get out.**

It doesn't matter whether it is marital, family, work, or social conflict. Life is too short to be in a situation that is draining your health and emotional energy.

There is nothing more rewarding than a happy family or a job you enjoy. There is nothing more emotionally draining or destructive of life's energy than unhappiness in either of them.

I was the director of the outpatient department of a hospital. I thought my neck was bothering me because I was doing too much exercise (really smart psychologist, right?). Then I realized that the problem had nothing to do with the amount of exercise I was doing.

The director of the facility treated people terribly, but it did not occur to me that the stress of the situation was causing me physical pain. To say he was a "pain in the neck" is so polite as to be nauseating. The words I learned in the steel mill are far more appropriate for him (see the chapter, "Greetings to You"). Many people wanted me to stay, and the administration asked me to help get him out.

I left. I decided I wanted to put my energy in a positive direction, rather than put any more effort into what could have become a blood bath. That would have benefited no one. It worked out very well. I went immediately to a marvelous organization. The place I left managed to put out the !*#*|! director three months later.

When a conflict can't be resolved, one positive solution is to accept the situation as part of life, and move on.

This next comment probably sounds ridiculous after the illustration I've just given; however, since I am unwilling to allow inconsistency to distract me from the truth, I will instead emphasize it boisterously: **Sometimes self-love or love for someone else demands that you must not only stay in a conflict, but that you must start it.**

There are instances when someone starts a conflict and relentlessly keeps it going. If you can't get away from it, then fight with all your might to win. Some people find themselves in conflicts with a vengeful ex-spouse who expresses anger by withholding children. A child held as a hostage is a tragic conflict, and seldom one to walk away from.

What is important with any conflict is to be kind to yourself. The common tendency is to blame yourself. Blaming can be a way of staying negatively connected to a miserable situation. It keeps you "stuck" in the past, burning energy that could go into positive projects or relationships.

Just as important in conflicts where it is possible, is to be kind to the other person. To do so may make a good friend or keep one.

In the first chapter, "Greetings to You," I discussed how blame benefits nobody and can cause a lot of pain to the blamed and to the blamer. This is especially true if you are being blamed, and are also blaming yourself. Blaming is an intellectual exercise. It is far better to face and release your feelings about the situation, and then—let it go.

Objectivity is essential. It is painful to take conflict personally. It is crucial to *deal with conflict as a task* to be accomplished *rather than as a personal affront*.

Let me add that it is important to assist your children to understand that conflicts are a part of life, and discuss with them ways of resolving them. It is not a question, in any human relationship, of *whether* there will be a conflict. It is a question of *how does the conflict get resolved?*

In the final analysis, it is not essential for a conflict always to go well. It is crucial, however, for the conflict participants to have sufficient respect for each other that, when a fight is not resolved, they have enough trust and affection to risk coming together again to restore their friendship.

Working with couples in therapy has confirmed for me some things that must be avoided for conflicts to be creative.

First, it is important to avoid getting into issues about the past. Every time somebody starts to bring up the past (even if "the past" was only an hour ago), the memories of the situation are different, and both people get buried in divergent verbiage.

When the past is interjected into a conflict, it is often to blame the other person. Even if its purpose is to defend a point of view, it is usually perceived as an attack. Bringing up the past seldom solves a conflict. In fact, it usually interferes with the resolution of the conflict.

Second, it is also important to avoid getting into discussions of the future during a conflict. If you are discussing an issue and trying to find a solution, you may at times need to include some information that relates to the future, but that is different from getting into fears about the future.

One of the problems with bringing the future into a conflict is that no one knows what is going to happen in the future. It only serves as a distraction from the main topic to be resolved.

When you bring the future into a conflict, it is a deterrent to problem solving because it is often brought up as a club-like weapon with which to try to beat the other person into submission—which seldom brings submission and certainly not resolution! Talking about the future is just as much a block as is discussing the past.

Third, it is important to avoid responding to a question *with* a question. This is often a way of deflecting the issue by throwing up a smoke screen, because you are either losing the argument or are trying to avoid exposing your feelings or needs.

It obviously does not lead to a mutually satisfactory solution when one of the participants in the conflict uses questions to trap the other so they can "nail him/her to the wall."

There is one exception to what I have just stated. It may be necessary to ask a question to clarify what the other person meant by what they said. Then a question is very important so that misunderstandings can be avoided.

Fourth, it is frustrating to try to resolve a conflict when one person is using a power position in an attempt to overwhelm or overpower another.

Further frustration arises when a person uses passivity during a conflict. People often do not realize that there can be tremendous power in passivity, especially when they give in quickly to "your" solution, will not discuss it, and clearly let you know they are angry and that, if you proceed, you will pay. To be in that kind of setting can create tremendous feelings of helplessness.

Fifth, for you to describe to someone how you perceive their actions will also be disruptive. The conflict will go nowhere, because the other person will probably get on the defensive. If a situation is heated, people usually feel attacked if you tell them your perception of them, or ways that you see them maneuvering. Even if you do not intend your comment as an attack, the person you describe often feels hurt, frightened, or frustrated and will defend their position or attack. Discovering a solution to the problem is thwarted.

The above are five things that you should **NOT** do during a disagreement.

What you **must do** is to express your needs, feelings, and thoughts clearly, precisely, and directly. The more accurately you can express them, the more accurately the other person can respond to them.

It is at times interesting to listen to some couples. I will realize that what is being said is different from what the speaker is thinking. I then hear the partner respond. What the listener heard is different from what the speaker said, and also different from what was in the speaker's mind! The response from the listener was filtered through past experiences, and is not connected to anything the original speaker said. (If you find this description difficult to grasp, imagine how confusing it is for the unfortunate couple in the situation.)

I then tell each of them my perception of their thoughts and my impression of what they intended to say. They each confirm that my assessment is accurate. Then I tell them what they actually said. They are amazed to learn the discrepancy between their brain and their mouth. Often there is such a contrast that everyone laughs.

With this type of interaction, it is no wonder that settling a conflict is difficult.

It is necessary to express your thoughts, feelings, and needs clearly, precisely, and directly.

It is also essential to listen. When I emphasize listening, I am including **listening to yourself** to be sure that what you are saying is what you intend.

Often the emphasis is on listening to the other person. This is a natural place for the emphasis to be. If you don't hear what the other person said, you can't put your heads together to come up with a creative solution. Nevertheless, you must also listen to what *you* are saying.

What gets in the way of effective listening? Fear does.

If you are afraid that you will hear judgment, condemnation or attack, it is very difficult to listen to another person. Your response will generally come from your fear, and you will attempt to block out the other person by talking while they are talking, or you will mentally block what they have to say. It is necessary to keep your fear in perspective so that it does not get in the way of your listening.

When you hear a comment that hurts you, it is possible that the pain is coming from your family of learning, or from other experiences. Being aware of your own "rawness" from built-up pain inside allows you better to assess how to respond to what people say. It is wise to give them the benefit of the doubt, unless you know that they are a vicious person.

When the fear of getting hurt surfaces, the tendency is to attack or to withdraw. If you instead hang in there and listen, you may be surprised to discover that what is being said is not an attempt to hurt you, but is a caring comment directed to please you. You will totally miss it if you only respond by anticipating a painful remark. I have had many people in therapy with me drown out my praising words because they had expected to hear criticism.

Another feeling that can get in the way is **helplessness**. If you start to feel helpless, remind yourself that it is only a feeling. You will experience less helplessness and more of a feeling of being in control if you focus on listening to the other person. You can deal with the reality of the situation much better if you know what is being said. Take charge of your mind and emotions, and you can then absorb the information that comes from the other person.

Anger is still another feeling that gets in the way of listening. I have already mentioned that anger may be a layer over another feeling. Anger wants to protect you, yet you must take a moment to be sure it is pure anger rather than a knee-jerk response covering fear, helplessness or pain.

I might add that **excitement**, pleasure, and joy can sometimes get in the way of listening, because you are so excited that, if the other person does not share the same enthusiasm, it interferes with your hearing what the other person is saying.

Affection will generally not deter listening. Affection for the other person causes you to want to listen, because you want to respond with caring.

The point is: In order to be a good listener, you must be aware of what is going on inside of you. You need to know what your feelings are, and where they are coming from.

Self-insight is a significant ingredient for good listening.

The next major component to listening is to listen not so much to the words, but to the meaning the person wishes to convey. When you really become a sophisticated listener, you can not only listen to the meaning, you can also absorb the feelings behind the words. Emotional vibrations can be the most accurate way of assessing the message. "Vibes" are more truthful than words.

If you think the other person's emotions are in the way of a clear message, or are indicating a mixed message, inquire sensitively as to what they are feeling. Many times, simply asking that question will not only neutralize a conflict that is going nowhere. It can even swing it in a positive direction. Because you ask kindly about feelings, the person recognizes that you care for them. This recognition provides the person with an opportunity to express themselves. If no criticism or judgment follows that expression, the friendship remains intact, and the process toward resolution can continue.

If the person doesn't know what they are feeling or thinking when you ask "What are you feeling?," the suggestion to take a break from the argument to allow their feelings to surface may be useful. Tell the person that you want to know their needs, wants, and wishes and will wait until they themselves know them and can express them.

When you ask about the other person's feelings and express your own, it can help break down barriers of fear and distrust. When you are aware of your emotions and express them at the right moment, it can move a conflict to a constructive conclusion. When you emphasize that you value hearing the other person's thoughts and feelings, it can lead to finding a solution that will please you both.

Even though you are afraid to be vulnerable, it is invaluable to take the risk of expressing your feelings to help the other person know what is going on inside of you, and to build trust. I am encouraging you to be as open as possible when you want to build a friendship.

Another way you can build trust is to make it clear that you have heard what they said by stating what you have heard. It can be valuable for people who have a hard time resolving conflicts to replay to the other person what you heard them say, to make sure you heard it accurately. Listening is crucial to resolving a conflict.

Listening is essential in order to take care of yourself. This is especially true if someone is trying to overpower you, or manipulate you. By hearing what they are saying, you have a better opportunity to respond in a manner that effectively protects yourself.

This idea has seldom been emphasized, and it is therefore worth repeating: *Even though listening to the other person is important, it is just as important to listen to yourself, to be sure that what you say is what you mean.*

I am encouraging you to express yourself as openly as possible in any setting where you want to build a friendship.

I must also add a word of caution: When I have encouraged you risk being open, I have been referring to situations in which you would like to build a friendship, especially one in which you would like closeness and intimacy with another person. To risk openness may not always be in your best interest. If you are being open with someone who appears to use your openness to take unfair advantage of you, then it is wise to "test the waters" to find out if that person has integrity. If they do not, then protect yourself. For you to continue to be open and honest is to be self-defeating, if not self-mutilating.

For me, buying a car is usually a frustrating experience. Even when someone I trust has recommended the salesperson, the next thing I know, I find myself facing a variety of maneuvers, strategies, and often, outright lies. Car salespeople must think we are so stupid that we don't see through it all. They must think they are so shrewd that, when we do see through their manipulation, we won't be offended and leave, never to return, or that we won't try to turn the tables on them.

It is amazing that car dealers have not realized that they can make just as much money, feel just as good, if not better, about a sale, and have other people feel good about buying a car when they are direct and honest in their dealings. Instead, they often try to squeeze every possible cent out of one person and then, when things are not working out on the next sale, give that next person a break. I believe in paying a fair price, so that everybody can be happy. What I resent is having to be on guard against all the attempts at manipulation. What I would appreciate is for someone to stop playing the frustrating games.

When somebody is trying to take advantage of you, is trying to squeeze everything possible from you, or is lying —be they family, social, business, or sales settings—to be open is to your *disadvantage*. Sometimes directness and honesty will neutralize them but, in other situations, you often must play it safe and use whatever weapons you have in your armament. It is to your advantage to learn as much as possible about how to handle yourself when someone is attempting to maneuver you. You may need counterstrategies of manipulation or intimidation. If so, be glad you have them. Having the skill to take care of yourself with a greedy or unethical adversary can be very satisfying and build trust in yourself.

One of the really nice experiences I have had occurred in real estate. I was referred to a realtor who was a person of integrity. We put the life of our family in her hands. She found a house for us and dealt with us honestly and fairly, and everybody was happy. The people who owned the house became and remained our friends long after we bought the home, the realtor became our friend, and everybody benefited from the creativity of the experience. It turned what could have been a trauma into joy.

Later I discovered that this particular realtor had been in business for only one year. Within that year she had created the top agency in the area. The reason for her success was that she approached people with respect. She did her best to respond to the needs of each person who was involved in the transaction.

I encourage you to face conflicts head on.
Be combative or withdraw when either is wise.
Have the courage to use Creative Conflicts in your personal and business settings. Those uncommon skills and attitudes lead to friendships that are of immeasurable worth.

I believe that if each of us:
1. will risk openness and honesty,
2. will give others the benefit of the doubt until they show that they don't deserve it, and
3. will assert our personal power with a commitment to creative caring,
then our marriages, our families, our industries, our country, our world will be increasingly safer places to live—to trust—and to relax.

Affection is an emotion.

Caring is a decision.

Affection

"I love you!"

These are the most precious words we can ever hear. They can convey the deepest sense of affection, caring, and passion that one person can share with another.

They are also the most confusing. "I love you" can mean that a person is expressing dependency, sexual attraction, manipulation, infatuation, pain, anger, or attraction to a myth. It can be coming from the unconscious as transference or as superimposing. Because the word "love" can have so many meanings, it is wise to evaluate seriously the quality of the person who is verbalizing those words to you.

When someone tells me they love me, I don't automatically know what they mean. I have heard people say, when I asked them why they were staying in a relationship that appeared to be destructive to them, "I *love* her" or "I *love* him."

My response is: "Love is irrelevant." What is relevant is caring. Caring is a decision. It is a decision to be kind, to share or show affection, to be considerate of another person and their needs. Caring is to think and act in the best interest of the other person. It is to be considerate and responsive to their needs.

The word *love* is wonderfully sentimental, but is not sufficient information on which to make a commitment of your life. If another person is feeling love toward you, or if you have love toward another person, you need to illuminate the burning emotional embers with the light of reality. While

71

the words "I love you" can carry a powerful emotional impact, they do not necessarily make for a caring relationship.

My thought is, if someone loves me—that is wonderful! If they tell me they love me, but treat me poorly, that is not wonderful—and I don't want it! If someone tells me they love me and is kind, affectionate, considerate, and responsive to my needs, then I believe they truly love me.

How I am treated is far more important than what I am told. The point I am making is this: The word *love* is only that—*a word*. It can intend a variety of different, sometimes conflicting, meanings. It only has meaning within the context of a relationship.

I have heard many people, with pain in their voice, say to me, "I love him" or "I love her." What they mean is that they "love" someone who is causing them pain, or who is not returning their affection, or that they are loving someone whom they cannot realistically have.

That is not love. That is self-torture.

My reaction is totally different when a client says, "I really love her. I want to give her the best of myself and meet her needs. I enjoy being with her, and want to share the joys and trials of life with her. It feels so good to know what she wants, and to do it for her." My perception of him is that he is a loving, caring person. One half of the friendship has potential. It doesn't mean that it is a good relationship. It means that one person has the right perspective.

If the woman to whom he wants to give his caring is not a kind person, or vacillates between being affectionate and being hurtful, all that love is wasted on her because she can't receive it. He will be confused, and probably hurt and helpless, when he is with her.

However, it is really exciting if his partner, or the person he would like to be his partner, says, "I love him so much. I want to do things for him that he likes. He is so wonderful to talk to and play with. I love giving myself to him in every way." When they both have the attitude expressed in these words, they have the potential for a commitment that can be fulfilling and lasting. That is a loving friendship, in the best sense of the word—when two loving, caring people want to share their love with each other.

My excitement turns to ecstasy when they both say, "It is so wonderful when we are together. We can express our feelings to each other. S/he is so kind and open with me. S/he tells me what s/he is feeling without overwhelming me or attacking me. I feel safe to be myself. There is no crisis so upsetting to us that we can't go through it together and find a solution to it. We play together and we have so much fun. As we face our difficulties together, it seems to deepen our love for each other, which adds to our joy of being together. Our love for each other is so wonderful."

Does all this seem like unrealistic, heavenly bliss? It may be that, but I would rather have a vision and be with someone who can envision the same thing, and strive for it together, than have whatever other options exist. **The unbelievable is far more likely to become reality when we picture it, than it is when we dismiss it as impossible.**

I don't in any way mean to play down the importance of verbalizing your affection. It is absolutely essential that we say caring things such as "I love you" to the people we love. This in itself is a very caring action. Saying words of love is exciting, and hearing them feels terrific!

I knew a man who did not think his father loved him. His father did many caring things, but his message never really came through, because he never said "I love you!" to his son. It is essential to express caring in every way available.

It seems to be more common for men to hesitate to verbalize their affection. Women, therefore, find themselves questioning whether or not a man really loves them when the man has not SAID it. I must add, however, that women can have the same inhibition about expressing their affection.

It is pleasing and satisfying to hear positive things. Perhaps you never realize how much someone cares about you, until they tell you. If you are like me, when someone tells you they love you, it is exciting and thrilling to hear.

Let me also emphasize the benefit to the friendship you have with yourself of expressing affectionate, caring thoughts to YOURSELF—even out loud.

Having mentioned affection and caring, let me clarify some distinctions. Affection is an emotion. Affection is the emotion that accompanies attraction, warmth, tenderness for someone or for ourselves. It is experienced with the wish to be close to someone whom we enjoy.

Affection may or may not be based on how someone acts. We may have warm feelings toward a person, even though they are not acting lovably—they may, in fact, be acting terribly. Our emotion may come from an attraction. It may also be familial, because it is possible to have maternal or paternal feelings for our children, or fondness for our mates, or for our parents, even when they don't act the way we would like them to act. Affection is an emotion, a feeling. Affection can be love, but love is not necessarily affection. Love is not affection if the "love" is uncaring.

Caring is a decision. We can decide to be caring, even when we don't feel affection. We may even feel anger, and yet respond with caring, because we decide to.

There are times when someone says something to me that hurts. When that happens, I can instantly think of a response to retaliate that would hurt them. I then have a decision to make.

Most of the time, especially with people about whom I care, I make the decision NOT to say the phrase that would hurt them. Instead, I respond in a way that will attempt to neutralize the attack, or I will express my pain about what they have said. The other person has the option of answering me in kindness or hostility. Then I can decide about my next response.

There are times when I will choose to unsheathe my stiletto tongue. (A stiletto is a knife with a point so sharp and blade so slender that it goes in cleanly and deeply and you cannot feel it until the pain explodes inside. A stiletto tongue has the same effect.) If a person is being outrageously obnoxious, I cherish having the option to knife them verbally, even if I don't exercise that option.

Since it is not common to think of caring as a decision, let me repeat it: **Love expressed by means of caring acts can be directly the opposite of the emotion the person performing the caring acts is feeling at the moment. The feeling you experience may be pain, may be anger, may be fear, but you can pick a compassionate comment or action for the sake of friendship.**

I encourage you to give the other person the benefit of the doubt. They may be kind, but have made a comment that triggers pain that is from your past. I try to discover the other person's intentions, assuming they intend to cause no pain, unless previous dealings with them have shown them to be mean and nasty.

If you are unclear about the quality of a person because you have had no previous contact with them, you run the risk of being hurt. If you know how to take care of yourself in such a situation, it's no big deal. (The chapter "Conflict" will assist you with this.)

If you keep your stiletto tongue ready to attack someone at the least perceived provocation, you will be hurt far more often than if you give the other person the benefit of the doubt. I have found that, by overlooking someone's initial abrasiveness, I have made a lasting friend who will forever after be loyal and kind to me.

It is possible for a person to be caring and to feel angry at the same time. An example is an adult who has left their family of learning, but is in the position of taking care of an aging parent or having to visit a nursing home. This can be a major intrusion in their life, and they experience anger because of it. It does not mean that they lack caring and affection. All it means is that there are two emotions involved in the situation. Both feelings are natural.

The anger may intensify, however, if the infirm parent has not been a caring person to their child or was abusive to them. The child who, as an adult, has the responsibility for that parent may not feel any affection, only resentment. The adult offspring may decide to act caringly toward their parent anyway, either simply because the aged person is *their* parent, or because the adult offspring has made a life-decision to be kind to anyone who is in need. You can experience anger and choose to be gentle nonetheless. They are not opposites. **Anger is an emotion. Caring is an action.**

Superimposing

One reason why the word *love* is so confusing to people is because the word is tied to transference or what I like to call **superimposing**. Let me now elaborate. Love can be transference. Transference is a technical, psychological term. It means you have an emotional tie with a person or event in the **present**, yet the emotions you experience are connected to, or even caused by, a person or event from your **past**. It's as though you superimposed a picture of another person or event onto your present experience. The problem occurs when you are not aware that you are superimposing and believe that the emotions you have now are caused by the situation in the present moment.

Transference can be either negative or positive.

Here is an example of negative transference: Your mate says something to you and you are really angry with them, but sense that they don't deserve your anger, or especially anger that is so intense.

When this happens, you can be sure the emotion is connected to somebody in your past who has hurt or abused you. You would be wise to discover who that person—or what that event—was. Then you can decide what to do with the emotion, based on your awareness of its origin.

If your mate is a caring person, explain what is occurring inside you. They can support, and possibly help, you to understand yourself more.

Positive transference may be a feeling of enormous attraction to someone because at a subliminal or unconscious level the person has characteristics that create a familiarity tied to a kind person from your past. It is not specifically connected to the present person.

An example of how subtly this can occur is when I was shocked by a physician who, at the end of my visit with him, rose angrily from his chair, exclaiming, "Well, now that you have completely blown my schedule for the day, we had better stop!"

I was stunned. I had seen him previously with my wife who was ill. He had spent a great deal of time with us, and was very kind.

I apologized to him and walked out of his office. For a while I felt guilt that I had done such a terrible thing. Then I realized that, unlike the doctor's expectations, and schedule, I had planned the visit to last for an hour. It dawned on me that I had expected to spend an hour with him because the doctor resembled—by virtue of his previous attentiveness, appearance, and ethnic background—a wonderful psychologist whom I had seen for therapy when I was in graduate school. I was relieved to realize that my unconscious had played a transference trick on me. I was not a total dunce who had been bad because I took more time than the doctor had intended.

It also crossed my mind that he could have said something earlier, before he got so angry, and before his day was demolished.

Another example, closer to home: I was tremendously attracted to a woman. She was a nice person, but the way she treated me at times did not warrant the degree of commitment I was prepared to give her. She had several positive characteristics in common with my Mother, which I enjoyed. It was evident, after some painful experiences, that the intensity of the feelings I had for her were precipitated by the past, and not totally by the present person. Sometimes being *perfectly human* can be painfully confusing—even for a psychologist!

There are also times when feelings of attraction for a person can be affected by some traits of your father or mother that were hurtful. You may be drawn to this person out of a sense of familiarity, rather than because they treat you in a caring, sensitive way that deserves your caring in return. In that instance, it is negative transference, even though it feels like a positive attraction. You may feel "love" toward a person who abuses you.

Sometimes you may experience feelings that are connected to more than one person—for example, to both parents. To cite an example, some men become frightened if a woman is upset. They expect to be reprimanded. This expectation and feeling may be coming from their past. A client told me about his family of learning. When his mother became distressed, his father punished him as a means of trying to protect his wife. The son carried into his manhood a fear of contributing in any way to a woman being unhappy. He would at times become frightened when he had done nothing to precipitate a problem, even when the woman who was upset wasn't blaming him.

He was shocked when friends were kind to him instead of blaming him when he was with a woman who was miserable. His fear in such situations was intertwined with the enmeshed actions of his parents in the past. (This example can just as easily apply to a woman who is frightened by a situation in which the dynamics are the same.)

You need to acknowledge your fear, identify its source, and then act with an awareness of the distortion from your past. This will free you from your past and give you control of your present.

Let me reiterate with a friendly warning. When some people say "I love you," that *love* may be connected to some form of positive or negative superimposing. When you experience attraction for someone, your attachment may stem from positive or negative transference. When a person stays in a destructive relationship, it is often because there is negative or positive transference attached to a negative person. It is common for people to be in an abusive relationship when they have been abused themselves as children.

I hope the concept of transference or superimposing is now clear to you. I hope it is obvious that both positive and negative transference can get in the way of authentic friendship. It is imperative to distinguish between transference and reality in order to have positive companionship within your family, with friends, at work, and in social settings.

Dependency

Another factor that can confuse "I love you" is the issue of **dependency.** The more the dependency stems from childhood deprivation, the greater the conflict it causes in adult relationships. When an adult looks to another adult to offset or fulfill the needs for affection that went unmet when they were a child, it places an impossible burden on their mate. It becomes an unrealistic expectation that can only lead to anger or resentment on the part of the dependent person and the person on whom they unrealistically choose to depend.

I have seen this fusion of dependency with love create a different problem. A woman had intense dependency on her husband. In therapy, as she grew to become less emotionally dependent on her mate, she then came to the conclusion that she no longer loved him. She began to think she did not love him because she was no longer experiencing the same dependency that had been intertwined with her love. Actually, she had much affection for him. What had diminished was the dependency that to her had "seemed" to be "love." Once this distinction between love and dependency was clear to her, her marriage improved.

It is not surprising that love is confused with dependency. Our first experience of love was as a child dependent on our parents. They were all we had to rely on for food, clothing, shelter, affection, life training.

The complication occurs because infantile dependency is a matter of life or death. If our parents did not provide for us the security of a home, food, and protection, then we would die. So, for a child, depending on one's parents is a matter of life or death.

A problem with dependency emerges when you bring what I will call **survival dependency** (the type of dependency infants have on their parents) into your adult relationships. If you are in a caring friendship and you bring survival dependency into it, the relationship will be diminished by the fear that you will die if the relationship ends. If you put pressure on the other person because of your fear, it is easy for them to believe that they are not loved, but merely an object you are using to ward off your fears.

If you are aware that it is your fear of dependency that is the problem, then you can share those feelings in an open, nonpressuring, or unaggressive manner. If your friend is a secure, caring person, they will respond with kindness. Then your fear will be reduced and you can move forward with your affection for each other.

It is crucial to distinguish between emotional dependency from your past and affection toward a person in your present. If you can get beyond the survival dependency that has come from your child/parent relationship, you can achieve power and freedom to establish fulfilling relationships.

When you grow through the survival dependency, you have the freedom to love another person in a positive way.

That love becomes not only self-affirming, but also others-affirming and mate-affirming.

When you grow through survival dependency, you also have the freedom to exit from a negative relationship. You develop the objectivity to see that to stay is to die, to leave is to live.

Let me quickly add that I am not demeaning or negating dependency in a relationship. It is essential, and can be fantastic. Love and caring means allowing another person to depend on you, and depending on them. Love that has dependency in the relationship can be beautiful, if each person can shift roles freely, and allow flexibility in responding to each other's needs.

Permitting another person to "mother" or "father" you when you need it as an adult can feel wonderful. The opposite is also true. To allow someone to depend on you to "mother" or "father" them can also be wonderful. This experience can lead to affectionate feelings toward yourself because you are giving and increase the other person's affection toward you because you are giving to them.

Dependency in a relationship can be a beautiful thing. A woman can be both fatherly and motherly. A man can, too.. Gender is irrelevant when needs are being met.

Responding to a friend's need, or having a friend respond to yours: that is **love**! Both giving or receiving can lead to feeling good about yourself. This is what I call **cooperative dependency** in a friendship. Cooperative dependency can be heavenly.

I alluded previously to a dependency that has unrealistic expectations in it and inevitably leads to resentment and anger for the person who cannot live up to the expectations of someone who has unrealistic "needs" (actually, "wants").

The following are some unrealistic expectations.

1. Expecting your mate to provide you with the caring or affection you did not get as a child. I mentioned earlier that being a parent to each other can be really beautiful—but

constantly expecting your mate to be a parent to you becomes destructive, and will lead to resentment in you both. **Dependency without reciprocity is deadly.**

Neither can you give to yourself what you did not get as a child. However, you *can* nurture yourself, be affectionate toward yourself, physically and emotionally hug yourself. All of these can provide what you now need. To nurture yourself with your emotions and actions can be fulfilling.

This is far more secure and less vulnerable than totally relying on someone else. Depending on yourself reduces the fear of being consumed by depending on somebody else, and makes selective dependency comfortable. Selective dependency can be defined as wisely choosing caring persons on whom you can depend.

2. Another unrealistic expectation is wanting the person to be someone they are not, or to achieve what they cannot, or to provide for you what they are unable to provide. In a relationship, caring means allowing the other person to be who they truly are.

To be constantly critical of the other person because they are not what you want them to be is to be unfair to them *and* to yourself. This will lead to resentment in both people.

Also, to criticize a person about past failures, mistakes, or neglect only leads to hurt feelings, and possibly a fight. **It is far more constructive to tell your friend what you need or want from them at this moment, than to tell them what they did not do.** They can respond to what you need now. There is nothing they can do to change the past. They can do something for you in the present moment, even if it is simply to comfort you as you experience the pain that he or she previously unintentionally inflicted.

Pain Disguised as Love

I have mentioned that superimposing (transference) and dependency may be experienced as love. Let us now look at pain that is perceived as love. When some people experience pain in relation to another person—or have a painful yearning for someone—they believe it means they are "in love." People who have grown up in a family where there was much pain, or where there was abuse, often connect the emotion of pain with love. It is similar to the blending of dependency and love that I explained earlier.

When the primary experience of "closeness," "love," and attention received by a child was verbal, physical, sexual, or emotional abuse, the result in later years will often be an unconscious belief that love is connected with pain.

These persons usually fail to recognize or receive affection that comes to them in a direct manner as warm, genuine caring. They may only respond to attention that is painful. They perceive abuse as "love." True caring and genuine affection, if perceived, are not believed or received, and thus caring is not a positive experience for them. Instead, they connect "love" to pain, and this leads only to more pain.

I have worked with clients who seem to be only attracted to people who are destructive to them. They believe they have been experiencing love, but are only repeating negative patterns from the past.

I encourage them to spend time with someone who is not attractive to them or who is unattractive, someone for whom there is **no spark** or **charge**. The purpose is to bring into their awareness the barriers they erect to positive friendships, and to show them that kind people are available to them. Spending time with someone whom they do not find alluring, and toward whom they have no romantic inclination, provides the possibility of shifting their pattern away from the one of choosing people who are not good for them.

By doing this, they may find a real caring, responsive friend with whom they can share common interests. Everyone needs people like that. They may discover that the person is not someone to whom they want to make an exclusive commitment, but it is one step in the direction of finding a person whom they deserve.

A person who has been abused may stay in a relationship that is negative for them because they can identify with the other person's pain. If you have been hurt deeply in a physically or emotionally abusive family of learning, you know how excruciating that pain can be. You may stay in a present relationship because you don't want to cause pain to the other person by leaving. This obviously adds to your pain. It is a double bind. If you leave, you are hurt because you identify with the other person's pain. If you stay, you experience pain in the relationship.

You may believe that if you stay, you can provide comfort to the other person, therefore, alleviate your own pain. This does not work; you get disappointed and hurt.

The best solution is to step back, identify your own pain, separate it from the fusion with the other person. Then realistically assess the relationship, and decide what to do about the situation based on the objective evaluation of the other person's traits and your needs.

Let me emphasize that being in a friendship with someone who has a lot of pain is not necessarily a problem. If two people have pain, they may have much empathy for each other and thus develop a very understanding, caring friendship in which each responds with sensitivity to the other's needs. When kindness prevails, the pain can be a glue that forms a lifetime bond. Problems arise only if one or both have perpetuated their parents' abusive style.

The Love/Anger Blend

To continue with the idea of love combined with another feeling, let us focus on the **love/anger blend**. This is often connected to superimposing, mentioned earlier, but it should be examined separately.

When you have a lot of resentment toward one or both of your parents, and it is superimposed onto a person who unconsciously reminds you of them, you will experience anger toward that person. If you express your anger with hostility, the person will be surprised by your anger, because they have done nothing to deserve it. However, if they are an understanding person, they will respond with compassion.

On the other hand, you may be surprised that they will not tolerate such treatment. The response depends on how you tell them about your anger, and how comfortable they are with the feeling of anger in general.

It is essential to question the qualities of the person you find yourself "loving."

It is wise to question the type of lover you are, and the quality of love you give and receive.

One way to take good care of yourself is to raise questions about the people who tell you they love you. Having questioned this "love," the only way you can really assess whether or not a person cares about you is to spend time with them to see how they treat you. If you are treated with kindness, caring, and sensitivity, and the person responds to your needs, then there is a good possibility that they do, in the best sense of the word, love you!

One of my earlier experiences with such things came when I was in the fifth grade. I found myself with my knees and elbows skinned, lying at the bottom of the steps in front of the schoolhouse. When I came to, I was told that a girl had come through the door behind me and pushed me! I learned later she did this because she really "liked" me! That is very common with eleven-year-olds. They are uncomfortable or shy around people of the opposite sex to whom they are attracted.

As an adult, I have on several occasions experienced a woman being hostile to me for no apparent reason. Later on, I am told by a friend who knows the other person that the woman was abusive to me because she "liked" me.

In these instances, the women realized I was not "interested" in them, therefore they were hostile to me. I do not know what you call that, but it certainly is not caring and affection. Such actions may be quite natural for someone who is eleven or twelve, but it is not appropriate in adult life.

Self-love

So far, I have talked a lot about the meaning of the word *love*, and about love in relationships. Now I want also to discuss **self-love**. Most people have heard the saying attributed to Jesus, "Love your neighbor as yourself." This is important from the perspective of loving your neighbor, but it also focuses on loving yourself.

I cannot find where the statement is located in Sigmund Freud's writings, but for years I have been giving him credit for a comment: "If people loved their neighbors as themselves, they would kill their neighbors!" This is humorous, but sad.

This points to a significant truth about people. Many really don't love themselves. They are not affectionate and caring toward themselves. They are self-abusive, self-defacing, self-blaming, and self-hating.

I would like to explain why this exists. Our self-image comes from the teachings we have been told about ourselves. In your family of learning, did you hear the words: "I love you." "You are so wonderful." "You are a fantastic basketball player." "You surely do speak well." "I am proud of the grades you got," or "Your grades are terrible, and I love you." "The slippers you knitted were beautiful." "The clothes you made look very attractive on you." "You didn't play a very good game today. I know that nobody is good all the time. Were you tired or were you just having a bum day?"

Or was what you heard something like this: "You are so stupid." "I hate you." "You dummy. You let them beat you. You shouldn't do that; you are better than they are." "What's the matter with you?" "Can't you do anything right?" "Here, let me show you, stupid."

If you heard the first set of comments, then you begin to believe it is fine for you to make mistakes. It is okay to be human. For you to be yourself is great. It's wonderful to have the talents you have. You are loved. It is acceptable for you to love yourself. You believe in the talents you have, trust your brain, like the way you present yourself and that you as a person are appreciated. That leads to an attitude of self-worth, self-confidence, self-caring, and self-affection.

If you heard the second set of comments, it is natural for you to believe you are a bad person. You have "put-down" messages running through your mind. You experience shame about yourself. You have feelings of guilt, self-blame, self-hate.

Each of us internalizes either the positive affirmations or the negations which we hear about ourselves. This has a lot to do with how we feel about ourselves.

At one point in my life I gave a celebration—a dinner and a "laughing, loving evening"—for the special people in my life. There were over one hundred people there from several states. I began it by singing "You Are So Beautiful," and ended it by singing "Perhaps Love," which ends with the words, "My memories of love are of you."

My Mother, who gave the first talk at this celebration, began—with a big grin on her face: "It wasn't easy having Jay for a child."

After mentioning numerous, humorous anecdotes, she concluded her talk by smiling tenderly and saying: "We have had some difficult times together, and we've had some wonderful times together, but we're glad we didn't give him back!"

There was a lot of truth in both comments my Mother made.

I received many positive things from my parents. I believe few people in their families experience any more caring than we had for each other. Yet, we have also had difficulties and pain from each other. I am sure there were times when they thought it would have been much easier if they had given me back, because I was not an easy child.

There is a story that my mother took me to the family doctor, concerned that I might be hyperactive. Good old Dr. Welluver (fortunately for me) responded, "He's not hyper-active. He's just a boy!" Hurray! Thanks, Doc!

I might also add that my parents were not always easy to have as parents. There were times when they did not respond to my needs. There were times when the way they treated me came from their own unresolved issues and conflicts, of which I became the focus.

That is inevitable. People are who they are.

What I value in my parents is their uniqueness, their negative traits as well as their positive traits. What I cherish in them is that they love me, in the best sense of the word, including my positive traits and in spite of my negative traits—but most important is that I know they love me! We have disagreements and conflicts, and our love for each other is the foundation for resolving them.

I have spent a lot of time, energy, and money trying to know how my family has affected me. I constantly attempt to be aware of the experiences from my past that influence me now, and to distinguish between them and the present reality.

I was once with a client who was particularly sensitive to rejection because of the abuse she had received in her family. She told me about a personal experience. Fortunately, she felt safe enough with me to ask, "Are you angry with me?"

I replied, "No. I am not angry with you. But you are right, I am feeling anger. It has nothing to do with you. What you said triggered some anger from my past."

It was comforting for her to know that my anger would not hurt her. It was crucial that I knew I was feeling anger, and knew its source. If I had been unable to accept my anger, I wouldn't have let myself experience it. Had I said, "No, I'm not angry," she would have been caught in the confusion between trusting her own perceptions and believing me.

If I had known I was angry and did not know it came from my past, I could have easily believed it was caused by her. If I had reflected it back to her with a question, without giving her an answer, she would have been frustrated and frightened by not knowing what was going on inside of someone on whom she was depending to help her. She would have also missed an opportunity to build trust in her own perceptions. Denying my anger, attaching it to her, or deflecting it back to her would have compromised her trust in me and in herself.

This anecdote happened in a therapy setting, but often there is this same type of experience in social, in work, or in family settings. When a person recognizes why they overreact they can then say, "I am sorry I laid that trip on you. It didn't have anything to do with you. It was coming from my past."

What a tremendous sense of relief I have experienced when someone is aware of, and acknowledges in our friendship, the feelings they bring from their past into the present.

It can be frustrating and enormously painful when a person you have chosen to depend on focuses their upset on you, and accuses you of doing or saying something wrong, attacks you, and you get blamed for something that has nothing to do with you, but is instead connected to their past. It is even worse if that person refuses to trust your explanation and your positive motives, and insists on attributing negative motivation to your actions.

In one such situation, I felt totally helpless because the person insisted on attributing negative intentions to me, allowing no opportunity for us to resolve the disagreement. She took it to the point that it appeared to be a desire to have an argument. There were other indications that she was afraid to be close, and conflict was one way of keeping distance between us.

Another friend and I were on a sailboat with friends of hers. The captain told us to cleat the sheet and, in the process somehow, she hurt her finger. She was angry at me, because she thought I had intentionally done something to hurt her.

I was surprised, because that was unlike her. After some discussion, I said, "I suppose I could lie and agree with you, that I intended to hurt you, or I can tell the truth and have you stay angry at me. I guess you can continue to be angry, because I'm not going to lie. I had no intention of hurting you." She decided to believe me, and we had a wonderful time.

I am trying to make a case for the importance of being sufficiently aware of yourself so that you are clear about the origin of your emotions.

How is this all tied into loving yourself or hating yourself?

If you don't like yourself, then it can be difficult—and even painful—to look at yourself introspectively for the purpose of self-improvement. If you feel guilty about yourself, then you carry a lot of pain inside. When you believe that you are bad, you expect to be blamed by others or you emotionally beat up on yourself.

Perfectionistic expectations and harsh treatment of ourselves prevent us from looking at ourselves.

The more affirming and the more caring we can be toward ourselves, the safer we will feel to take the risk to assess or analyze our actions and our emotions objectively. It takes a sense of safe objectivity to be able to realistically evaluate ourselves.

When we do look at ourselves and see that we have made a mistake, have done something or said something we dislike, it is crucial for us to realize it does not mean we are bad. If we walk around with the belief that we are a bad person, it is probably the result of what we were taught about ourselves.

If, on the other hand, we can look at our actions and acknowledge, "Yes, that was wrong," we can then say, "I'm sorry I did it, and I really appreciate myself for having the courage to see it. I will attempt to do it differently the next time." By having an attitude of gentleness toward ourselves when we need to be self-critical, we can learn from our mistakes.

When you apply what you learn from your mistakes or your "bad" actions, you can change your future actions. To assess your own actions with kindness can be an opportunity to learn about yourself. You will therefore be more kind and caring, both to other people and to yourself, in the future and you will increase your ability to function with greater competence.

Sometimes I tell clients that therapy can be like a professional football skull session. Monday morning, after the Sunday afternoon game, the players and their coachs have a meeting to review tapes of the game to learn from their mistakes so they can improve their performance in the next game.

At times when I provide therapy, I function as a coach. I assist a person to review a recent experience so they can handle it better the next time a similar incident occurs. I help them to understand themselves and other people so they can master the tools of constructive interaction in future family or job situations. When they become good at it, they can even anticipate challenges before they arise, and develop strategies for coping with them as they unfold.

Quarterback Joe Namath did that in the Super Bowl between the New York Jets and the Baltimore Colts. Many of the plays during that game were audibles, selected spontaneously and called at the line of scrimmage as Namath saw the changes in the Colt's defense unfold. It was masterfully done and exciting to watch, unless you were the Colts.

Introspection can be a skull session. You, with the courage to view your life tapes, to look at your mistakes and your successes, can learn new patterns and new skills for living your life. You can have the same mastery and excitement in your life as Joe Namath exhibited in the Jets/Colts Super Bowl. The difference is that there is no loser. Everyone wins!

I would like to distinguish between self-love and selfishness. Self-love is a way of treating ourselves that helps us to feel affection for ourselves. Self-love is an attitude of kindness and respect for ourselves.

Selfishness, on the other hand, is a person's attempt to grasp at things as a substitute for affection. When you dislike yourself, one way of attempting to offset your distaste for yourself is to acquire people in your life. If you have a lot of emptiness inside, a way of attempting to alleviate the emptiness is to acquire things in your life.

These do not work.

Selfishness, when recognized for what it is, deserves empathy instead of rebuke. It calls for understanding the person's actual needs, setting realistic limits on their grasping at us, and giving thoughtful caring to the selfish person.

Self-love can be attractive.

I was at a brunch having a good time enjoying the people. Someone asked me a question about my work. I explained the therapy I do and the results in very positive terms.

I later received a call from a woman who overheard the conversation, asking if she could meet me. We established a meeting time and place to have dinner. She told me what attracted her to me: She had heard me speaking well of myself. She concluded that, if I could feel that good about myself, then I would no doubt feel good about other people, and treat them as well as I treat myself. (I hope it is true.)

The incident is included here because, when I have mentioned it to clients to encourage them to think well of themselves, they have been surprised that anyone would think in this way, and they have benefitted from that realization. It is a different perspective from the one most of us have been taught. I was taught by my mother that I should never talk about myself in a positive light. Most people have difficulty believing they can be attractive if they express self-respect—self-love.

This principle can be applied in another way. A client gave me a bow tie that looks like a monarch butterfly and my mother made a black cape with a red/orange lining to match. I wear it with my tuxedo trousers and shirt. I refer to myself as "Count Monarch Butterfly."

A friend and I went to a costume ball. She wore a crown and a dress befitting the companion of a count. All night long, people were stopping to talk, or saying things as they walked by, like "Beautiful cape!" or "I love your butterfly bow tie!" On the dance floor many people commented about how nice we looked together. A woman who was studying in Boston had a picture taken of the three of us so that she could send it home to her family in Turkey.

As we drove off into the night, my friend commented, "You certainly got a lot of attention tonight."

I responded, "I surely did. Wasn't it great how many people enjoyed our costumes! They seemed to get a lot of pleasure from them, and they were comfortable to talk to us because of them. It was really fun!"

When we are playful, it is contagious and others join in the fun.

The opposite is also true. The following example had very different results from the ones mentioned above. I was at a tennis party. I was really hurt, and feeling terrible about myself. I walked over to a woman who was standing nearby. After a few minutes of conversation, I realized she was inattentive. Then she walked away.

This is not what I generally experience, but I understood why: It was because I was in a very negative place with myself.

I sought out the tennis pro, whom I didn't know personto be a decent and receptive man. I asked if I might speak with him in private. He agreed. **I took the risk to tell him I** ally, but I had observed him on other occasions. He appeared **was feeling hurt, and explained why.** He was responsive, supportive, and affirming of me, and I felt as though somebody cared. It totally shifted my attitude about myself. I left him feeling "good" about myself.

Immediately I found that other people were attracted to me. I met another woman who was friendly to "the feeling-good-about-myself" me. We became friends, and our friendship lasted over many years.

Had she met me when I was so down on myself, I have no doubt she would have walked away, too!

If the other woman, who walked away, had met me when I felt good about myself, she might also have been willing to be friendly with me.

The way you feel about yourself affects how other people will respond to you.

A further example of this: A friend described to me a situation relating to the time when she was a teenager. She realized she was walking with her eyes cast down, always looking at the ground. Once she realized this, she decided to look up and start looking at people. She found this made all the difference in the world in the way people responded to her. This change also began to make a difference in how she felt about herself.

How can you tell if you really value and enjoy yourself? The answer is: You are kind to yourself, you take good care of yourself. You treat yourself with respect, both physically and emotionally. You eat nutritious foods, sleep well, drink healthy beverages. You surround yourself with people who are affirming, affectionate, and caring. You encourage other people to treat you in a positive manner.

If this description resembles you, I celebrate your self-love. If you do not have these attitudes about yourself and do not follow this lifestyle, please do not judge yourself.

Most people are a combination of the two. They vacillate between harmful and helpful self-treatment. Hopefully everyone is on the road from self-abuse to self-affection.

If you tend to be low on the continuum, then it is even more important for you to treat yourself well, so you can move upward toward self-affection and self-caring.

If you abuse yourself, have a lot of guilt and shame, have difficulty receiving caring and affection, then you need to purposefully be kind to yourself.

Because you believe yourself to be unlovable does not mean that you *are* unlovable—or unloved. My experience with people is that, at the core of their being, they are both loving and lovable.

The people who make themselves difficult to love have covered that core with a self-protective wall. That wall can vary from being aloof and withholding to sarcastic, antagonistic, and attacking as ways of keeping people at a distance. Their actions are only what they show to the world, and perhaps are all they know about themselves.

Inside, however, at the core of their being, they are not that type of person at all. They are beautiful. This means that their beautiful core has been covered with distortion caused by the way they were treated as a child and in their experiences as they were aging.

Do not judge yourself, do not be negatively critical of yourself, because you lack confidence or self-love. That attitude can become a self-defeating downward spiral. If you dislike yourself because you don't like yourself, then you will continue to dislike yourself!

It is like pounding a nail. If you pound yourself on the head because you are down, you are only going to go further down as you keep pounding.

If you are willing to put the effort into shifting your attitude by praising yourself, you can elevate your self-esteem to a positive level of self-relating. An example that comes to mind has a lot to do with love, but also has to do with faith: John Wesley, who was the founder of the Methodist Church (or came to be, even though it was not really his intention), was having a struggle with believing he was lovable or was loved by God.

In the midst of his struggle he went from England to Germany, to talk with a man named Peter Böhler. The instructions he received from Peter Böhler were these: "Preach faith until you have it."

John Wesley followed the instructions. Even though he did not believe in God's love for himself at the time, he preached faith as a universal truth.

Some time later, he went to a religious society meeting in a house on Aldersgate Street in London. He felt his "heart strangely warmed."

By preaching God's love, he came to believe that God did love him—just as he was. It became believable to the core of his being that he was both lovable and loved.

I encourage you to do something similar to that which was successful for John Wesley. John Wesley preached it to others, but you can preach it to yourself. **Each day say to yourself: "I am a loving and lovable person." Even if you don't believe it, do it anyway.**

To paraphrase Peter Böhler's recommendation: **Express love to yourself until you believe it, then, because you have love, you will live it.**

I encourage you to make a list of the things you like about yourself. People often find this difficult. It is much easier for them to list the things they don't like about themselves. Some people find it hard to think of even one good thing.

I want you to make a "self-love list" of characteristics that you like about yourself. If you can't do it, ask other people (people at work or in your family) to tell you one trait they like about you. You may be surprised to discover that they will gladly respond with more than one.

Perhaps you will find someone who will not tell you something they like about you. Don't be discouraged. Realize that they have a problem with giving!

Enjoy your list as it develops. When it is finished, stand and read it out loud, perhaps in the privacy of your room, perhaps to members of your family. They can add to your list what they like about you and read it to you.

Reinforce each item by including the phrase "What I like about myself is..." with each statement. Or you can begin by saying, "I like...about myself." For instance: "What I like about myself is that I am a loyal friend." "I love myself for the caring person that I am." "I like my sense of integrity." "I like my body." "I like myself because there is a lot of me to hug." "I enjoy my beautiful voice." "I like my self-awareness." "I am thankful that I know my feelings and can express them well." "I love my sexuality." "I like myself because I am such a good cook." "I like my anger." "I like my earthiness." Whatever is on your list, preface it in a very personal, self-affirming way.

Then add, "I am glad that I am me!"

If this seems like overkill, it is just the opposite. This brings life. People usually kill themselves—emotionally and physically—with negativity. I want you to heap tons of weightless love on yourself.

When you are reading aloud to other people, instruct them to clap and cheer after each item. This may be uncomfortable, or you may find it exciting. Whatever happens, it will be a way for you to experience yourself with a different perspective, and get positive reinforcement for it.

Invite your friends and family members to make a list of traits they like about themselves and have them read it aloud to you. Give them the same opportunity that you are giving yourself.

If you tend to be negatively critical of other people, or you have difficulty finding things that you like in others, start by trying to discover things that you can like about each person as you encounter them during the day. You may be able to think of only one, but that is a beginning.

Say to yourself, "I like you because ...."

As you become more adept and comfortable, you can actually tell the other person your thoughts by saying, "I really like the way you...." Or "I like...about you."

Notice how people respond to you. Notice how you feel about yourself for having said it. Some people will be uncomfortable, others, receptive. You may find people a lot more friendly than you thought.

A client told me in the process of therapy, "More and more, I'm feeling good about myself. I don't even have to think about it anymore. I just feel loved. It's like it is a part of me now. It is an experience rather than something I have to think about or be conscious of. It's integrated, rather than the pieces it used to be. The pieces of myself are more acceptable. There is more kindness and softness. It's great."

Another client sent me a note between therapy sessions. She wrote: "I'm so excited about my discovery that I need an incredible amout of love and that I am human, and it's OK! Yippee!"

I have friends whose shower in their home is like a car wash. It has water faucets on the wall that spray you on both sides from head to toe. *I encourage you to shower yourself with affection and caring. Then invite others to share the shower with you.*

I have been mentioning my thoughts about love. The most important point I would like to make is this: **Please open yourself to give and receive love.**

The question arises, "What is the result of openness, caring and affection?" The answer is, "You get closeness and intimacy with others and with yourself." Phrased another way, "You receive wonderful friendships that lead to more pleasure in your life."

The most satisfying experience anyone can ever have is to be deeply intimate, to share yourself at the core of your being, with someone who can truly value and appreciate the beauty that is in you. That intimacy does not need to

be reserved only for friendships with other people. It can also occur in the friendship you have with yourself.

Please sit quietly and receive this affection for you.

I love you.

When you have absorbed this affection I give to you, continue to give all the caring that you can create, both to yourself and to others.

*Anger is a powerfully
productive emotion.*

Anger

Many people are afraid of anger. When I mention anger, they respond with a lot of fear, because they think of violence. Anger, to me, is not violence. **Anger is an emotion. Violence is an action.** Unfortunately, anger can lead to violence, but the feelings of fear and pain can also lead to violence. You may decide to be violent when you are angry, but that is *your decision.* You may also decide to withdraw. I am using the word *anger* in a broad sense, as a generic term that describes anything from mild irritation to rage.

To understand this chapter, you must think of anger as an experience of a type of energy, neither negative nor positive—just energy. Anger is an emotion. It just happens. It is a part of being human. Anger, therefore, is not an ethical issue. It is not a moral issue. The feeling of anger is neither "good" nor "bad." The way people express their anger often hurts others, thus is "bad," which is why anger has such a bad reputation.

Let me clarify the differences between sensations and emotions. Emotions are a form of energy. Sensations are a physical experience. Emotions may cause physical sensations. Anger can provide the thrill of energy surging through our body, giving physical pleasure as it is released in constructive ways. Anger can also cause physical pain or illness when the energy is locked inside our body. I will explain this later.

Anger is merely a feeling that is related to the flow of energy in our body. This feeling comes from a variety of sources. It can come from an encounter in this very minute.

For example: Someone says something really hostile to you. You immediately experience anger. That anger is a response to the present moment.

There are also times when anger comes from the past. For example: you are with a person who makes a comment to you and you experience the feeling of anger. As you ponder what happened, you realize that it is not the comment of the present person that angered you, but something said by a person from your past. It could be your father, mother, brother, sister, teacher, first "love," friend, enemy, or a past anyone, who triggered the feeling of anger that you now experience. The anger toward past persons leaps into the present moment and becomes focused on the person with whom you are engaged.

There are times when anger blends with another feeling. You take a taxi or beg a ride to get to the garage to pick up your car. It hasn't been repaired. They need another day to finish the work. Most people will feel frustrated. Frustration is a combination of helplessness and anger. The anger is that they did not meet your need to have your car. The helplessness is that you can do nothing to change it. The frustration is related to the inconvenience that you cannot leave the garage with your car.

Why is it important for us to accept anger as a feeling that is natural? It is important because if we can allow ourselves to be aware of the feeling of anger, we have the opportunity to decide whether it is connected to the present, or to the past. With that information, we have the option to decide how to manage the anger.

When we recognize our anger and its source, we have much more control over our lives.

Anger is a part of being human. If we do not accept our anger, we are rejecting a part of ourselves, and that is very painful. (Please see the chapter "Winning the War Within.")

Why does a person experience anger, and feel uncomfortable with it? The answer is that we are trained in our family of learning NOT to feel anger. Many parents teach their children not to express their anger. The parents fear their child's anger, and are probably afraid of their own anger, as well. If our parents were abused as children when their parents were angry, they will fear anger. Their fear will prompt them to stifle their child's anger.

Another reason is that the parents never learned how to express their anger in constructive ways, so they couldn't teach their children to manage anger constructively. The children who are unskilled at expressing anger have experienced difficulties in school and/or with friends. It has brought them pain and frustration, which they bring with them into adulthood.

In either of these instances, we are not taught how to deal with anger or may be taught not to express anger.

Unfortunately, we learn that anger is bad. We learn that anger is not safe to show to anyone. We may jump to the conclusion that it is even bad to have the feeling of anger exist in us.

Women in particular have this problem. In a moment, I will explain how the training men receive about anger creates problems for them. For now, however, let us focus on women.

Those women who have been taught that "little girls should be nice," and it meant that "females should not be aggressive," have learned never to express themselves in any forceful way. This is really unfortunate. It accounts for a lot of the cases that are labeled Depressive Neurosis by psychologists.

Let me explain my opinions about depression. I refer to it in two different ways. What I call "sadness depression" is the feeling of sadness connected to a loss. For example, when someone you love dies or moves away, when a child leaves home, when you lose a job, change jobs, or move to a new town, there is a sense of loss or sadness, because an important person or place will no longer be part of your life. When you cannot or do not release sadness, it will intensify and will disrupt your life. I call that "sadness depression," which is different from what I refer to as "anger depression."

"Anger depression" occurs when a person turns anger in toward themselves. When a child is taught, in their family of learning, that they should not express anger, the child—and later, the adult—tends to turn the anger in on themselves.

If either of these forms of depression progresses to an extreme degree, it is labeled as Depressive Neurosis. This is an *un*necessary progression. Families, friends, employers, and our culture as a whole need to recognize that feelings are energy. Feelings are a natural part of being human and as energy, they need to be experienced and released in constructive ways. **If people would provide support for each other through the temporary emotional upsets that are a part of life, the depression, the need for mental health clinicians, and the ridiculous overuse of medication would be greatly reduced.** Unfortunately, the fear of feelings that prevails in our culture—and the resulting repression—reinforces, even increases, the intensity of the depression. The result is greatly extended depression within the troubled person, accompanied by physical, emotional, relational, and vocational problems.

When a depressed person has sadness depression, they need to be permitted—even encouraged—to talk about the happy memories that are related to their loss and to sob out their sadness. The support of caring loved ones to face the pain of sadness and release it brings relief and lifts sadness depression as the fog leaves the meadow brought about by the warmth of the morning sun. (For more about pain and sadness, see the chapter entitled "Pain.")

Anger, and therefore, anger depression, is best released by some form of forceful expression, some form of aggression. If you have been taught that you should not express your anger, then you swallow the anger into yourself, and feel depressed.

Now, I don't mean to insinuate that this only happens with women, but I think that there has been some selective gender training in our culture, which has been detrimental to each sex.

What happens with women—and some men—who are suffering from anger depression is that they cry. To look at them from the outside, you might think they are hurt. Well, they *are* hurt. The reason they are hurt is that the first feeling was anger, which they felt unsafe to express outwardly, so they turned it inside. It becomes pain, and they cry.

A person with anger depression seldom feels relief from crying, and often feels anger toward themselves because they cried. Since anger is best released through aggression, crying does not release it. So, the crying continues and continues and continues. Every time the person is somewhat angry you will see some tears trickling—but it doesn't vent the feeling. The feeling is anger that is being "stuffed," so the depressed person carries all this pain and anger inside themselves, and then gets more angry at themselves because they are depressed, which adds to their depression.

Let me offer an analogy to show what happens when feelings are stuffed. If you increase the pressure of gas in a container, the container will inevitably give way at some point. The container will either become disfigured or explode.

Because anger is a form of energy, it operates in the same manner. If you intensify the pressure of the anger in your body by forcing it inside, it is going to do something. The body and its organs—as containers of emotions—will become distorted, disfigured, or dysfunctional in some way that may or may not be visibly apparent, but will nonetheless be experienced as pain. It may also take the form of a physical illness.

You may experience tension inside yourself when you are around a person who internalizes anger, because it almost seems as though the anger comes out through the pores in their skin, or it comes out in the form of subtle pressure toward you, or in sarcastically cutting comments.

You will also find some people who appear to be very remote, mild-mannered, and unflappable. Nothing seems to bother them. All of a sudden they "blow" like a pop-off valve on a boiler with too much steam. These are some examples of what happens when people turn their anger inside, onto themselves.

The point I want to make is this: Both in nature in general and in human nature, matter and energy interact. Gas, as a form of energy, can be transformed, but not destroyed. Feelings, as energy, can be redirected, but not eliminated.

There are only two options available. One option is to experience your feelings and choose their direction. The other is to block your feelings and give up control of them. The second option usually results in some form of emotional, physical, vocational, or social destruction. The only wise option, then, is to experience the feelings, and then choose to direct your life for yourself.

It causes many complications when a person turns anger inside. Introverted anger will very definitely affect you physically. What I have observed in my clinical practice is that some people stuff their anger in their back, or they get what is called a migraine headache. The migraine headache is often caused by blocked anger. The nausea that may accompany a headache can come from the fear of their anger. (Fear often affects the stomach.) The migraine headache goes away once you give a person permission to experience their anger and to express it in positive ways.

One client called me between sessions with a migraine. Within a few minutes, I helped her to recognize her anger and to identify the person at whom it was unacceptable for her to be angry. I gave her permission to experience her anger and suggested ways to release it—and the headache left.

When a person has a back problem, they will often say, "I hurt my back when I bent over to pick up the paper," or "I was working in the garden and I hurt my back."

Many times, it is not bending over or picking up something that causes the back problem. The physical exertion is the final straw of stress on the muscle. The back muscles can no longer tolerate more tension, because the tightness caused by stuffed anger prevents the flexibility they need to expand and contract. The backache is caused by the person holding the anger in their back. The two muscles down the spinal column become like iron rods. Therefore, the muscles cannot flex when the person bends over. A stressed muscle tears, goes into spasms, or hollers in pain, "Ouch, don't stretch me."

I use my arm as a way to demonstrate this principle to clients. I show how soft and flexible my bicep muscle is when my arm is straight. When I bend my arm at the elbow, I ask the person to step back a distance so they won't get hurt by my bulging biceps (which is so totally ridiculous that they laugh), and I "make a muscle." Even though I'm being silly, I also make my point, because my muscle becomes hard and rigid when I tighten it.

This is what happens when we hold in anger and it goes into our back muscles. The muscles get hard, lose their flexibility, and when stretched, cause pain.

People have flown me long distances to alleviate excruciating physical problems that had existed for years, even after a variety of medical resources had been explored. After I have lived with the family for a weekend, included several generations of family members in therapy sessions in the home, used a variety of healing modalities, and helped them to experience and release the feelings, the patient has the first relief from the symptoms in years. On follow-up with the person, the remedy has been lasting.

Energy will go somewhere. Anger, as a form of energy, will go outside or it will go inside. If it is turned inside, then it is either going to give you some kind of pain, psychosomatic illness or body problem, or it will come out in another way.

The way some people express their anger is to use a passive appearing approach that renders their foe helpless, but brings suffering on themselves.

Here is an example of expressing anger passively. Picture a teenager who refuses to study because they know their parents want them to do well. The student expresses their anger toward their parents by coming home with D or F grades. Eventually it will backlash in their own life. They cannot get into college, or they are unable to have the vocational opportunities that would enhance their life.

Another example of expressing anger passively is a mate who needs orderliness, yet will not keep things neat, or purposely disrupts a living or work area. The messiness—which is really a means of expressing resentment—may distress this person's partner, co-workers, or employer, but the end result is discomfort and disruption for the person making the mess.

You can translate this principle to any other kind of situation. Employees who are often late, or will not do their work, because they are angry at their boss wind up fired and cannot support themselves or their family.

These are examples of ways in which people attempt to express anger indirectly. The problem with expressing anger in this passive manner is that whenever we do something indirectly to hurt someone, it backfires. It boomerangs to hurt us.

There are other ways that people express anger very subtly. They learn to do this so they will not get punished for expressing anger directly. They use sarcasm or "kidding." Now, there can be times when people kid around affectionately and it is not painful; however, sarcasm is the kind of comment that leaves you confused as to its meaning.

I refer to a sarcastic person as someone who has a stiletto tongue. Let me repeat for anyone who is reading this chapter first: A stiletto is a knife with a long, slender blade and a sharp point. Stiletto sarcasm slides in so subtly that you know you have been knifed, but you don't know what it means or how to respond. A person who is really talented in the use of stiletto sarcasm uses it in such a way that it leaves the recipient of the sarcasm confused, helpless, and hurt.

Obviously, if you are expressing anger through sarcasm, you are putting other people off. You are not allowing people to come into your life. This blocks personal and social relationships.

You may also jeopardize your work. For instance, you are at a meeting in a situation that is important for your future. If you let your anger come out as sarcasm toward your employer or client and you cause them to be uncomfortable, upset, or feel helpless, it certainly is not going to enhance your opportunities for vocational growth.

Here are some thoughts about freedom and bondage as they relate to anger. The original hippies had a statement to make about life. Their actions represented a philosophical perspective. They were challenging our culture's values and systems. Their beards and dirty bodies and unkempt clothing were an attempt to confront the inequities in our society. The significant contribution the hippies made at that time was to confront us with the way human beings are mistreated in our country.

There were also hangers-on among the hippies, people who were just angry. By directing their anger toward the broader community, they avoided their personal issue, which often was anger toward their parents. Because their anger was connected to their past, they were locked into a position where they did not have the freedom to choose what to do with their anger, so they did not have the freedom to choose what to do with their lives. They did not have the freedom to take a shower, to shave, or dress up. Unlike the philosophical hippie who had a social consciousness and was angry at the way human beings were oppressed, the hangers-on were mired in unresolved personal rebellion that was misdirected anger, and were, therefore, in bondage to their past.

At the risk of appearing to be a male chauvinist, let me say that a similar thing has happened in the women's movement. There is a difference between the "liberated woman" and a "women's libber."

The liberated woman can be a beautiful sight to behold. She has the freedom to choose after a man tells her what to do. She can say, "I am not going to do it, because it is not in my interest, or because it is not positive for this situation." Or she can say, "Yes, I will do it," even though she knows the man is a total *@%*. She will do it because she knows it is the best option for the situation, even though the source of the positive suggestion came from a man. She has the freedom to decide and act on her own behalf, unshackled by her anger at the man or at men.

Women's libbers are locked into their own anger. If a man tells them to do something, they have to defy the man because of their anger about previous terrible treatment from men. They refuse to do what a man tells them, even if it is in their own interest.

The unfortunate plight of men is that, for many, their oppression is so subtle and insidious that it goes unnoticed. At least women are trying to improve the injustice that exists.

The point is for you to be aware of the source of your anger. To discover the origin of your anger gives you the freedom of choice to defy, comply, or seek an alternative solution for the situation. In the example of the liberated woman, although she may be angry at the man, the anger does not prohibit her from taking care of herself and responding to the needs of the situation in the best way that she can. Men can learn from a liberated woman.

I think it would be great if we had a men's liberation movement that would encourage men to express their caring, sensitive, kind, softer side. I believe it has already begun. I know many kind, thoughtful, caring men. The shift in men's attitudes about self-expression has not, by the nature of its gentleness, been as conspicuous as the women's movement.

I have indicated some of the indirect ways people learn to cope with anger because they were not allowed, or taught, to express it in constructive ways. I mentioned the cultural training women get about aggression. Let me now illustrate what happens to men.

Males are taught that it is natural to be aggressive, even necessary to be aggressive. Boys are told to fight. Men are taught to be aggressive in business, to be the aggressor with dating women, and aggressive in protecting women.

Men are not only taught to be aggressive. They are also taught that they should not show pain, fear, or helplessness—all of which are considered weaknesses. They are taught that it is unmanly to be weak or vulnerable. A man therefore has always to look powerful and in control.

Men are taught this attitude in their families of learning and by other males, but it is also reinforced by women who are uncomfortable with—and attempt to interfere with—a man's revelation of his pain, fear, or helplessness. Men learn to avoid the hurt of having their feelings rejected by not showing them to a woman. This statement is contradictory to the popular opinion that some women have, that men are uncommunicative and will not express emotions. I know men who express their feelings to other men, but who hesitate to be vulnerable to women because they have had their feelings rejected by women.

I have experienced women who were angry at me, and other women who were frightened, when I cried during a movie. Some women have thought that I was weak because I cried. I thought I was simply being human. In fact, I believe that I am far more solid, durable, and strong because I can release my pain.

As a result of all these factors, a man learns to express aggression, but he expresses it at times when anger is not what he is truly feeling. When he is feeling hurt or helpless or vulnerable or frightened, he will often express anger. He may not even know the actual feeling and only be aware of anger.

He will not get his needs met this way. When he appears aggressively angry, people will either attack him, withdraw, or leave.

If he is already feeling frightened or hurt or helpless, what he really needs is to be comforted. What he gets is attacked and hurt more, or people withdraw, and that hurts, and he is even more frightened and feels more helpless. He will, then, become more self-protective, more cautious of appearing vulnerable, often more aggressive. It becomes a vicious circle.

I do not mean that only men do this. Women can also be aggressive and attack when they feel frightened or hurt or helpless. I do, however, think it is more true of men.

I am emphasizing the importance of being aware of your true feeling. When the feeling is anger, you need to express it in some constructively aggressive way, which I will explain later. If it is another feeling, it is important to express what the feeling really is. If you say "I am really hurt," or "I am feeling frightened," or "I feel helpless in this situation," the other person can respond to your true feeling. You create the opportunity for the person to comfort you, and the possibility of getting your needs met.

What are some constructive ways to express anger? As with any feeling (you will hear this often throughout this book) breathing is crucial. One way to release anger is by breathing. Breathing relaxes your body and allows your emotions to flow. I have already mentioned that anger is a form of energy. Breathing keeps your energy moving. If you block the flow of energy you create a lot of needless tension.

One way I have seen people "stuff" their anger is by smoking tobacco products. If you want confirmation for this point, ask a smoker either to not smoke or to blow their smoke away from you. Many people who smoke will show a tremendous amount of anger when you request smoke-free air. Sometimes you can even tell how angry a person is by the way they suck on their cigarette or blow out their smoke.

Some of you, as you read this, may become angry that I would suggest such a thing.

Once, with the encouragement of the leaders of an organization, I made a motion to have no smoking during the meetings of the organization. One woman dramatically, defiantly lit up a cigarette as I was making the motion. When I finished, another woman—who I thought was a friend —walked up to me and blew cigarette smoke in my face.

People block anger by smoking. A less aggressive example made this clear to me. A client, who had not yet got to the place where she could express anger directly, smoked. She also could not cry. She would get to the point where she was about to cry, and she would light up a cigarette.

I knew that behind the smoke were tears, and behind the tears was the anger. I decided to limit smoking in my office, because one purpose of therapy can be to release feelings, and I also needed to protect myself from the physical harm of smoke. I announced this to her at the beginning of the session. She could no longer stuff the feelings, and she cried for the whole fifty minutes of her session. Then it was a matter of helping her to move beyond that, so she could allow herself to be aggressive, and vent the anger.

A former client called me to say, "I haven't smoked for years, but I have been craving a cigarette for about two weeks. You seem to know a whole lot about smoking. Can I come see you?"

She did. Within a few minutes, we found out at whom she was angry. I helped her to release the anger. We set up another session.

She telephoned me and explained, "I don't need to see you again. I haven't had the urge to smoke since about twenty minutes after we started the session in your office. When you focused on my anger and I released it, the desire to smoke went with it."

Now, why do I mention the smoking and breathing? Because smoking forces you to breathe. Many people reach for a cigarette when they get tense. I believe they feel tense because, underneath the tension, there is a feeling of anger that is unacceptable to them.

They find that by smoking they relax, which is not surprising to me, because when you smoke, you have to breathe. If a person breathes *without* the cigarette, they are going to relax. I mentioned this to one of my clients, who is a chain smoker. During the next week, instead of reaching for the cigarette when he was angry at his job, he went out for a walk, did some deep breathing, and he felt no need for the cigarette. Breathing is a way of relaxing—even without a cigarette. So **breathing is a way to keep your energy flowing, to release anger, and to relax.**

Another way of constructively releasing anger is to confront the person you feel anger toward, and expressing, "I am angry at you about...." That opens the way for resolution.

Get ready for a Uhlerism: **Unexpressed anger is a barrier to affection.** When we hold in anger toward someone, it is difficult to experience affection toward that person. The other side is: **Released anger makes space for affection.**

One example: I had a person doing some typing for me. I had given her several pages. There were lines across the pages to divide segments of my project. I gave her several more of the completed papers to be typed. Then I noticed that she had put a line in as a divider where it did not belong. When I called it to her attention, she was angry, naturally.

As an angry person, she had several options. She could have stuffed the anger inside and continued to type, probably making a lot of mistakes. She could have slammed down the typewriter lid and said, "I'm not going to type for you any more if you don't give the material to me in a proper manner." She could have screamed and hollered, which might have helped her in some ways, but does not generally help relationships—unless the other person happens to be a psychologist. (I hope you laughed as much as I did when I reread this.)

Or she could have done what she did. She told me that she was really angry because I had caused her to make a mistake on the material she was typing, and now she had to do it over, and that was irritating.

When she expressed her anger clearly and directly, it worked out well. She had a chance to get it out of her system. I had an opportunity to explain that there was no attempt on my part to cause problems for her. She went typing merrily on her way.

That was one incident where it turned out to be a positive experience for both when a person let out her anger to another person.

Anger can be responded to by humor. This can be a plus and a minus. If we are angry about something, and somebody makes a friendly joke or comment that has humor in it, that can relieve a lot of tension, and it's terrific. We can also experience acceptance of our anger by warm, affectionate humor.

If, however, every time we express anger to someone, such as a mate, they make a joke out of it, that leads to more anger and helplessness—the combination that I refer to as frustration. There are times when we need to have our anger accepted and responded to directly by the other person. Humor can be a pleasant way of releasing tension, but it can also be a way of keeping a person at a distance. It can be a way of avoiding an issue.

We need to be aware of how we use humor in situations with someone who is angry.

In a really solid, safe, and secure relationship, in which both people know there is an enormous amount of caring, just shouting and hollering at each other to get it out of their system can benefit both people. It can also be fun to make up afterward.

In some relationships, each partner needs to take turns. The relationship breaks down if both people shout at the same time. However, if one person "blows their stack" while the other person calmly lets them vent, the ventor can get it out of their system. If the other person loses their cool and begins to shout, it can add fuel to an already blazing fire, and escalate the conflict into the stratosphere. This benefits neither party. By remaining calm, the flame is fueled only by the ventor's own anger. It will burn out quickly, once discharged.

One value of expressing anger to a safe friend or mate is that you have the advantage of assessing what is behind it. This is especially helpful if the anger is from some source other than the present situation. It can help you to understand where the anger is coming from, then provide an opening to deal with it in a positive way. If you feel safe with the other person, they can accept your anger and, if necessary, help you understand it. You can trust that their observations are intended to benefit you. When you are accepted and enlightened, you can deal with the anger in a constructive way.

There are times when the relationship is not the type that will permit this to happen and there are situations that are neither safe nor constructive.

An example: I was playing a tennis match with a man. I was a better player than he was, yet he criticized me every time I missed a stroke. I was getting more and more angry, but did not believe he could deal well with my anger. I knew that some of the anger was not connected to him. It was coming from my past. I held it inside until later, when I knew I could release it.

I did what some people would consider crazy. I went to a store where they had tennis racquets on sale. I found some inexpensive ones, took them into the woods near my house, and smashed them on a tree!

It got the anger out of my system. It didn't harm the other person in any way. It didn't disrupt the tennis match. It didn't damage the tree. I didn't stuff the anger into my back or head, and didn't have physical or emotional agony afterward. I felt relief.

My sons had a good laugh when they looked in the bag to see the pieces of broken wood and tennis racquet strings. I felt fantastic, and it was a lot cheaper than seeing a therapist! There are a couple of ways I suggest to people to help them release anger. Often, simply hollering in the privacy of your car, your room, or some other safe spot is a way to get it out. Hollering gets the energy moving. The most important part of getting feelings out of your system is to keep your energy flowing.

It can be useful to throw in a few slang or swear words when you are hollering. One of the ways we have been controlled or limited in expressing our anger is by being taught that we should not say certain words. To use those terms can be a way to release anger. I don't need to mention them in this book. If you ride on a school bus, go to work, listen to television, or go shopping, you hear these terms. They can be effective in releasing your anger.

Another way to release anger is to pound on pillows with your fists or a tennis racquet. Some people with physical problems prefer pounding with a racquetball racquet, which is lighter than a tennis racquet. Instead of using pillows, you can use a mattress (preferably with no one on it). These are aggressive ways to release the energy we call anger without hurting anyone.

If you are an adult with children, it is a good idea to explain to your children what you are doing when you do this. I have encouraged some of my clients, when they are angry, to explain to their child, "I am going into my bedroom. I will be pounding and shouting. When you hear it, don't be alarmed. It is just my way of releasing some anger."

When I have seen the client in the next session, they would often have the following story to tell. Their child came running home from school or the playground, and said, "Where is the tennis racquet?"

Then they headed into their bedroom, pounded away, got it out of their system, and came out feeling great. By explaining to your children what you are doing, you can warn them, so they won't be frightened. You also teach them a constructive outlet for their own anger, which benefits them and harms nobody.

Some women enjoy another way more. I have suggested to them that they seek out a yard sale or some other place where they can get some inexpensive dishes. They should then take them down into their basement and throw them against the wall. They love it. (How about men doing the same?)

If you are married and have a friendship with your husband, it can be even better for you if you ask him to clean up the mess after you have thrown the dishes. That way, you don't have to "pay" for having expressed anger. There has too often in our lives been some form of punishment for expressing anger. If your mate will cooperate, it will be a more delightful, freeing experience.

I'm sure this sounds quite scary to some of you, especially if you have been taught not to be aggressive. It sounds ridiculous to others. Try it. You might like it.

Let me emphasize that, in some situations, it can be tremendously constructive to express anger aggressively. Sometimes I use my anger to accomplish something. I think of my anger as a laser. It is not loud or violent. It is just focused energy. When I release my anger, *things move!*

There can be times when you are in a situation in which you need to protect yourself from getting hurt. I recall walking down a street on a dark night. I heard the feet of a running dog kicking up stones as it rushed down a driveway in my direction. It was so dark that I couldn't see the dog, but I said angrily, "Stop right there!" The dog did, and I heard the gravel flying as he headed in the other direction.

Do not think anger is unkind. It can be very caring. There are times when I get angry at a person for hurting themselves with some stupidly self-destructive act. In such a situation, I sometimes feel only anger, sometimes helplessness mixed with the anger. Sometimes the anger needs to be expressed in a forceful way, other times, in a gentle way.

When a person knows without a doubt that you care for them, they know that your anger is there because you care. To tell the person pointedly of your anger can be more than caring. It can change lives. I have seen people turn their lives around because of the combination of love and firmly expressed anger.

I have hit people verbally. Once in a therapy session I saw a couple who, during their first session, were mercilessly vicious in their attacks on each other. I watched this a bit. They continued. After a few minutes, I bellowed, "Shut up! If you want to treat each other that way, go home and do it. Don't do it in front of me, because it makes me sick. I can't stomach seeing you treat each other that way."

They stopped.

Another time, a mean male client, with whom I had been very understanding and kind, made a really cutting, snide remark to me. I swore and hollered at him for several minutes with every word I had learned in the steel mill, and finished it off by shouting, "If it weren't for the wonderful woman who's with you, I'd throw you to #/*(%\@#^! out of my office!"

He was much bigger than I, but he sat there and took it. His mate apparently decided that, if I wasn't afraid of him, she did not need to be, either, and she never let him hit her again.

Several years later he saw me on the street. He came running up all smiles, to tell me how well things were going between them, and how happy they were together.

Let me give you another example of how anger can be caring. Quite a few years ago, I was driving on a four lane highway. There was a car turned over, sitting on its top. There were a lot of people standing around it as I drove up. The driver was still inside his car. I parked my car. Then I went over to help the man get out of his car through the smashed rear window and helped him off the highway.

I encouraged some men who were standing there, watching, to help me roll the car over. After righting it, we began to push the car into a large parking lot along the side of the road. As we were pushing the car, the proprietor of the store adjacent to the lot came running out, screaming, "You can't put that car in here. Get that thing out of here."

I turned to him and said firmly, "Back off! I am helping this man who is hurt. We are going to put his car in this lot."

The proprietor backed right down. He became polite, and offered to help. That was plenty aggressive of me, but it was also constructive.

I am attempting to convince you that: (1) anger definitely is an acceptable emotion; (2) aggression can be a very positive expression of yourself; (3) withholding anger can be uncaring; and (4) expressing anger can be kind.

I am not encouraging aggression to be hurtful or harmful, but I am encouraging you to express anger to assist someone who needs help, or for the purpose of limiting other people who would attempt to hurt you. Anger can be a motivating force for positive accomplishments. Combined forces stemming from anger have constructively rectified injustices (See "Helplessness").

In the first chapter I mentioned that underlying every one of the thoughts I present to you is the idea of caring for other people and for yourself. Aggressive caring can be a powerful, positive force—when used properly. **Caring anger can empower people to create constructive change**

If you do not allow anger to be an acceptable experience for yourself, then you are going to stuff it, and it is going to come out in some indirect way, with destructive results. If you hold it inside, it is going to cause you emotional and physical harm.

The value of accepting anger as an emotion is that, once you are aware of it, you can clarify its source. Then you have the option to choose how to release it, or to hold it in, until you can release it in the future.

I have seen women who were absolutely gorgeous when they were angry. They became alive, expressive, elegantly forceful. I wish that kind of beauty and power for men and women alike.

I encourage you to enjoy experiencing your anger and the opportunity to choose satisfying outlets for it.

PLEASE, express your anger with caring.

Cherish your anger, and cherish yourself for learning how to express it.

Your anger is beautiful—and so are you!

***C**rying is <u>not</u> breaking down.*

It is LETTING GO.

*P*ain

Pain is often more painful than necessary.
Few people understand pain. They don't know what to do with it. They are taught to hold it in—not how to release it. Holding pain in your body intensifies the emotional trauma that will get turned into, or add to, the already existing physical pain.
Internalized pain intensifies pain.
Released pain provides relief.
During the separation at the end of my marriage, I was driving to a clinic where I worked. I was feeling sad about the end of my marriage. As I drove, I sobbed out the pain for about three minutes. I felt relief, and went on to have a wonderful day.

If I had kept the pain inside and blocked it, like a lot of people do, I would have felt "bummed out" the rest of the day. I would have experienced a headache, a feeling of heaviness in my chest, and probably would not have been much good for anybody, including myself. As it turned out, I felt really chipper and had a great time.

I want to emphasize the value of understanding pain, and knowing what to do with it.

It is possible that reading this chapter may bring to the surface some pain you are carrying inside of you. This may be happening even though you are not aware of experiencing pain. *If you have difficulty reading this chapter, it may be because you are experiencing pain. You might want to turn to the end of the chapter and read "How to Release Pain."*

Just as the last part of each chapter teaches you ways to release the emotion, the end of this chapter suggests ways to release your pain.

Don't let this frighten you. You will probably find it comforting to read this chapter. I know, however, that many, many people have a lot of pain in their life, and I want to be sensitive to that fact as we embark on our journey through it.

For some of you, it may be comforting or enlightening or just plain fun to read this chapter with someone with whom you feel safe, so you can share your thoughts, feelings, past events, and joy of learning together during the course of your reading.

Let me explain what pain is. Some people say "pain" is physical and "hurt" is emotional. I do not want to make that distinction. Physical pain that people experience can be very closely connected to emotional pain. Each of these two types of pain can create the other.

A person who is hurt physically, and unable to do the things they would usually do, will experience emotional pain. When a person has emotional pain from the death of a loved one, it causes physical pain. When emotional pain is held inside for a period of time, it causes chronic physical pain. I do not make a distinction between pain and hurt, so I will be using the terms interchangeably throughout the chapter.

Some people think that psychosomatic conditions are not physical pain. They say, "It's all in their head." Let me emphasize that psychosomatic pain is physical pain.

I had a client who could barely get out of bed because she had so much pain. I sent her to a chiropractor, whom she had seen previously, just to determine how much of the pain was physical and how much was emotional. He alleviated about half of it, and said the rest of the pain was emotional.

She and I already had an appointment scheduled for that day. I saw her and we dealt with the emotional causes. She walked out of the office pain-free.

It is important to recognize the source of the pain, and to be as clear as possible about the cause of both the physical and the emotional suffering.

Having said that, I want to emphasize that **the worst kind of emotional pain is pain that comes from self-rejection.**

Many people think the worst pain is the hurt that comes from somebody else. That is certainly painful. For instance, if someone you love throws up a wall against you, blocking off the affection you have for them, that is enormously painful. When you love someone and they attack you, that hurts tremendously. When you see someone whom you love doing things that are self-destructive and hurting themselves, the pain can be nearly unbearable.

To reject yourself, however, is the greatest affliction a person can experience. The treatment we receive from somebody else can obviously be very painful, but the most devastating and debilitating pain is that which comes from hurting ourselves by rejecting our self.

Let me expand on that. If somebody says to you, "You are selfish," it can hurt a lot. Many people have heard as a child, at one point or another, "You are selfish."

What does the word *selfish* actually represent? It is a "put-down," to put you off. If you ask for something and are told that you are selfish, it means that the name caller doesn't want to give you what you request. Telling you that you are selfish is intended to make you feel guilty about asking. The hope is that you will stop saying what you want. Then the name caller can go on their way without responding to your needs. Who is really the selfish one? Are you, or is the person who put the "selfish" label on you?

If you have often in the past heard from your parents that you are selfish, you will probably believe the person who is presently accusing you of the same thing, and you will feel hurt. If you have been called selfish in your family of learning, it is possible that twenty years later, when somebody tells you that you are selfish, you will accept the label and believe you deserve it.

The reasons it hurts are: (1) your needs are not met, (2) you feel rejected by the other person, and most significantly, (3) you have internalized the rejection received from the past and reject yourself. **Self-rejection causes the most pain.**

If somebody says to you, "You are weird," are you going to feel hurt by it? You will probably think they are joking and laugh about it. I like to have fun and make comments that cause people to laugh. Sometimes I'm told that I am weird by my kids, clients, and friends, so I get to laugh with them.

If somebody indignantly says that you are a Martian, you think, "I wonder what their problem is?" It is clear to you that you are not from Mars, nor of Martian ancestry, so you don't hurt yourself with it. (If there are any Martians reading this, I do not mean to be offensive.)

A lot of the pain you experience when somebody accuses you comes from self-accusation. It is the result of indicting yourself. You experience pain when you believe the other person's accusations, accept the label, and judge yourself as being bad. Self-rejection is the most painful wound.

Another form of self-rejection is guilt. Everyone suffers from guilt sometime in their life. **Guilt is a feeling which occurs when we turn anger in on ourselves. Guilt is turning anger into the pain of self-blame—a form of self-rejection.**

There are times when we feel guilty and there is no just cause. Often this occurs when someone dies. One of the feelings that accompanies grieving is guilt.

An example: I was visiting a man in a funeral home just after his mother's death. I sat down beside him, and asked, "How are you doing?"

He replied, "I'm really hurting. I am feeling a lot of guilt."

I asked him, "What are you feeling guilty about?"

He replied, "I don't know. I did everything I could for my mother."

I responded, "I know you did, but I am not surprised that you are feeling guilty, because guilt is one of the feelings we have when someone dies."

What happens inside when someone dies and you feel guilty, even though you have done nothing wrong? Our mind does not like ambiguity. It likes a focus for our feelings, so it becomes like a police scanner. It goes: "beep, beep, beep, beep," picking out something from the past as a peg on which to hang the guilt feelings. When your mind finds a suitable peg, a past omission or a negative action, you will think, "Oh, that's why I am feeling guilty. I didn't tell him I loved him." Or, "I told her that I hated her" (twenty-five years ago).

When we feel guilt, it is imperative to realize that the guilt says nothing about the quality of person you are. It only says you are feeling guilty.

Guilt is pain that comes from turning anger toward yourself about things that you think you should have done for, or should not have done to, the person who died. It is only a feeling of "badness," not a realistic indication that you are bad. It only means that you are having the natural feelings that occur when someone you love dies. If you feel guilty and believe you are a bad person, you will feel the pain that is already a part of any loss or death, plus the undeserved pain caused by the feeling of guilt.

The truth about this feeling of guilt is that it is not truthful. It tells you lies, saying that you are bad, which is untrue.

When your guilt lies to you as your mind finds an omission or action from your past, you must remind yourself of your innocence. Review your positive qualities to dilute the guilt and to renew your appreciation for yourself.

If you made a list of the things that you like about yourself, as I encouraged at the end of the "Affection" chapter, you can look at that list to remind yourself of your lovableness. If you do not have a self-love list, you might want to glance at the last few pages of that chapter to give you ideas or to start your own list.

Pain is unnecessarily increased when it is intensified by other feelings that accompany it. Guilt is one of those feelings. By disbelieving guilt's attempt to show that you are bad, you can alleviate the additional pain that does not need to co-exist with the pain you already have.

Any time you feel guilty, for any reason, is a good time to get out your "Self-Love List." (See pages 96-97.)

Many people have found it a tremendous relief to know that guilt is a typical feeling that occurs during certain events, and indicates nothing about their goodness or badness. It simply exists.

I hope that I have said it enough times and in enough ways to make that point clear to you. Understanding that feeling guilt tells you nothing about the kind of person you really are can be a matter of emotional and physical life and death. Gnawing guilt can eat away at your body, drain your vitality, and put you in a living hell, often ending in an early death. Managing guilt is important for creating a healthy life.

I do not say this to scare you, only to emphasize the seriousness of this message. If it still doesn't make sense to you, please contemplate the previous comments until you comprehend the contents and can apply them to your life.

How to Release Pain

Let us now look at the best way to vent pain.

Breathing is a great way to release stress connected with any feeling. To breathe deeply in and out relaxes your body, and releases the body tension that accompanies pain.

Another way to release pain is by sobbing. Crying can be wonderful. Many people think they are crying if they let a few trickles of tears run down their cheeks. That is not what I mean. I mean SOBBING! Through sobbing, you are breathing deeply into your stomach. Deep breathing helps you to sob more freely, and to let out sobbing sounds that go with it.

I teach people who have difficulty crying to exercise what I call the "crying reflex." People who have been taught not to cry, use their muscles to block crying. By getting the crying reflex going, even if you don't feel like crying at the moment, you are training your body to move as though you are sobbing. You are flexing and loosening your muscles so you can cry when you need to cry. This preparation can lead to liberating your body from pain.

Practicing the crying reflex uses the same principle that applies to perfecting a sports activity or athletic skill, except that you are practicing perfecting the game of living life to its fullest. This is the most worthwhile aspiration of all.

The tears that come with crying are a way of washing out pain. Sobbing is a way to get your whole body to free itself from the pain. You have perhaps heard the statement, "What you need is a good cry."

To see what real sobbing is, I suggest you observe a young child who is experiencing a few moments of sobbing. They cannot speak, they gasp for breath between bursts of sobs, their shoulders and chest heave and shake, and tears flow in seemingly endless waves. *That* is **sobbing!**

Sobbing children are not out of control. They are letting go. I was sobbing at the funeral home in front of my grandmother's casket. I stopped immediately when some strangers came to say goodbye to her. Contrary to some people's belief, it is very possible to sob and still have control of yourself.

Let me describe sobbing more clinically. Your diaphragm moves when you breathe deeply and sob freely. Your diaphragm is just below your lungs, and extends into your stomach area. By breathing deeply into your diaphragm with your diaphragm muscles flexing and by relaxing into sobbing, you get your whole body to release, and you thereby free yourself from pain.

What happens if you don't do that? The chances are that you will have "sinus difficulties." Sometimes what people label as sinus problems are actually blocked tear ducts.

You might also have a lot of tension in your neck and shoulders, from the fear of expressing the pain.

Another physical symptom caused by emotional pain is an ache in the heart or chest. Pain is the feeling most often stored in the heart. It seems as though men have more heart attacks than women. Men also have more difficulty releasing their pain. They are taught to hold it inside, which creates stress on the heart muscles. Holding hurt in our heart muscles makes the muscles lose their flexibility.

You provide relief for your muscles and allow them to regain their elasticity by releasing the pain, which allows the muscles to move as they were designed to move. Heart muscles were not made as a storage tank for feelings. They work best when they are sufficiently relaxed to pump blood.

You have heard the common expression "died of a broken heart." This colloquialism is an accurate intuition connected to holding sadness, the pain of loss, in your heart.

If you are able to sob, you can eliminate much of the physical pain that gets labeled heart or sinus problems.

Many people have been told not to cry. Men, especially, hear this: "Men should not cry," or "Big boys don't cry." People get told, "Stop crying or I'll really give you something to cry about." This is unfortunate. People learn it is unacceptable for them to release their pain by crying. You would not be crying if you did not have something to cry about.

It is disastrous when parents, or anybody else, tell children to stop crying because "Big boys don't cry." What this message precipitates—especially for men—is a lot of stress. If a man feels hurt, he doesn't show the pain for fear of rebuke. He holds it inside, or expresses it by what looks like anger. When others see the anger, they respond by either withdrawing or attacking. That causes more pain. What the man really needs is to be comforted.

I am not saying that this is strictly a male trait. Women do the same thing, but it is more common for men to be blocked from expressing pain.

Whenever you see someone (particularly a man) who looks as though they are angry, it is a good idea to ask yourself if pain is underneath the anger. If you do that, you can respond to what the person is really feeling, rather than respond to what they are showing.

Or, if you find yourself angry, you can ask, "I wonder if there is pain underneath this anger? Perhaps my true feeling is pain and my anger is masking it." To search for and discover the core feeling is crucial to understanding yourself and to understanding others. Acquiring this skill will contribute to enjoyable friendships.

An action that disrupts relationships is when a person expresses one feeling, but is really experiencing a different one. It is confusing when someone diverts attention from pain by attacking. What is necessary is to share the true feeling. When you share the core feeling, it can build closeness in a friendship.

A friend once angrily attacked me for about twenty minutes when we were driving home from an event. Knowing that I had done nothing to precipitate the attack and that the accusations did not apply to me, I simply stayed focused, objective, and waited quietly. (Don't jump to the false conclusion that I always wait quietly!)

My friend then began to cry. As we discussed it, it became clear that the actual feelings were pain and fear. Her willingness to express the bottom line feelings provided her with the opportunity to receive comfort and closeness. My caring patience with her, and my clarity that I had done nothing to instigate her wrath, turned what could have been a fight into a time of tenderness.

This is a marvelous opportunity to declare, shout, quietly emphasize, bellow, or do whatever else is necessary to get your attention.

It is wonderful to be close, receiving and giving affection without first having a fight. **I encourage lovers to treat each**

other as though they are making up after a fight, without having the fight!!!

Many years ago, a friend showed me a line in a book, the title and author of which I have long forgotten. I have not, however, forgotten the words, written by a woman social worker in Canada: "Women *respect* men for their power; they *love* men for their vulnerability."

One of the ways of being truly close in a friendship is by expressing pain and crying together. It can be one of the ways of becoming more intimate. It can lead to sex in a truly loving, caring way. A man who is unable to express his pain misses a tremendous amount of closeness and comfort.

A man must also avoid jumping to the conclusion that a woman is feeling pain when she cries. Even though you see her tears, do not necessarily believe that the true feeling is pain. Due to the training a woman receives, she may be crying when she is angry. In the relationship of a woman with another person, or with herself, it is essential to discover the actual feeling. Whether the tears indicate pain or anger, the important message here is to invite the crying person to talk about their feelings and the precipitating factors that led to the tears.

It can help a friendship for a person to express anger constructively. Caring expressions of anger can lead to closeness. Both sexes benefit when a person of either sex *shares* authentic feelings.

Most of you have heard the saying "You are just feeling sorry for yourself," when you were showing pain. What that usually means is that the person labeling you is uncomfortable with your pain. They don't know what to do with it. They don't know how to respond to it, so they try to "guilt trip" you into stuffing it. I believe it is natural to feel sorry for yourself, meaning to feel sad about your involvement in a painful life experience.

If somebody pushes you away when they see you are hurt, often it is because they feel helpless to do anything about your pain. Seeing pain in someone else can cause us to feel helpless, because we want to eliminate their pain. Seldom is there a way to alleviate the pain for somebody else. They must do it for themselves by releasing the pain through crying. What we can do—which is a lot—is to be there, accepting the feelings and providing whatever comfort the person wants.

Another reason someone will push you away when you are in pain is because they have a lot of pain inside themselves, which they have learned to stuff, or at least have not learned how to release. They try to avoid their own pain by getting you to stop expressing yours.

I cannot emphasize this too much. If you have learned that you should not express your pain, or if you were told that you're just feeling sorry for yourself—don't believe it! You *need* to express your pain. You **must** express your pain!

You do not need to express your pain alone. What you do need is to find somebody who has enough comfort with your pain to allow you to show it and to support you while you release it.

For myself, I find it is wonderfully comforting, when I am hurt and need to cry, to have somebody hold me. The physical warmth of a caring person can be enormously comforting.

Let me follow up on the phrase "just feeling sorry for yourself." Let's make a distinction between "suffering" and "facing pain."

Some people get into the habit of suffering. They have learned that the only way they can get attention is by suffering. Other people have, for other reasons, adopted a position in life where they suffer. You might get clubbed to death if you try to take away their suffering.

Everybody has undoubtedly seen someone who clings to their suffering. It can be easy to believe that you are just like that person when you are in pain.

Let me suggest a way to make a distinction between yourself and the cling-to-their-suffering kind of person. If you face your pain, sob to release it, and feel better afterward, you know you have released pain in a constructive way, because you feel a sense of relief and relaxation. After you release your pain, you may feel like sleeping. That does not mean that you are tired. It means that you are relaxed. That is great.

When some people move into their pain, they "wallow" in it. They feel more pain, and then more pain, and more, and so on. It is a downward spiral. The pain only leads to more pain! That can be a warning sign that you are moving in a negative direction. When the downward spiral happens, it is just suffering. That benefits nobody, neither yourself nor those around you.

However, when you avoid pain, it can have very destructive physical and emotional consequences. It is important for you to "move into" and deal with the pain you feel.

You need to assess what your pain or suffering means. It may mean that you need to really let go by sobbing, not just trickling a few tears. It may mean that you need to find new interests or friends. It may mean that you need to shift your thinking to something other than your suffering—to pleasant, productive, happy thoughts. It may mean that you must take action to change something. It may mean that you need to talk to a minister, or other mental health professional, because you need assistance to make the changes necessary to alleviate the pain.

Move through the pain in whatever way is useful for you. You certainly do not need intense suffering in your life.

There are times when people invite or bring on pain, such as listening to a really sad song. They purposely play it to feel sad. It can be a way of suffering, or it can be a way of remembering someone you have lost, bringing the sadness into focus and crying out the pain.

Once again, the way to know if you are constructively focusing on pain and releasing it, or are merely suffering, is to assess your intent and to observe how you feel afterwards. If you just continue to feel worse the longer you listen to the song with no relief, it means you are into "heavy suffering."

If you find, when you listen to the song, that you sob and feel better, then you have used the song as a way of moving into the pain and releasing it.

Let's look at a variation of this: A person who sobs and feels worse has been taught that crying is negative. At some point in their life, they were punished for crying. Now when they cry, they experience what I refer to as "afterburn."

The afterburn may be fear from the past, because you were punished for crying. It may be a fear of "breaking down." It may be anger at yourself for being "weak," an attitude that you acquired from your family of learning. It may be pain from having internalized other of your parents' attitudes about crying, so that now you punish yourself when you cry. It may be the "emotional memory" stemming from previous times when you were punished after you cried, so that when you cry now, you feel the old pain plus the present pain, which doubles your pain when you cry, instead of bringing you relief.

Perhaps you have been taught you are "bad" when you cry—then you will feel guilt. If you have been taught that only weak people cry, then you will feel shame. Both attitudes bring pain.

If you do not feel relief after crying, it may be because of afterburn relating to something you were taught earlier in your life about crying. If you are not more relaxed after crying, then another unpleasant feeling has slipped in. It can be beneficial to discover why you do not have a sense of peace after you cry. Consider any one of the reasons I have mentioned.

Here is something to remember when you are experiencing pain. My mother has often reminded me of it in my life: "This too shall pass." There are times when you are really hurt, but the next morning the pain will be reduced, if not fully allevi-ated. Sometimes it is gone the next minute.

It helps to realize that pain is just a feeling. It is like the New England weather. It will change shortly. Even though it is important to take pain seriously, it is also very important not to take it too seriously.

Recognize that "THIS TOO SHALL PASS."

This is different from "Time heals." Time does not necessarily heal. Releasing pain heals, which takes time. To say that time heals can be a way to avoid facing pain.

Let me conclude by encouraging you never to run away from pain.

People try to avoid pain by drinking alcoholic beverages, or by taking street drugs or prescribed drugs. That creates more serious problems for themselves. When a person drinks and does drugs, they may temporarily avoid some pain, but cause a lot more pain in their life, and an enormous amount of pain for the people around them.

Other destructive ways of avoiding pain are work, food, shopping, sex, and cigarettes—as in workaholic, foodaholic, shopaholic, sexaholic, and smokeaholic. (See the chapter "Anger".)

Another way of refusing to face pain is to push it down inside and pretend it is not there. When you won't share pain, or refuse to share it, you block a major way of connecting with other people. If people want intimacy with you, expressing your pain with them is going to benefit them as well as you. They will appreciate your trust in them, and cherish the closeness.

The main point here is the importance of facing pain. When you face pain, you then have an opportunity to decide what to do with it. I hope you will decide to release it.

A value of being aware of your pain is knowing you are alive! If you live in this universe, you are going to have pain. You are going to have your own pain, and you will have pain when you see it in other people. If you don't have pain, either you are medicated, are walking around like a zombie, are "numbed out," or are dead inside—hardened and cold. If you face pain, then you are alive—and human.

Going over this chapter to edit it has been painful for me, as I have reflected on hurtful events in my life and thought of the pain in the lives of people for whom I care deeply.

I commend you for your courage and tenacity in reading this chapter, and hope you have been able to cry as you have experienced the need to do so. I hope you have people in your life to share your tears with, and who will comfort you.

For me, I choose to experience the pain of my life. I choose to embrace my pain, risk sharing it with trustworthy people, and enjoy the comfort and intimacy that follow. I want to be an emotionally expressive, alive, and vibrant person!

I wish for you a life full of the depth and richness of your emotions, and a total awareness of the radiant beauty that is in you.

Tears can be beautiful. Shared tears can be *exceptionally beautiful!*

You are *beautiful!*

*F*ear does NOT predict the future.

Fear

Fear tells you only one thing—that you are afraid.
The task then is to discover the origin of your fear. Sometimes the fear comes from the past. Sometimes it is from the present situation. Sometimes it is a warning about the future. The trick is to discover which of these is the source of the fear.

People tend to believe that their fear is caused by people or events in the present moment. Based on my observations, I am convinced that in most situations when people are frightened, the fear comes from past traumatic experiences. Such misconceptions complicate their relationships and confuse their lives.

When feelings from our past or feelings in anticipation of a future event are perceived to have their source in a current predicament, we will usually choose a response based on inaccurate information. This not only will not work—it often works against us.

An example: You meet a nice person who is potentially a good friend or mate but, because of your fear, you keep them at a distance, or tell them that you don't want to see them again. Another fear response is the yo-yo version, where you get very close, then get very distant, then close, then distant, and on and on, until the other person has had enough of being treated like a yo-yo, and ends the relationship.

Here is an example of the way we blend the past and the future with the present: If we have been abused in the past, we learn to protect ourselves when we think we are being attacked in the present. What we believe to be self-protection can be an overreaction, because we do not separate past and future from the present.

An example of the effects of fear can be the image of a Native American looking into the water for fish as he slowly paddles his way up the river with his bow and arrow lying in the front of his canoe. He suddenly finds himself barraged by cannonballs. Looking up, he sees a fort in the distance. The fort is inhabited by people who were frightened, so they showered cannon balls on this innocent, peaceful man as though he were the whole Apache Nation attacking their fort.

This kind of situation can occur when a person brings fear connected with past experiences into the present relationship with their mate, children, friends, colleagues, and coworkers, or even passersby. Although the fear is coming from their past, the person perceives the threat of attack in the present, and responds totally out of proportion to the reality of the present situation.

The reality testing of the fisherman in the previous example is wholly intact if he perceives the threat to be a present danger. Those are real cannonballs splashing around him. He had better respond to the present or he will be wounded or killed.

The people in the fort may have precipitated a realistic fear of attack in the future. If the fisherman escapes, he may bring his tribe to attack the fort, in retaliation. The tragedy is that the people in the fort are seldom aware that their fears, based on past experiences and expectations of pain, are preventing a potentially positive friendship with the Native American. The people in the fort are even less aware that they have brought the possibility of an impending attack on themselves.

If we believe we are being attacked and are not aware that the perception is based on past fears, or fears of the future, we either unnecessarily drive people away, or needlessly invite attack by them.

Where do the fears connected to the past come from? They come from previous experiences of neglect or abuse. The first place we live is within our family of learning. If our needs were not met in our own family of learning, we begin to fear that no one else will respond to our needs. We operate with that negative expectation in mind in our contacts with other people. Unless we are with a particularly astute and caring person, we will not get our needs met, because the other person is not aware of the fear that is our barrier. Even if the other person recognizes the fear, they probably do not know how to overcome it. The fear from the past therefore interferes with our present life, blocking us from getting what we want or need.

The fear related to our past family can also come from physical abuse, from emotional abuse, or from incestuous activity within the family. It can come from competition for affection. It can come from unsuccessful attempts to be loved by one or both of our parents. It can come from having experienced rejection as a child because of a divorce, death, or a parent leaving for some reason. It can come from expectations our parents placed on us, our inability to measure up to their often unrealistic expectations and the feelings of fear, rejection, and pain that followed.

Fear can come from playing sports in which we are pitting our talents or physical strength against someone who is better. When we have competed with somebody and have been scolded or scorned because we did not overpower the other person, we will dread competing again.

School is another source of fear when teachers use fear rather than caring to try to motivate students.

Obviously, all through our early lives, and continuing into vocational life and relationships, **fear is a part of our existence as human beings. To deny that part of ourselves is only to create internal confusion, conflict, and complications.**

Let me emphasize that fear is a natural part of life. We cannot live in our world without being afraid, any more than we can live in our world without having some prejudice. Prejudice is a form of fear. I remember, probably twenty-five years ago, listening to Woodie White, now Bishop White of the United Methodist Church. He was speaking about how pervasive prejudice is in our culture. He asked a question that has stuck with me all these years. It was: "What color is a skin-colored Band-Aid?" This brought to my awareness the point that, at that time, the only "skin-colored" Band-Aids available were pink. This is just one subtle form of prejudice. It is impossible for a person in our culture not to be prejudiced. It is also impossible to be free from fear.

There have been times when I have disliked myself and felt guilty when I would become aware of my own prejudice against a person of a different skin color. I would need to remind myself that it didn't mean that I was bad. It simply meant that I was smart enough to learn well the wrong information. If we treat other people harshly or unkindly because of our prejudices, we deserve to feel guilty about our actions. To judge ourselves for our thoughts or feelings on which we do not act, however, is harsh and unkind to ourselves.

I remember experiencing my own prejudice when I was in college. There was an African-American man with whom I had become friendly. At that time at Union College in Kentucky, there were no black students living on campus. They all commuted to campus.

One day he came up to me really excited and told me he had received an A on one of his tests. I was excited for him. I shook his hand and was happy for him. However, the rest of the day the thought kept invading my mind, telling me to wash my hands. Each time I would become aware that the reason for this thought was because I had shaken hands with a black man, I felt really angry with myself. I did not want to be prejudiced toward anyone, yet I had always been taught that when my hands were dirty from being in contact with something black, I should wash them.

The point I am trying to make is that **previous lessons learned well in the past, which made an impression on us, have a powerful impact on our present life.** To be angry at yourself for having any thought or emotion, regardless of whether the feeling comes from the past or the present, does an injustice to yourself. **Fear is a natural part of being human in our culture.** Whether the fear came from your family of learning or from the present setting, **you need to embrace it—and yourself.**

The past can be a powerful force in relationships with a mate. It is very seldom that a person can get into an intense, committed relationship with someone without it's being complicated by feelings connected with their relationship with their parents.

This is especially true in the area of fear. If we were excessively controlled by one or both of our parents, we will have the fear of being "controlled" by our mate. If we were rejected by our parents, pushed away, punished by seclusion in a room, it is probable that we will have a fear of rejection. If a parent died, or we lost a parent through divorce, it can lead to an apprehension that our present mate will abandon us for some reason.

If our needs were not met by our parents, we may have a fear that our new mate will not respond to our needs. We may even fear expressing our needs. Some children learn that they should not express what they want or need, and are told that they are selfish for asking. The result is that, when they grow up, they still don't directly express their needs, wants, or wishes to others. This is a handicap that can interfere with their relationships. People who cannot express themselves can become resentful that they don't get what they want from their friend, mate, or coworkers. Other people—who want to give to them—become frustrated, because they can't get the information they need to provide what the fearful person wants. Either scenario leads to rupture in relationships.

The belief that no one will respond to our needs can lead to what psychological jargon refers to as a "self-fulfilling prophecy": A person brings about that which they fear.

Here is an illustration of a self-fulfilling prophecy: Tom is working in his yard, mowing his lawn. His lawn mower suddenly breaks down. He can't fix it, so he decides to ask to borrow his neighbor's mower. On the way across the yard to his neighbor's house, Tom thinks: "There is no way he is going to let me borrow his lawn mower." As he continues to his neighbor's door, he is convincing himself that his neighbor will not let him use the mower. He arrives at his neighbor's house and knocks on the door. When the door opens, Tom says angrily, "I didn't want to borrow your lawn mower anyway," turns on his heel, and leaves. Tom blocked himself from getting what he needed because of his fear that he could not have it.

Another disruption to relationships that stems from our family of learning arises if our parents told us we were responsible for them and for their feelings. We can then have the fear that, if someone we are with is upset, we are responsible and will get blamed, or we may even blame ourselves without any thought of rebuke coming from the other person. We then create a lot of tension in ourselves, and often in our relationships, by our attempts to keep everything running smoothly so no one will get upset. The result often is that other people resent what they experience as being controlled. They do not realize that we are trying to protect ourselves from the painful self-blame we anticipate if anything goes "wrong" and someone is upset.

All through our early lives, and continuing into vocational life and adult relationships, fear is a part of our existence as human beings. To deny the fearful part of ourselves is only to create internal confusion, conflict, and complications.

Many of our experiences cause fear in our current relationships. I think it is imperative to be aware of our past, so that we can be aware when it sneaks into the present. It is especially important to be aware of the dynamics of the relationship between our parents—and how our parents treated us—so we can manage the fear that was created back then, and can see our mates and friends realistically, rather than clothed in the emotional garments of our parents. When we are familiar with our family's influence on our present life, we can separate our mate as the focus of our fears.

Let us now consider how fear is connected to the present. An example: I was mugged some years back. I was standing on the sidewalk reading a newspaper article on business dynamics in which I was quoted. I had not been able to buy the paper, so a friend, who was also quoted in the piece, had made copies. As she was bending into her car to get them for me, I felt an arm around my throat.

My immediate reaction was to think, "Who do I know here?"

My friend reacted similarly, thinking, "I wonder who Jay knows in this neighborhood?"

Both of us believed that the world is a relatively safe place. Neither of us expected for me to be mugged on a main street.

I slowly reached for the man's arm, to lower it gently from my neck. He gradually released it. I think the reason he moved his arm was that he sensed there was no fear or tension in me; therefore, he didn't need to defend himself.

He reached for my hip pocket. I then became aware that he wanted my billfold. Had I been consumed by panic, I would not have made choices. Fear would have been controlling me. However, since he had lowered his arm, I managed to control whatever fear I did have.

He'd tried to get the pocket flap open, and couldn't.

He said, "I've got a knife in your back." I could feel a pointed object. Who am I to question the word of a stranger with his arm around my throat and a knife in my back? He pushed me over against the car, but he did it gently.

Because I was comfortable with my fear in that situation, I could think about what to do. There was a possibility I could come around with a well-placed elbow to his head, because he had to use both hands to get into my pocket. It seemed as though he wasn't in total control of the situation.

The thought then occurred to me that he might have an accomplice. My decision, since I didn't want unnecessary pain, was to assure him, "You can take my billfold. I'd appreciate it if you would leave my driver's license."

Needless to say, he did not leave my driver's license. He tore open my pocket, took the billfold, and ran away, leaving me standing there feeling as though this was the nicest mugger anybody could ever have. I've had "friends" who've hurt me more than he did.

The police told me that two people had been knifed on that street that same week. The lesson from this is that my friendly mugger did not have to fear me. He didn't have to protect himself, because there was no tension or resistance from me. Whatever fear was in me was completely under my control. Since the fear was an acceptable feeling, I based each decision on the present reality. I also based each decision on my priority that health and well-being are more important than money.

One of my fears has been the fear of being alone. Fortunately, at this point in my life, that fear is minimal.

I was lonely after being divorced. There were times, especially when I was heading home from work, that my foremost thought was, "Who can I call to have dinner with me?" (Dinner was always a fun family time when I was growing up.) I realized it was not a matter of needing to be with somebody. I had been with people all day. It was more a matter of the fear of being alone.

As I realized that, I began to see how I could have a great time being alone in the evening. I could enjoy dinner alone. I found ways to offset loneliness that were enjoyable and entertaining to me. I realized that I had so many interests, it could be fun to be alone. At times, it was even a preference.

Fear said nothing about whether or not I would enjoy the evening. It was only my *fear of* being alone that was a problem—not the being alone itself. My fear did not predict the future.

Having come to this realization, I put myself in the position several years ago of vacationing in an isolated family camp setting for a week with my children. They had other companions. The other people in the camp were all in family groups. I was the only person who had no guarantees of companionship. I had nobody but myself. It was gratifying that there was only one time during the trip when I was uncomfortable about being alone.

One evening I began to feel upset. Everyone had something to do and people with whom to be—except for me. When I realized what I was feeling was just fear, I relaxed. It turned out that I enjoyed practicing music and reading a book. I had a wonderful evening just being alone with myself. The whole week was marvelous—including my time alone—even though there had initially been discomfort because I had feared loneliness.

Again, let me emphasize the importance of listening to our feelings. By accepting my fear, I could realize that it did not predict the future. It only told me that I was afraid. Then I could choose ways to cope with the fear, which, in this situation, included selecting some activities I could enjoy by myself.

What about the fear of the future? As I have mentioned, it is a warning. When we realize that the fear is related to an anticipated event, then it can be a warning to prepare for that event. I don't think fear is a great motivator, but it can be an indicator that we need to do something to prepare for the future.

I learned at the New England Speakers' Association that most people list the fear of speaking in public as their number one fear. If that is true (or even if that is not true), it is a good example of what happens with fear. The fear may be coming from the past, if we have been criticized or otherwise told we do not talk well, or that we are stupid, or that we should be "seen and not heard."

Fear might be coming from a situation when we had been induced to be in front of people to speak. It might be caused by remembering receiving a poor grade in school for public speaking, or recalling that we were told we spoke poorly and did not live up to the image our parents wanted us to present.

That kind of fear clearly is coming from the past. It is not a fear that tells us what will happen in the future.

If the audience to which you present is hostile, the fear of speaking in public is connected with the event. I had a colleague who came to me because he had to make a presentation to a difficult group. This man was absolutely brilliant and meticulous in his preparation. He had gone to several other colleagues before meeting with me.

After hearing the information he intended to present, I praised him, saying, "You really know the material well. That's great!"

He said, "Thanks, but I'm really anxious!" He went on to say that, each time he had met with his other colleagues, they had assured him he really knew the information well; but he was still afraid. Again, they assured him he had no reason for fear. Every time he heard this, his level of anxiety increased.

By the time he had been to five people who told him he had nothing of which to be afraid, he was nearly in a panic!

When he told me that he was anxious, my response was, "Of course you are anxious. The only reason you wouldn't be afraid of those hatcheteers you're presenting to would be if you were numb or dead." He began to breathe again.

I knew his audience was an extremely critical group, often attacking people. Fear is completely natural and appropriate under those circumstances.

When he received confirmation for his feelings, and permission to have them, my friend could then relax. He didn't need to be terrified of being afraid, or concerned that he was "crazy."

When he faced the audience, he was comfortable with his fear, let his natural humor and brilliance show through, and received many accolades for his presentation.

Fear of fear is unbearable. It drains our energy. Comfort with our fear allows us to place the focus where we choose.

In the mugging story, the focus was on the mugger. In the hatcheteer story, the focus was on presenting the material.

Let me offer a scenario that contrasts with the previous story: You are going to speak before a marvelous audience, but the topic is one on which you have little information. In that situation, the fear you feel can be a warning: "Look, if you are going to do this well, you need to get the proper knowledge. You must prepare your talk so you can present it to your audience in such a way that they will appreciate the accuracy of your facts and your delivery."

The fear says, "Prepare!"

Fear is a natural part of our existence. You need to look at your own fear objectively and kindly, and use the opportunity to decide if it is coming from the past, if it is connected to the present, or if it is a warning to prepare for the future.

Let's now consider anxiety. I view anxiety as a form of fear. The difference is that anxiety is unfocused, and fear is focused. It is an intense or subtle discomfort of some unknown impending danger. We don't know where the anxiety is coming from. There seems no reason for it. The anxiety is out of our control.

Anxiety can come from several sources. One source is the result of having been taught that a given feeling, sensation, or thought is "bad." We will probably experience anxiety if that feeling or sensation occurs in us. For example, when we have been taught that we should not be angry, and we begin to be aware of being angry, anxiety will kick in and may even eclipse the anger, making us aware only of the anxiety and not the anger.

This can happen with any feeling: pleasure, pain, affection, fear, helplessness. When we have been taught, directly or indirectly, that sexuality is unacceptable, we will usually experience anxiety when we have sexual sensations. When we have been taught that we should not express our personal views (children should be seen and not heard), we may be anxious when we are put in a position where we are required to express our opinion. When we have been taught that we should not even think "bad" thoughts (whatever those thoughts are), we will usually experience anxiety when we think them.

If we have a lot of guilt or shame, and/or believe that we are "bad," we can feel anxiety when we are successful, because we can't believe we "deserve" the recognition. We might fear we will be "found out," so we take away our success to reduce our anxiety.

If we have been taught that we are not to succeed, we will feel more and more anxiety the more success we attain. Some people do something to block their own success because they cannot tolerate the anxiety that builds along with the success.

If none of the members of our family went to college, and resented college-educated people as "snobs," or "intellectuals," or people "living in the clouds," or who "only care about books," or who "don't understand real life," we probably will feel anxious even thinking about going to college. We will probably feel anxious when we are attending college, when we are studying, or when we achieve good grades. The anxiety occurs because we are going beyond the limits that have been defined by our family.

Anxiety may also be a vague anticipation of some form of punishment. It is connected with punishment in the past. It is a strong sense that something bad will happen, or that we will be hurt—somehow! We don't know how or when, but it will surely be terrible, and inevitable.

If we develop the habit of connecting the past with the present, look at past events and their effect on our present emotions, we will discover patterns that will explain and clarify the source of our anxiety. (See also "The Hurtful, Frightening Family.")

Now the question arises, "What shall I do with my feelings?"

Well, one important thing to do when you are afraid is to breathe.

The first thing most people do when they are frightened is to hold their breath. It may be somehow related to the belief that, "If nobody hears me breathing or sees me breathing, I will be invisible, and what I fear will not be able to happen."

Whatever the reason, when you stop breathing because you are afraid, you increase the fear. That is exactly the time when you most need to breathe. Breathing can help you to relax.

Watch a high diver. He stops on the diving board, takes a deep breath to relax, then goes into his dive. Relaxation is always important, but it is most important of all when you are in a frightening situation.

There is the tendency to tense up all of your muscles when you are afraid, bracing yourself against that which you fear. Breathing deeply is a way of relaxing your whole body.

The first step, then, is to BREATHE.

The second step is to discover the source of the fear. Is it coming from past experiences, which you are bringing into the present? Is it connected to the present experience, which is truly a threat? Or is the fear telling you that you need to prepare for something in the future?

Once you have decided where the fear comes from, you can decide what to do with it.

If the fear is coming from the past, you have several options. One is to remind yourself that it was in the past, and this is the present. Then open yourself to the other person or people, and share your fear. That can help those on the other side to relax and be open to you. If it is someone whom you know well and trust, like a good friend or safe mate, you can tell them your fear and past experiences. They will appreciate your trust, and may see things in your experiences that you do not. This approach can reduce your fear. It can also lead to greater closeness.

If you find the fear is connected to the present, you can assess what is the actual threat. If you are immobilized by your fear, you cannot think clearly to assess the danger. If there is a possibility of bodily harm, you decide on ways to protect yourself from it. If there is verbal abuse or intimidation from someone, you decide how to respond to that person.

One way of reacting to verbal attack is to remain neutral. This gives the other person an opportunity to vent their upset feelings.

For instance, if someone is really angry with you and you do not get caught up in their anger, you will not contribute to escalating the situation. If somebody is really upset, there is no point in feeding their flames by getting upset with them. If you remain detached, they will have to fan their anger with their own energy. It will burn out more quickly than it would if you add fuel to the fire. By remaining emotionally neutral you can let the person get it out of their system. You may have the opportunity, once the anger is discharged, to discuss what is upsetting them, and to resolve the issue.

In some situations, you may decide to attack the other person, catching them off balance. That puts them on the defensive, and protects you. At other times, you choose to withdraw. That may be the best solution for you and for the other person.

Some people have difficulty giving themselves permission to use these three tactics.

Some people always attack, and do not have the flexibility to remain neutral or to withdraw.

Some people always withdraw, because they have been punished for being aggressive or for expressing anger. They do not give themselves the option to attack.

Some people stay stuck in the situation, and can neither withdraw nor attack. Their own fear immobilizes them. This is very different from remaining calmly neutral and staying connected to the other person.

I want to emphasize the flexibility of your options, and the importance of picking one that, based on your assessment of the situation, fits best.

When your fear relates to the future, you need to realize that the fear does not predict the future. It only tells you that you are afraid.

It may be a warning that there is something you must do to prepare yourself for the future. It can be a warning to arm yourself for a threatening situation. It is crucial for you to gather information as a way to gain control.

Frightened people worry about or prepare themselves for disasters that never occur. A client was distressed for two weeks because of fear that the upcoming holiday was going to be miserable. I brought to his attention the point that he had already been suffering for two weeks and the holiday was still two weeks away. Therefore, he would be putting four weeks of suffering into the anticipation of the one "bad" day!

He realized that it was hardly worth it. He relaxed for the next two weeks. As it turned out, the day wasn't terrific, but it wasn't as bad as he had feared, and it was only one day.

I mention this anecdote because I see a lot of people who get very upset in anticipation of an event that only will take a few hours. The event generally turns out to be not nearly as upsetting as expected. They suffer greatly beforehand.

When we take the time to get a realistic assessment of our fear of future events, it can greatly reduce the upset and suffering in our lives.

"So," you ask, "what do I do with anxiety?"

The greatest difficulty with anxiety is to recognize it. Many people, especially men, don't even know they have anxiety. It seems ridiculous to tell an extremely successful, highly intelligent person, "You have anxiety, and you won't know what it is until you have less of it." Fortunately, they believe me. Later they tell me, "I had no idea what you were talking about. Now I know, because I can experience the difference."

Once you become aware of the anxiety, the next problem is to convince yourself that you can function well without it. People fear that if they are not driven by anxiety, they won't be productive and will fail to achieve, possibly losing what they have.

They can begin to let go of the anxiety and relax when they realize that anxiety needlessly drains energy. The kind of anxiety I am referring to here is the chronic anxiety that constantly coexists with a person.

Let us now assume you no longer perceive anxiety as a productive companion and have therefore reduced the time you spend with it. You have begun to enjoy being competent and productive without the constant pressure of anxiety badgering you. You find there are various aspects of living from which you now take pleasure. Other people seem more at ease with you, and more attracted to you. You are generally relaxed, but experience anxiety from time to time. What do you do with that anxiety?

Let me widen my reply to that question to include some other folks. Some of you have lived as I have just described for all of your lives. Anxiety was never constant, but appeared to you every now and then.

This is the message to each of you: **Your anxiety can be a friendly informer, if you listen to it.** It can advise you to discover the lessons you were taught as you were growing up. It can let you know what you were punished for, or taught not to experience. Anxiety can call your attention to feelings of which you are unaware. Anxiety can say, "Look at what feelings are underneath me. Discover what you were taught about these feelings, and then decide what to do with them."

By following anxiety's suggestions, you can proceed with your life in a positive direction.

Please do not conclude that a person gets anxious only about "negative" feelings of pain, anger, fear or helplessness.

For some people, "positive" feelings of pleasure/joy or affection produce anxiety; at the very least, they can be experienced as negatives. These people were taught not to express affection.

Other people were punished for being noisy or excited or enthusiastic.

Others were told that they would lose their joy (if by some freak of nature it crept into their life). They were taught, "If it's good, it won't last." People thus learn to fear their feelings of affection, or happiness, or relaxation, or success, and they become anxious.

Your anxiety may be a sign that things are going well for you. Anxiety may be a signpost telling you, "Everything is great! You are only experiencing me because you were taught that it can't be this good."

Take a deep breath, relax, and enjoy yourself.

Let me repeat: **It is natural to be anxious. It is natural to be frightened. Be kind to yourself when you become aware of these feelings. Enjoy the messages these feelings can bring to you. Revel in the fact that feeling fear is *perfectly human.***

...And B-r-e-a-t-h-e!
It may not be—and probably is not—as terrible as you fear it to be.

*H*elplessness is not terminal.

It only seems that way.

*H*elplessness

Unfortunately, an increasingly common life experience is one parent keeping a child hostage from the other. Over the years I have known fathers who have been prevented from seeing their children for months, including during major family holidays. The sense of helplessness and pain is excruciating.

It is a helpless feeling when your children live with someone who has custody of them and has values very different from your own. When you love your children, you want to be with them, you want to show them all the affection they deserve, you want to show them what you have learned about successful living, you want to create an atmosphere that nourishes them and in which they feel safe. You want to provide them with opportunities to experience new adventures and to expand their horizons. You want their physical and emotional needs to be met. When you observe that this is not done to your satisfaction, you feel helpless. It would be impossible to feel otherwise.

I spoke about family dynamics at an organization's annual meeting. The majority of the audience were elderly men and women. I was surprised at the questions they raised for discussion after the presentation. They wanted to know the effects of divorce on children. The questioners were grandparents whose children were divorced and they were concerned about their grandchildren. Grandparents feel helpless when their grandchildren need them and they either don't know how to respond or are prevented from meeting the grandchild's needs.

Helplessness is a feeling that occurs when we seem trapped or confined. It is experienced when we are dependent on someone or some situation that seems unsolvable. We feel helpless when we are unable to get our wants, wishes, or needs met. We feel helpless when we are prevented from being with those whom we love. We feel helpless when we cannot meet or are prevented from fulfilling the needs of someone we love. We feel helpless when we have several positive options and can choose only one.

The feeling of helplessness can be immobilizing. We must remember that helplessness is merely a feeling. We are not necessarily helpless. However distasteful the options may be, we are not helpless as long as we have choices. We can take action.

Pick Your Options

To choose is to be free. Choosing options in the midst of feeling helpless reduces or alleviates feelings of helplessness.

One of the choices you have when your children live with someone else who has custody of them is to avoid contact with your children, because the situation is so painful. Another option is to kidnap the children. Another option is to maintain contact as often as possible, even though that in itself may stir up painful, helpless feelings and possibly bring abuse from your mate when contact occurs. Another option is to move your residence a distance away, so you can easily rationalize lack of contact. Another option is to seek custody, which usually means a battle that can be emotionally upsetting to everyone involved and financially devastating. Another is to kill their other parent, but going to prison has a way of limiting access to the children we seek to be with.

None of these alternatives is completely satisfying. Some are better than others. We must, however, do something. We must pick an option, then pursue it. This does not always reduce our feelings. Even when our choice does ease our feeling of helplessness, our helpless feeling may be replaced with other feelings that are just as intense. Options, however, make it obvious to us that we have a choice. **To feel helpless is not to be helpless.** We DO have control over our own actions.

You can feel just as helpless and powerless when you have several options that are all good! Each of them is something you want, or each would be a wonderful opportunity. By virtue of time, money, and/or circumstance, you must pick one. The feeling that results is helplessness.

Let me give you some examples. You enjoy both your work and your child. There is a meeting with a client in another city which is significant to getting a major contract. It is being held at the same time that you have been invited to present your daughter or son with the Outstanding Scholar and Athlete of the Year Award by the school they attend.

Or you are asked to give the keynote address at two major conferences on the same date.

Or you have been told by your parents that you could stay up late to watch your favorite program, only to discover that your most favorite, *favorite* is scheduled for the same time (and nobody in your family knows how to set the VCR).

Or your two favorite boyfriends call to ask you out for the same night. (This used to apply to fifteen-year-old girls. Now it applies to females ranging from ten to one hundred, and also applies to men who are asked out by women.)

Or in your final semester before you are to graduate from college, six of your favorite professors are giving their best courses which fit with your life work. You have always had a scheduling conflict, therefore were unable to take them before, and now the most you can take is four. (I can picture you students thinking, "Come on. Get real.")

Sometimes we will feel helpless when we can only have two or three things when we need ten. Now, don't start getting judgmental that such a person is selfish and should be contented to have something nice, even if they can't have the other nine things. Remember, feelings just happen. They are neither good nor bad. They just are. They are a part of being human. It is okay to have feelings of frustration (which is a combination of anger and helplessness) when there are limitations on what we can have.

Helplessness is usually associated with being in a position where someone else has control. I am expanding that meaning to include situations where you are in control, but where it is not possible to have all of the positive possibilities that are available—all the "good stuff."

You can feel helpless until you make a decision. You can go "crazy" trying to make a decision between wonderful opportunities and feel terribly helpless when you either don't know what you want, or when any choice you must make is affected by many unknowns and variables. You feel relieved when you make your decision, and the feelings of helplessness are alleviated.

The point is: When you clarify your options and make a decision, feelings of helplessness subside. That is the focus of this chapter.

Helplessness Is Not Reality

Helplessness is only a feeling. It does not describe the external reality. It does not mean you must give up whatever power you have, even though it may not be much. There are usually ways in which you can exert power, if you are willing to pay the consequences.

Helplessness is much like fear. It is a feeling that does not tell you the reality. All it says is that you feel helpless. The trick is to discover whether helpless feelings are the result of past experiences, whether the present reality is the source of the feelings, or whether you feel helpless to cope with future events.

My assessment is that helplessness seldom discloses the reality. All it does is to tell us that we are feeling helpless.

This may be difficult to believe; however, there are few situations in which we can be totally confined physically, and even fewer in which we can be mentally controlled, if we choose otherwise.

It is also possible to change the "reality." The unreal can be made real. The not-yet-real can become real.

There is a difference between helplessness and hopelessness. The analogy is the same difference that exists between fear and anxiety.

Helplessness and fear have a present focus.

Anxiety is more global. Hopelessness is also a global feeling. Anxiety is the anticipation of disaster. Hopelessness is the anticipation that nothing can or will change. Hopelessness is a sense of despair. It is the feeling that terrible things will continue to occur and that nothing will ever get better.

Helplessness is much more immediate. It doesn't have the same long range scope as feelings of hopelessness.

As my Mother says, "This, too, shall pass!" It can be a great perspective when you are feeling helpless, or when things seem to be hopeless.

Let me suggest some situations where helpless feelings occur. You will feel helpless when you are "born to" or choose to be dependent on someone who will not respond to your needs. Helplessness is a very strong feeling in "The Hurtful, Frightening Family." When your parents misunderstand, or lack the desire to understand, your ideas or actions and call you "stupid," or make other rebukes, you will feel helpless. When you attempt to express your feelings and you are interrupted, dismissed, discounted, or punished, you will feel helpless. You may be aware of anger, but the core feeling is helplessness to be heard or to be appreciated or to have your needs met.

When you speak to someone and their response is unrelated to what you said, you will feel helpless if miscommunication persists. You will feel helpless when you are unable to penetrate another's wall.

You can feel just as helpless when you are striving to meet another person's need, and they deny your attempts. It is a helpless feeling when you want to be kind and considerate to another person, but their response is to attack, divert, or withdraw, rather than to appreciate.

You can feel helpless when someone is attempting to control you. This is especially true if they are in a position of power, by virtue of physical or psychological leverage.

You may say, "Absolutely. When I am in any one of those situations, I *am* helpless."

I want you to understand that helplessness is only a feeling. It does not necessarily say anything about the situation in which you find yourself.

Most children believe that what they experience in their own family is true of all other families. It's as though their life would be the same, even if they changed families.

When children are abused or oppressed, they will feel helpless, and they often are helpless to do anything about it. Children are at the mercy of adults. Children are hostages in an abusive family because they depend on their parents for food, clothing, shelter, all of which are necessary to survive.

Some children even try to leave home, only to return in order to avoid dying, or because they are returned by others.

The childhood experience, carried as the "child within," will perpetuate the helpless attitude in an adult, which will be expressed either by a martyr or victim position, or by seeking external power in an attempt to be safe. Either of these life-styles contains a great deal of helplessness, fear, and pain.

In the event you, my tenacious reader, are in the midst of feeling helpless, let me encourage you to assess your situation from the perspective of "The Hurtful, Frightening Family."

Often our past has become the yardstick by which we measure the present reality. The dilemma is this: What is accurate? It is as though the past were measured in inches, but the present is measured in centimeters. When we continue our learning from the past and, therefore, measure the present in inches, we get a distorted reading.

Let me illustrate ways in which past experiences in your family lead to feeling helpless in the present.

If, in your family of learning, your basic needs go unrecognized, or if your parents fail to respond to your needs when you express them, you develop a sense of helplessness that carries over into adult life. You avoid asking anyone to meet your needs. You develop an attitude such as, "Why waste my time asking for things, when I won't get them anyway?" Your adult expectation, based on your childhood experience, results in the belief that no one will respond to your needs. You do not trust anyone, so you learn to rely on yourself. You either attempt to meet them yourself, or else you use manipulation to get others to meet your needs. Each of these approaches creates difficulties in your relationships, as well as isolation for you.

If your family members did not put any effort into trying to understand your ideas and your thoughts; if they discouraged your creativity or—even worse—if you were told, "Children should be seen and not heard," then it is easy for you to develop a sense of helplessness, believing that no one in the present cares about you, or wants to know what you feel or think.

If, when you were a child, you cried in an attempt to let someone know what you needed, but nobody responded and you were left to cry alone, the experience has the potential for instilling a sense of helplessness. If, as an adult, you don't believe that anyone is interested in your needs or ideas, then the old feelings of helplessness have continued into your adult years.

When you project to others that you expect them to reject you and your needs, you contribute to that rejection by the way you approach them or by the way you present your needs to them. You present your needs, wants, or wishes vaguely, or cloaked with anger or fear. Others, then, don't know how to respond to you.

If you do not try to express what you need, or cannot express it, you will continue to have a feeling of helplessness about getting your needs met. **The reality is that there are responsive people around you if you look for them and if you approach them in a sincere, direct manner.**

If you have grown up in a family where you were dependent on people who did not seem to appreciate what you did, but instead put you down for what you were doing, you will find it difficult in your adult life to believe people are pleased by you, and will feel helpless to please anyone. If your attempts to meet your parents' or siblings' needs went unrecognized, and they scolded you, you will probably become bitter and feel worthless.

Often people feel helpless in school or work settings where someone else has authority. If your parents taught you that they were always right, and society taught you always to respect your father and mother, and if you were punished when you did not obey parental or school authorities, then you as an adult may feel helpless to go contrary to, or even to question, anyone in a position of authority over you.

I am very much aware that there are times when it is in the interest of everyone to do what we are told, and to do it quickly. I believe, however, that under most circumstances cooperative means of arriving at decisions are better than decisions by one person's decree.

I am convinced that, if you as an adult are feeling helpless with another adult, you need to assess the situation seriously. Your decision may be to do something different from, or the opposite of, what you are told to do. You may choose to do exactly what you are told, granting another person authority. You may make that decision because of their experience, because the danger of the circumstance demands it, to avoid a fight that makes no sense, or for the sake of having fun and enjoying yourself.

Let me illustrate those last two reasons why it is wise to decide to obey an authority. I was invited to go for a weekend trip on a sailboat. The friend who invited me warned me about the abusiveness of the owner and captain. Shortly after we set sail, he instructed me to cleat the sheet (a rope attached to the sail) in a way I knew was wrong. I knowingly complied, following his instructions. Then he rebuked me for doing it wrong. I simply changed the knot on the cleat without saying a word, but laughed inside because I knew his game. I had decided, before we boarded the boat, that I was going to have fun, and with that attitude I had one of the best weekends in my life.

I chose to give him authority, even though I did not respect his demeaning style. I mention this because I believe people are **given** authority. They do not have it by virtue of their position. Authority must be earned or gained in some way.

Acquiring Authority

I, as a young man of eighteen, worked in a brickyard as a way of earning money for college. My father was the superintendent but, being a smart man, he did not have me report to him. There was another foreman to whom I was accountable.

I was responsible for quality control of the products, and for five to ten men. All of these men were older than I. Some of them were in their fifties.

After I had been there over a month, one of the older men who had befriended me said, "You had a lot going against you when you started here. You've overcome a lot, with being a Yankee in a Southern plant, a college student working with laborers, your father the superintendent, working for the company rather than for the union, and being only eighteen." He praised me for what I had managed to accomplish in winning the respect of the men.

I know the reason I earned their respect was because I treated everyone the same and put myself above no one. We were all just human beings working together. If a particularly offensive task needed doing, I would pitch in with the others even though it was not part of my duties. They appreciated that "nasty work" was not "beneath" me, and that I liked them enough to work alongside of them.

When I had to tell the men what was to be done, or what needed correcting, I was direct about the orders and clear as to why it was essential that they be followed. Most important in earning their respect, I was fair and I appreciated them.

This assessment is hindsight, because at the time I was not thinking in those terms, but was merely doing what was natural for me. I see now why it made a difference.

There are some situations where it would not be wise for anybody to do as I did, but I had earned respect on this job, in spite of the fact that I was so much an "outsider," therefore was granted authority by older and more experienced men.

There was another situation that happened in the brickyard, where I had a certain amount of authority, but was only able to use that authority because it was given to me by the other people involved.

The men would throw brickbats (flawed bricks) in a container that could only be removed by a lift truck. There was a problem one day because the grinder that reduced the brickbats to sand for recycling had broken down. There was no place for the lift truck operator to put the bad bricks.

One of the men, who was gauging bricks and checking for brickbats, overstepped his bounds by yelling to the lift truck operator, "Get those bats out of here!"

The lift truck operator became frustrated, and said, "If you want them out, pack them out yourself!"

The man gauging bricks retorted, "You come down off that tow motor, and I'll pack *you* out of here."

The tow motor operator stepped down off his truck. A fight was inevitable.

I stepped in between them.

"You get back on your tow motor," I said emphatically, pointing toward the lift truck, "and you go back to gauging bricks," I directed, pointing to the gauger's machine.

The brick gauger argued, "If I want a boss, I'll go get one!"

I turned squarely to him and said, "You go back to gauging brick." They both saw that I was determined, and decided to do as I said.

Why was I, an eighteen-year-old, able to exert this authority over a man in his early forties and a man in his mid-thirties? The reason is because it was in the interest of neither man to fight, as they would both have been suspended, lost pay, and possibly fired. However, it was in their interests to do what I had told them to do. They gave me the power in the situation because the control I was exerting was in their best interests. Had they not given me authority, they would have "had to" fight.

I mention this example because it illustrates how and why a person will give away power. I learned later that the man gauging brick had twice previously knifed someone (not in the brickyard), and he might easily have turned on me more aggressively than he did.

I believe one reason he did not was because his first day on the job he did not have the necessary equipment. I went out of my way (unknowingly violating company policy) to meet his need. Remembering that I had shown an interest in him and his needs, he later came over to apologize for his comment about "getting a boss." His apology was not because of authority that I had in the brickyard, which was essentially none. His apology was to show respect for the authority I had earned by responding to his needs his first day of work, and by risking getting myself hurt preventing a fight to protect him from losing time or his job, and allowing him to save face.

There are times when it would be totally unsafe to attempt to prevent a fight, because one or both parties could turn on you and hurt you. You would be brutalized because they would not respond to your demands. I am sure you can imagine situations where it would be unwise to intervene, because you have no leverage, no opportunity to earn respect, and will not be granted credibility or control.

There are also times when it is in the interest of the "larger good" and of everyone concerned for you to refuse to use your authority, thereby allowing feelings of helplessness to intensify in other people so that leaders will emerge.

I once had the responsibility for a project that was mandated "by decree from above." I knew if I were to accept a major leadership role, even though I was the person who had "authority," it would be a flop, because it was perceived as the project of my superiors being imposed on others, which they resented.

We had a planning meeting of the women and men at the local level. They were insisting I be the lead organizer, emphasizing it would be wise for me to have control since I was responsible. They threatened that my position in the organization could be jeopardized if I did not see to the success of the endeavor.

I argued two points: (1) we had the option of choosing not to do the project, and (2) if it was not taken as a joint enterprise, it would be unwise to attempt it at all. I knew there were leaders whose talents were a better fit for this particular project, and who would be granted more authority on this project than I.

I listened to all of the reasons why I "should" lead, neutralized all those reasons, and then we sat. There were about fifteen people just sitting and looking at me, with me sitting, looking back. This went on for perhaps five minutes, which seemed like hours. Nobody said a word.

Ed ended the silence. He said, "I will head up the project if Jim will do it with me." Jim agreed.

Both were very capable and would bring success to the project. The two men, with the assistance of many others, carried it through to completion, exceeding the financial objective that had been "set" for us. Their leadership led to many completely unforeseen indirect positive results that grew out of the project.

Had I settled into helplessness, feeling I had to comply, the project would have flopped. Had I accepted the authority and told people what to do, not only would the project have failed, it also would have been disastrous for our organization.

Because I was willing to be patient and let other people feel helpless, they chose to invest themselves in organizing the program, resulting in a very productive venture.

Had they decided to scrap the project, that would have been okay, too. It would have been far better for us to put our skill and energy into another productive direction than to waste it on one that was going nowhere.

Often, when you are in a position of "designated" authority, it is most wisely used by sharing it. In most situations I attempt to include other people in decisions, whether it is in my family or in work settings. My sons, Jeph and Matt, were involved in decisions as little children, including whether or not they would attend nursery school, what shoes to buy, and so on.

When Jeph was not quite three, he wanted to go to the kindergarten down the street with his friend next door. The director knew Jeph, who was mature for his age, and agreed that he could attend. I felt proud but sad as we walked down the street to the school, holding hands. My son was old enough to go to school. Boo hoo!

Jeph had a terrific year. He had fun. He learned a lot. He had made a great choice.

We moved at the end of the year. Jeph started another kindergarten. After a few weeks he came home and said, "Dad, I don't like it there. I don't want to go anymore."

I said, "Jeph, if you decide not to go, it's okay; but I would suggest you try it another week or two."

He chose to do that, but after two days he told me he wanted to quit. My four-year-old son made the decision not to go to kindergarten.

My thinking was this: He had experience as the basis for comparison to help him reach a decision. I also concluded that he would be compelled by law to attend school in the future. If he were forced to go now, when there was more choice, he could carry that resentment into future schooling. By encouraging him now, when there was more freedom for him to choose, it would build his confidence and respond to his needs.

The main reason why I agreed with his decision was that I trusted my son's judgment.

Matthew, my younger son, decided he didn't want to go to kindergarten before he even started. This school was different from the one Jeph had attended.

I was firm. "Matt, you are going." I told him, "If you go for a few weeks and don't like it, then you can stop. Right now you have nothing on which to base your decision, so you are going." He went, and loved it.

There are times, in matters of health or issues of which I had greater knowledge by virtue of my age, when I would assume ultimate authority. Fortunately, in most of those situations, they would give me the power to make the decision.

On one such occasion Jeph protested a doctor's appointment from which he'd already returned, announcing, "I went because I thought you would tie me up and throw me in the car if I didn't!"

He must have been reading my mind. I told him, "I had considered that possibility, if it was necessary." There are times when authority is given to you because you are bigger.

In a clinic I was directing, we were having difficulty establishing a day for staff meetings and case supervision. I had decided that, since everyone's schedule varied, a combined staff decision would be best. We spent time on this for a few weeks, and nothing was happening. No one proposed a solution that would fit the requirements that were necessary to comply with the law, and would also provide the amount of supervision essential to meet insurance company regulations.

I realized that I had made a mistake by giving the staff the decision on which day the meetings and supervision would be held. They were not able to come up with a solution with which I, as the responsible person, could be comfortable. I issued an ultimatum, stating that the staff meetings would be on a particular day, at a certain time, for a designated length of time.

At this point they were all angry with me for making the decision, and furious that I had given them the false impression they had the power to make it. I let them know that I totally understood their frustration and anger toward me. I agreed that it appeared as though I had set them up and betrayed them. I told them that I had been totally sincere in my wish for them to seek a solution on the scheduling, but that, when the staff was at a standstill, the circumstances had changed. I explained that it was my original intention to include them, but then I made the decision to exclude them from the process and make the final decision myself.

The staff had options. They could settle into helplessness, be miserable or passively resistant, or they could find other options. Their choice was to cooperate and to have the staff meetings in accordance with my "decreed" wishes. They chose to give me power in the situation, but not without using plenty of opportunity to express their resentment.

They could have blocked my decision, resigned, or caused a lot of other things to happen. The point is: They had the power to defy my decision, but also had the power to choose to go along with it. This is an example of power and authority from the top, and how others respond to it from the framework of their own power. It is an example of choosing options when you are feeling helpless.

Anger Can Be Empowering

The following illustration shows the caring anger of a nurse in an apparently helpless position, who went against authority on behalf of her patient in a hospital setting and, as a result, gained authority.

Legally, a doctor is the only one who can prescribe medication, but a nurse is legally responsible if she does not catch a doctor's mistakes. The nurse often appears to have little power, at least under the law, and also little power when it comes to dealing with doctors.

A student in a nursing program began to assert her power and express her opinion to the doctors about what was being done with the patients. She believed that, because she had far more contact with the patients than the doctors did, her views should be valued. She expressed her observations of the patients' medical and emotional needs, whether it agreed or disagreed with the doctors' assessments.

Some of the doctors did not like it, but they had to contend with her as a force within that hospital. When a doctor would try to intimidate her, she gave back as good as she got. They began to appreciate her determination to stand her ground, and especially appreciated her wisdom about the patients' needs and her technical medical awareness.

The outcome of her actions was that, when she graduated, instead of being hired as a floor nurse, she became nursing supervisor in the hospital where she had done her training.

I mention this to call attention to a person who seemed to be in a position of little power, while other people around her had the designated authority. It shows how one's personal power, if used in an intelligent, constructive manner, can win respect and benefit many people in the process.

It makes sense to me for the nurse to have a significant say in the treatment plan. I think it is often wise to include the patient, also.

When I go into a school for a psychological consultation about a student, I rely on information from the teachers. The teachers have more contact with the students than do the administrators and psychologists within the school system.

My approach is to talk with the teachers who work with the students, and to include the students in the decisions about their educational plan. To include the teachers has been a tremendous source of information, and allows me to make a more reliable contribution to the case by getting accurate information upon which to make my recommendations.

Involvement: A Path to Power

One of the most significant contributions I have made during consultations is to involve the student in decisions that affect him or her, even if it meant arranging another meeting in order to have the student present. It is crucial to have the person most affected by the decision present to contribute to the outcome. The chances are great that if the student does not have a major role in developing the plan, they will undermine it in some way. At the least, it will not fit the student's needs and the student will not be motivated to perform to their highest level.

If the student understands the educational plan, and has been a part of developing it, they are more likely to enjoy the plan, and everything will run more smoothly for them, for the teachers, and for the administration.

This principle of including the person whose life is affected by the knowledge of others also applies to the patient/doctor relationship in the medical profession. A lot more healing will occur, and fewer malpractice suits will be filed, when patients are included in and understand the decisions that influence their well-being. I also believe that the cost of health care can be reduced if patients take responsibility for their own health care by asking questions such as "What are the side-effects of this medication?"

It can be a tremendously helpless feeling to have to depend on people in the medical profession who will not tell you what they observe and what they are doing to assist your body in healing itself. It can reduce both anxiety and feelings of helplessness to tell the patient and their family the details of the treatment plan, and to show you care.

My Father had open heart surgery at St. Joseph's Hospital in Lexington, Kentucky. The whole experience was just marvelous. One nurse was specifically trained to explain the procedures and answer questions. She met with my Father, Mother, sister Tina, my niece Laurie, and me in my Father's hospital room the day before the operation.

At intervals the anesthetist, the head surgeon, the assisting surgeon, the physician responsible for before and aftercare each came into my Father's room, introduced themselves, explained their part in the procedure, and answered questions.

After they had all been in his room, the nurse returned to answer any other questions. She told us the possible complications that could arise during and after the operation, and how the team would cope with them.

When she left, we felt completely secure that the operation would succeed and my Father would have many years to live.

My parents' minister drove over a hundred miles to be with us and to pray with us. We cried together, laughed together, then cried some more.

A man who had successfully recovered from open heart surgery and his wife came to visit us as volunteers to talk with us and to bring a pillow for my Father to hold onto while he coughed to clear the fluids from his lungs after the operation.

The lonely walk from my Father's room, and the drive to our motel for the night, knowing that my Father was facing a life threatening operation the next day, was made bearable by a medical staff who showed us they cared.

The total experience, which could have been horrendous, was made a positive one because of the technical explanations and attention to the psychological needs of my Father and our family.

Several years later, in his mid-seventies, my Father walks about four miles a day to and from work and home for lunch, and even mows the lawn. His body is healed and he does what he wants. He doesn't even squeal like a pig, as my niece Laurie had predicted, knowing that her grandfather was going to have a pig valve in his heart.

I believe that patients should be included in their own medical care. Doctors should be required to tell patients the possible side effects of the medication they prescribe. If the doctor tells the patient, the patient can assist the doctor with information to prevent the use of medication when it would harm the patient.

More harm can come from the side effects of medication than from the illness the medicine is treating. An allergic reactions to medication can weaken the body so the medication interferes with the healing process.

Caring anger led to action on the part of a family member who was upset watching his mother being destroyed by medication. The mother of one of my clients lived a long distance away and was under the care of her local psychiatrist. My client went to visit his mother. He came back really upset, claiming, "That's not my mother." His mother had been taking medication given by her psychiatrist. It was so disabling that she was practically a zombie.

A week later we learned she was in a general hospital because she was experiencing a lot of physical difficulties. The doctors were prescribing even more medicine to offset the side effects of the previous medication. My client felt helpless to do anything to help his mother.

I suggested to him that he bring her to the Boston area. Taking my advice, the man brought his mother to his home in Boston with the blessing of her local M.D. That doctor realized that her son was really concerned, and that his care would benefit her healing.

In the process of all this, her son was able to reduce his mother's medication. When I saw her a few days later, she was feeling better. I was then able to arrange a consultation for her with a brilliant Doctor of Naturopathy friend. He explained how the physical symptoms were the result of the medication she received for her emotional difficulties, and recommended non-medication methods to assist her body in healing the physical complications created by the medication.

In addition, I referred her to a hospital day-care facility, as she could barely tolerate being alone. Assisted by the administrative physician in that hospital, I was able to prevent her from being put on any medication.

One psychiatrist did succeed in putting her on medication in spite of our efforts. It came to our attention because my client's mother had problems sleeping. This alerted her son that she was again on medication.

I exerted influence with the higher-ups in the hospital, causing the medicating psychiatrist to call me. The doctor attempted to use guilt, manipulation, and intimidation to get me to consent to the medication. Finally, we agreed to let the family decide.

The son then ordered that his mother be given no medication. There was plenty of caring anger on the part of all concerned in these conversations.

The competency and caring of the hospital day-care staff (without the use of medication), the assistance and support of the doctors in charge, the healing knowledge of the Doctor of Naturopathy, and the decisive aggressiveness of my client led to his mother's recuperation.

Her therapy at the day-care facility ended within six weeks of her admission. She was well enough to do volunteer work in another hospital even before her release. Shortly after she left, she landed a part-time job. Soon she wanted a car, and began enjoying her mobility. She felt sufficiently confident physically and emotionally, within a few months, to return to her home state. She once again lives on her own. Now, several years later, she has a full, healthy life.

Had her loved ones failed to intervene, this woman would be dead. Because her family was willing to exert their power, take the risk of going against authorities, and call in other knowledgeable and powerful people in this cooperative effort, the woman now enjoys a wonderful life.

People who observed this story called it a miracle. It was not a miracle. It was a combination of understanding physicians and skilled, caring people with the wisdom, will, and ability to help her heal. People who had the courage to use their power and knowledge brought new life to this woman.

There are three points I am trying to make: (1) even though you do not have designated authority, you do have power; (2) designated authority does not necessarily give you power, whether it is parental authority, authority in a company, or authority in government; (3) helplessness is a state of mind, rather than a material reality.

If you find these points hard to believe, watch a parent who is trying to subdue a child having a "temper tantrum." Not easy! Look at a family in which the parents have given away control to their children. Look at the parents who have used their power to reverse roles by getting their children to take care of them.

Power, Power, Who's Got the Power?

Things are also not necessarily as they appear when it comes to determining who has power. In the vocational realm, the person who appears to have power does not always have it. I have seen executives who were completely controlled by their secretaries. The husband appears to the children to have all the power, but when you get to the real core of the family dynamics, you find that the timid, apparently powerless wife is the person really controlling the family. In some situations she even isolates the father from the children by portraying him as a "bad guy."

Do not misconstrue this as a prejudiced man blaming women, but instead as a statement that women in general have been told they don't have any power, so they have learned other ways of using power. This type of power is more subtle and elusive than the blatant power of men.

Mothers have had more opportunity to influence children in their early development than have fathers. Many fathers abdicate the joy and responsibility of child rearing, leaving it to their wives. Fortunately, this is changing. I enjoyed over-hearing some construction workers talking with each other over breakfast in a restaurant about how much pleasure they get from playing with their young children when they go home after work, and on weekends.

The point of all this is: **Appointed authority only has power when power is relinquished by a person or group. Power must be granted. Helpless feelings do not mean that you are helpless. Actual helplessness only exists when you give away your power.**

This means that if parents are caring and have integrity, their children will grant them power. Their children will trust them because they have learned from experience that their parents will not use that power in an overpowering way.

Most people have heard the Bible passage, "Honor your father and your mother that your days may be long in the land." Let me call attention to a little-known passage in the 6th chapter of Ephesians that begins by quoting that famous promise. The Bible then goes on to say, "And now a word to you parents. Don't keep on scolding and nagging your children, making them angry and resentful. Rather, bring them up with the loving discipline the Lord...approves, with suggestions and godly advice." The message to parents is that if you are going to be respected, you must be respectable.

It is wise to keep an open mind when you are faced with a person who is attempting to exert control. They may actually be in a more vulnerable position than you. Some people "blow up" and make demands or assertions—appearing very angry—when, underneath, their feeling is helplessness. Clients tell me of incidents in which they are intimidated by another's anger. As they describe the situation, it appears to me as though the "angry" person is feeling frightened, hurt, or helpless.

To recognizing the vulnerability in another person can totally change your own helpless perspective. When you feel helpless or intimidated, you are inclined to attack or withdraw. This inclination can lead to destruction in the end. When you acknowledge the helplessness and fear in the other person, you can respond with openness and kindness, thereby reducing tension. This approach allows for a potential resolution in which everyone benefits. This is true in human family, corporate, and international relations.

Take Control

You create the possibility of a positive outcome when you recognize the emotions that are driving the other person to be so controlling, abusive, or intimidating. The more a person needs to wield power in a negative way, the greater the possibility that they feel a sense of vulnerability, usually related to their previous experiences.

If you recognize the helplessness and/or fear of the intimidator, you can attempt to reduce their threat. If their response is to relax and stop their attempts at intimidation, you are headed in the right direction. If not, you can always reverse your direction and either withdraw totally, or attack.

I warn you not to apply this principle to every situation. There are some violent, vicious people in this world. It is important for you to sense the difference between decent and indecent people and to trust yourself to know the difference. My belief is: There is no way we can control other people. Our task is to control ourselves. We can only control others if they give us the power to control them.

The greatest power is personal power. There are stories about people in concentration camps who never lost their will-power because they had the power to choose what they would do with their minds. By keeping control over their minds, they maintained internal freedom and could endure, and survive, total confinement.

The point I am trying to make is this. If you have self-control, you have power in menacing circumstances.

Another point about helplessness is: It is the people who feel the most helpless who make it the most difficult for another person to connect with them. They stir up feelings of helplessness in others. Their apparent immobility and impene-trability give them a form of passive power that they do not recognize, but which is experienced by other people around them.

Sometimes I feel helpless as a therapist when I am with a person who has a "wall" around themselves. They send an S.O.S. requesting relief from their helpless predicament, yet block my attempts to show them an exit or prevent me from assisting them to remove the barriers they perpetuate—barriers that hold them in a helpless position. I can see that the helplessness they perceive stems from the helplessness they experienced as a child in their family of learning, yet the client denies that influence, and clings to their helpless perspective, perpetuating their own victimization.

It takes a strong belief in what "can be" for a therapist to see the hope that exists for such people, and much patience to convey quiet optimism to a person who is entrenched in helplessness, and frightened of the power that is there for the taking.

It can be especially trying when the client perceives the therapist as having power to alleviate their upset, in spite of the client's own, unperceived, obstructions. The therapist may be accused of being inept or uncaring. The client, in misery and anger, doesn't acknowledge that the therapist—as a human being—only has control over their own life, and no control at all over the lives of others. When the client does not grant the therapist authority to help, therapy makes little progress.

I have broken the impasse with clients by expressing the helplessness I feel. I tell them that I feel helpless to help them. I convey that if I'm feeling helpless, the helplessness that they experience must be unbearable. I emphasize that the only way to change that is for us to work together to improve their life.

When I'm working with a couple, I find that if one person feels helpless, the other usually feels helpless, also. The more helpless one of them feels, the more helpless the other one feels. The more powerless each one feels, and the more entrenched each one becomes, the more their feelings of helplessness are increased within their couple dyad.

Some people "throw in the towel" when a disagreement occurs. That can be an invincible move in blocking efforts toward a mutual decision. I find it enormously frustrating, in my own relationships, when someone will not confront an issue. It is even worse when the person compliantly "gives in." I would far rather they express themselves so we can struggle to a workable solution, than to have someone yield without agreement.

When you give away your power, it may be because you fear another person. You fear you will lose something, fail to gain something you want, or be punished for causing discord. **The greatest fear of all is the fear of losing the affection of a person who is important to you.**

If you were punished for "talking back" to your parents, punished for fighting, accused of starting strife in your family, you will have difficulty participating in disagreements.

If you observed conflict that was like a world war with brief truces (if any) but never any peace in your family, you will be afraid to be involved in a controversy. You will believe there is no point in attempting a resolution, because you believe no such thing as resolution exists.

If you have always lost every encounter you entered, you will consider yourself stupid to enter the fray. "The outcome is predictable," you think, "so I'll save my effort and give in. That way, I won't lose what I now have."

If you were rejected, given the "silent treatment," or ignored when you spoke your thoughts, you are probably afraid to express your wishes, and so you concede.

All of these experiences contribute to self-defeating attitudes that perpetuate feelings of helplessness. They lead to a "roll over and die" approach to dissension.

The opposite helplessness-inducing circumstance is to be frightened by your own feelings of anger or aggression. We have been thinking about the fear of others. Now let us look at the fear of ourselves.

If you have been taught that you should not express anger, you may have taken that lesson to the extreme of believing that you should not even *feel* anger. Usually a person will then block anger from their awareness. If you are in a situation in which you feel angry and you become aware of it, the fear is that you will express it and be punished.

There is often a fear that you will destroy someone or something if you express your anger. If you have kept it bottled inside, there is the fear of the intensity that has built. The fear is that if it comes out it will obliterate everything in sight. The problem is that if you repress your anger, you will feel helpless.

Anger can be an enormous asset for reaching a goal if you allow yourself to experience it and direct it to a purpose or cause. It is not necessary to have anger in order to achieve, but it is clearly difficult to overcome feelings of helplessness if you "must" turn your anger inside, instead of using that anger energy with a sense of direction.

Helplessness Masks Other Feelings

I have mentioned earlier that actions that look like anger often mask helplessness. I must also emphasize that seldom does helplessness exist without anger also being present. Fear of the anger intensifies the feelings of helplessness.

One antidote to helplessness is mobilized anger. By this I am not suggesting violent flailing or hollering. Such impulsiveness is usually rooted in helplessness.

I am suggesting that you explore the value of anger which leads to constructive activity. Caring anger expressed in the form of action precipitates more benevolence in our society than most people feel comfortable to acknowledge.

Sometimes attaining power is a matter of discovering what is lying underneath the helplessness, dealing with that, and then moving beyond it. Allowing anger to provide you with a sense of direction and power accomplishes far more than merely letting it fester and allowing yourself to become immobilized. Constructively directed anger can accomplish a lot for yourself and on behalf of others.

A woman who wanted a supervisory/director type of position within her company once came to see me. She was so angry and helpless when it came to dealing with the administrator that she was ready to resign. In the process of working this through with her during one of our sessions, I gave her permission to feel the anger, and helped her to release it. She left relieved and with a sense of her own power.

Two weeks later she was appointed to the advanced position she had wanted. The administrator had not changed. What had changed was that the woman was no longer immobilized by a feeling of helplessness and fear of her anger. Once she had developed acceptance of her anger and was able to express it, she had a different perspective of both the administrator and herself. This acceptance of her anger mobilized her to make the moves she needed to make, and to progress aggressively to a new position.

Dr. Spock, early in his career, devoted his life to children as a pediatrician. In his later years he exemplified caring anger by his actions as a person concerned about society. He expressed his anger in protest of the abuse of children and adults by military weapons and nuclear arms.

Caring anger in the midst of helpless feelings was exhibited by people who were incensed at the violent intervention the United States made in Vietnam and the toll taken both as American youths died overseas and as repression of freedom increased at home. Once people saw on TV the violence of police "riot squads" toward our own youth, they took a conscientious look at what was occurring in our own country, and began to put pressure on our government to end the war.

Compassionate anger can be a mobilizing force empowering people to create constructive change.

Martin Luther King, Jr., gave hope where there was no hope. He replaced helplessness with power—the power that comes from a dream and a mission of justice for all. He provided a model for people of conscience to stand firm for truth. His caring anger toward a brutal, racist system, and his caring kindness for the perpetrators of that system, gave courage to the system's victims and reduced their oppression.

Those who cling to helplessness as a way of life are attempting to cope with the pain and fear in their lives. Helpless feelings are reduced only when you face the fears and the pain that are so frightening.

Courage that can cope with helplessness and provide stability comes about only by the willingness to take responsibility for yourself. It means seeing the truth about yourself and speaking the truth to those around you. It means risking rejection and abuse. It comes from the determination to gain in spite of the risk of losing. It takes a trust in yourself that transcends the repressive experiences from the past, the intimidations of the present, and the fears of the future. It comes from the perspective of life as being a challenge, with a desire to live life to its fullest.

It helps, in the midst of the feeling of powerlessness that often accompanies helplessness, to be aware that there are people who, if you are willing to ask, will assist you with the predicament that is provoking your feelings of helplessness.

It helps, in the midst of the loneliness that often accompanies helplessness, to seek to be with kind, caring people and to ask for their affection.

It helps, in the midst of the despair that often accompanies helplessness, to believe there is an energy in the universe that gives you strength to move, when the circumstances surrounding you seem immovable.

Redirecting Helplessness

Let me suggest ways to cope with helplessness.

My first recommendation for when you feel helpless is to recognize that it is only a feeling. It does not tell you about the reality around you.

My second recommendation is to seriously assess the feelings you have. Look under the helplessness to see if another feeling lurks there. It is possible the feeling of helplessness may cover up another feeling, such as anger or pain or fear —especially fear.

If you have been taught you are not supposed to express anger, then you will feel helpless if it is necessary for you to be aggressive to get your needs met or to protect yourself. The helplessness is your barrier against expressing your underlying feeling, which is anger.

When helplessness is a cover for fear, you must get beneath the helplessness to assess your fear, to discover its source. By naming your fear, you can assess the realism of your fear. Then pick your options, fully aware of the frightening consequences of your actions.

I have attempted to make each chapter in this book self-contained; however, the chapter on fear is especially relevant to helplessness, because people feel helpless when they fear that they cannot get—or will lose—what they need, want, or desire.

The third thing you need to know is whether the feelings of helplessness are from past experiences that you have carried into the present, or from the present situation, serving as a signal that you need to do something—to act.

The fourth suggestion is to discover your options so that you can act wisely. Don't eliminate any of them. When someone appears to have control over you and you feel helpless, consider every option, even those you would never select.

The reason I suggest that you think about extreme choices is to encourage you to make a list that includes EVERY possibility, eliminating none. Then you can see the ridiculousness of some of the options. If you don't include the horrible or ridiculous, you will automatically exclude other apparently implausible, but preferable, choices.

The point is: **It is beneficial to consider every option to alleviate the feelings of helplessness.**

My fifth suggestion is to express your needs, wants, and wishes clearly and directly. Many people feel helpless because they do not express themselves. If you tell a person or group of people of your needs, you provide them with the possibility of responding by meeting your needs. Few people are mind readers, or even good guessers. If you never take the first step of expressing yourself, you are stuck, which feels helpless. If you ask and get your needs met—instead of waiting for a mind reader or good guesser—you won't feel helpless.

If you have clearly stated your need and no one chooses to respond, it clarifies for you that it's necessary to look elsewhere to find a new resource. Then you won't feel helpless.

It is unfair to others and unwise for yourself if you withhold stating your needs, wants, and wishes. It is unfair because there are many kind, caring people in this world who get much satisfaction from being nice to another person. You block them from a source of joy and self-satisfaction in giving by preventing them from knowing your wishes.

I do not mean to give a false impression. There are some people who cannot give, or who resent giving. One day Matt, Jeph, and I were in the bank, where I was making a deposit. Matthew, who was three at the time and who is loved by everyone and who is always courteous, asked the teller, "May I please have a lollipop?" It was a reasonable request, as he had always been given one before.

The teller snapped, "No, you may not! We only give lollipops to nice little boys, and they don't ask."

She trembled as my wrath fell upon her. "Well, I'm glad he asked," I said. "I encourage my son to ask for what he wants."

Flustered, she responded, "It's the bank's policy."

"That's a lousy policy," I spewed.

I took my money, put my arms around my kids, and left. It took three more times in the bank of being nice to her before she recovered sufficiently to relax in my "overwhelming" presence.

Saying no to Matt was not what infuriated me. Children need to learn how to receive "no" for an answer. It was the repugnant look on her face and the nasty tone in her voice and, especially, the helplessness-inducing message she was giving to Matt and to Jeph that "nice boys don't ask."

Having been born under the sun sign Libra, I must balance this incident a bit. This woman may have been taught as a child that she should not ask for anything, so her whole life she has felt helpless to get her needs met. When she was asked by Matt for the lollipop, she resented a child who could ask clearly and directly for what he wanted. This may be overly "shrinky," but please tolerate my idiosyncrasies!

Even if your parents taught you not to ask, most people find it a lot easier to be asked than to have to guess. Most people are pleased to respond to a clearly stated need.

Parents who teach their children not to ask may do so because they are uncomfortable saying no. Some parents were punished as a child when they said no. People have been rejected when they said no. To say no to their child raises in them a fear of punishment.

Some parents are have difficulty saying no because they love their child and want to say yes. They say no because they don't have the method or the financial means to give their child what the child wants. They discourage their child from asking for things so they won't feel the pain of saying no to them.

When you are the one being asked for something, it is better to say no, than to say yes and resent it, or to say yes when you don't mean it, or to say yes when you know that you will not follow through with the promise. I can deal with a reasonable—or unreasonable—no, much better than I can with the confusion and disappointment of an insincere yes.

The best type of no is the one said kindly, with a reasonable explanation. It is wonderful to know that we are understood and liked, even if our specific physical need is not met. After all, our basic need is for affection and caring.

The point is: It is much better to express your need and have the gratification of a positive response, or the pain of a negative response, than it is to walk through life feeling helpless and powerless.

My sixth suggestion is to select wisely the people with whom you associate. Surrounding yourself with kind, caring, supportive people reduces your feelings of helplessness. It helps you to be more creative, productive, and powerful. Plus, it is easier to deal with the oppressive people when your life is full of supportive people.

The older I get, the more patient I am with people in general, and the less tolerant I am with how I am treated by negative people. I expect to receive from everyone the best treatment humanly possible.

The message I want to impress on you is this. **Helplessness is a feeling. You are only powerless if you choose to give away your power.** **I cheer you on to tap into your inner source of power, and to seek dependable external sources of power, when you feel helpless. Whatever the external circumstances, take control of yourself.**

Your inner attitude can even exert external power. You can often influence, and at times even determine, the outcome of an apparently helpless event because you feel self-control.

Each of us has power within ourselves if we can grasp a realistic perspective on our present situation.

If you have grown up in a "Hurtful, Frightening Family," the inevitable helplessness distorts the present perspective of your external status as an adult. The experiences from your past eclipse your personal power.

My son, Matt, and I teach a course entitled "Projecting Personal Power in Presentations." It is exciting to watch people, in four weekly sessions, move beyond fear to experience a sense of confidence and personal power. Through the use of a video camera, and by highlighting each person's strengths, we help them to see their present reality as an adult, contrasted with the stifling images they learned in their family while growing up.

One man, after watching the videotape replay, said with his head bowed in embarrassment, "I know I have a terrible voice."

The facial expressions in the rest of the class ranged from shock to surprise to disbelief. Matt and I were stunned.

When we all recovered, the man explained that when he was a boy, members of his family used to tell him, "Your voice is too loud!"

The reality is that he has a deep, rich, full voice. It is not "loud." It has marvelous vibrancy. It has a quality that is soothing when he is with a few people, but could fill an auditorium were he speaking to a large audience.

It was exciting to see the smile on his face spread as he began to relax into the awareness that he has a magnificent voice.

One series of classes concluded with a comment from a man who had been tremendously frightened when he gave his first talk to the class. He glowed as he expressed his enthusiasm: "I have been asked to introduce two speakers to an audience of a thousand people. What is astonishing to me is, I am actually excited."

For people who have the courage to face their fear, our course has been a safe, quick way to see themselves in a new light.

All of us need assistance throughout our lives, either to improve our life or to get out of situations that seem helpless. For some people that means to read a book or listen to tapes For some, it means to take a course or to attend college. For some people that means to get involved in politics. For others it means to form a power group to create social change. For some, it means help to get away from an abusive male or female mate. For some, it means to gather family support to confront a boss and risk losing their job. For some, it means a career counselor to aid in finding a different job. For some, individual, group, or family therapy is the solution.

There are people in our society who consider someone who seeks help as weak, or even crazy. Those people can be especially critical of the person who chooses psychotherapy. The truth is that I have seen many people in therapy who have much more strength than those who avoid seeking the help they need. Often it is the most frightened and vulnerable people who are the most critical of those who seek assistance.

The doubters fail to recognize the amount of courage and strength it requires to explore family attitudes and teachings, to risk confronting lifelong beliefs, to face their emotions, to learn to release those emotions, and to endure the difficulty that friends and loved ones place in the path of personal change.

People who avoid facing themselves, sadly, miss the sense of integrity, the self-acceptance, the inner peace, the solidness that comes from the courage to know yourself and affirm yourself.

The resolve to know the truth, and to live it, gives a power that far exceeds external authority or the intimidation of others. The power that prevails over helplessness is the determination to face what is, and to *change it.*

I wish for you the insight to see beyond your feelings of helplessness, and the quiet strength to get everything in life that you, as a uniquely beautiful human being, deserve.

I hope you have a concern for others that will inspire you to guide them through the maze of their helplessness to a quality of life that every person, everywhere, deserves as his or her birthright.

Take joy with you wherever you go,

...And watch it grow.

PLEASURE AND JOY

Enjoy Pleasure. Take Joy with you wherever you go.
I have used both words, *pleasure* and *joy,* in this chapter's title because *pleasure* includes tranquillity, whereas *joy* is exuberant. The term *pleasure* seems to encompass a broader range of experience, but there are people who think of pleasure as sinful gratification. *Joy* does not seem to capture the quiet peace that the word *pleasure* carries with it. In an attempt to include the meaning of each of these words, I have used both.

Terms that expand the meaning of pleasure and joy are: happiness, ecstasy, fun, excitement, relaxation, delight, exhilaration, contentment, bliss, gladness, merriment, exultation, glee, gaiety, and especially, self-acceptance and peace.

From this point on, I will use *pleasure* and *joy* interchangeably, having already established their similarities and subtle distinctions.

A derivation of pleasure is the word *pleasing,* which can have several meanings. It can mean attractive or pleasing to look at.

A self-accepting, joy-filled person is attractive and pleasing to the eye. A person who enjoys life is a joy to behold.
If you like yourself and like other people, you will radiate joy.

A glamorous person doesn't necessarily have joy. A physically attractive person may be self-deprecating and have a lot of pain, if they come from "The Hurtful, Frightening Family."

Pleasing can also mean *to satisfy others*. A person who is always pleasing others may not have joy either. If you exclude joy for yourself, you won't have it to give to other people.

A person who pleases others and is self-pleasing can be very attractive to other people, and have much joy in their own life. Joy in your life makes you attractive.

One night at a dance, I was talking with a good friend during the music break. When the band returned, I asked him if he would like to dance. Even though he knows that I do not let rigid attitudes deter me from having fun with my friends, he was surprised.

He said, "Well, since it is a fast one, I will. If it was a slow one, I wouldn't." Most fast dances are like calisthenics to music, so a fast one seemed safe enough to him. We began "dancing" and two women and another man joined us. There were five people together on the dance floor, having a great time.

Other people just stood there looking on, watching us enjoy ourselves. They were too shy to make a move, but didn't want to miss out on watching our fun.

Later one of the women who had joined us asked me to dance. She commented that she didn't know what I was like, but she knew my friend was exciting. When she saw us dancing she wasn't about to miss out on sharing our energy.

If you do not have joy in your own life, it is unlikely that you can give pleasure to others. **When you have joy, it becomes contagious.**

I think joy is a choice we make. Some people think it isn't that easy. It's not.

Joy is as elusive as love.

Self-love is essential to joy.

You must make friends with your feelings if you are to have self-love.

It is essential to release anger and pain, to get perspective on fear, to cope with helplessness, and to express affection if you want to have joy in your life. Holding anger and pain inside is exhausting, and occupies a lot of space in your body. Unbridled fear drains your strength that could be used in more pleasurable ways. Helplessness is a heavy burden that binds joy.

When you release anger, you make space for other feelings, such as affection or joy, which leads to more joy. When you let go of your pain, you make space for pleasure. When you get your fears into perspective, you have freedom to make decisions that will be pleasurable for you. If you choose options that diffuse the helpless feelings, you can move beyond helplessness to joy. Expressing affection to someone you care for certainly brings pleasure when they receive it, and adds to your pleasure when they give affection in return.

I hope it is obvious why I placed "Pleasure and Joy" as the last of the chapters on feelings. How you deal with the feelings in the preceding chapters is directly related to the amount of joy you will have in your life.

This is also true: **To make a decision that you *will have* joy in your life affects the choices you make about how to manage your other feelings. When you choose joy in your life, you will cope with your other feelings in a way that ultimately brings pleasure.**

Please choose joy for yourself. My purpose in providing this book for you is to enlarge the amount of pleasure in your life. Have fun while you read it.

The Wisdom of Choosing Joy

Joy is a choice you make. If you make the decision to have as much joy as possible in your life, that affects all your other choices.

Most people don't know that it is possible to choose joy. They have been taught to suffer.

In the Hurtful, Frightening Family, joy is not popular. "Misery loves company" seems to be the operative phrase in this kind of family. If either parent is chronically unhappy, they will take the joy or enthusiasm out of their children's or mate's life. It doesn't take long after a child is born for the child to be as miserable as the other members of the family.

This misery is especially true of a family with an alcoholic member. Any ray of sunshine that manages to shine through the smog is quickly reduced to suffering.

An interesting situation often occurs in therapy. After I have seen a suffering person as a client for a while, I detect that things are going well, but they are blocking feelings. When I raise questions about the barrier, it becomes apparent that they are feeling joy in their life. A little further exploration makes it clear that they were afraid to tell me how well things are going and how happy they are feeling because of the fear that I will do or say something to take their pleasure away.

Because of the trust that has been building between us, my client knows intellectually that I would not take their joy away, but with their memory full of pain and fear from past experiences, the question arises: "Why wouldn't he?" The fear and pain answer: "He will. It has always happened in the past. I'm not going to risk losing this joy now that I've discovered it. I'd better not let him know how wonderful I really feel."

When I remind the client that a goal of the therapy is to bring joy into their life, the joyous feelings begin to flow! That is exciting to see.

The point is: It is common for people to be afraid to show their excitement or enthusiasm because negative people have been unkind to them when they shared it and their pleasure was taken away.

The more we know about ourselves, about our feelings, and about our experiences in our family of learning, the more choices we have.

One evening, a friend of mine called about getting together on Friday night. I had some other tentative plans that might conflict, so I suggested I would get back to her.

I was supposed to call her on Friday, but I couldn't reach her because she had been shifted to another part of the building where she worked. By the time I made contact, she had made other plans with other friends.

I was miserable. I laid on my bed and began to emotionally bludgeon myself because I hadn't asked her for an alternative way to reach her, although I had not known that I would need one.

Then I realized: This is ridiculous. I decided I was *going* to have fun. I picked up my tennis racquet, went over to the courts, met some friends, got some exercise, and had a great time. I returned to my apartment, fixed myself a nice dinner, and enjoyed the evening. I had decided to have a pleasurable time rather than be miserable. It happened!

Let me quickly point out that there are times when it is pleasurable to suffer. I was interested in dating a woman friend when I was in college. She decided she didn't want to date me. I went around for three days in "sack cloth and ashes."

There was another wonderful woman friend who tried to cheer me up, but I felt like beating her over the head with a club. Who did she think she was to try to take away my misery?

An interesting footnote to this story is that, when my parents came to visit me at the campus, I introduced them to the friend who was not interested in deepening our friendship. Later, my Dad commented, "She's a lot like your mother." Is it conspicuous to you that superimposing (transference) had much to do with the intensity of my attachment to her, and the degree of suffering that I experienced from her rejection?

It just occurred to me that her name was the same as my older, favorite cousin who used to baby-sit for me. That's a double whammy! Plus, she surely was nice, and pretty, too. (See "Superimposing" in the "Affection" chapter.)

I was once told about a mother in a Midwestern town who went to visit the grave of her son every day. The opinion of the storyteller in the town was that, if her son were raised from the dead, she would kill him so she could keep on with her suffering.

Contrast this *unnecessary* suffering with the *essential* suffering involved in positive grieving to let go of someone you love. Constructive grieving provides the opportunity for you to create a new enriching life for yourself.

Sometimes when someone dies, family members or the family doctor want to "protect" the grieving person from their emotions. This is a totally destructive attitude toward life. There may be occasions when a person for health reasons needs medication to buffer them from the intensity of their pain, but to constantly encourage people to avoid life's emotions is tragic. To avoid the emotions of grieving with medication, because we fear our feelings or because people around us are uncomfortable with feelings, is only to delay the necessary release that must take place. It may also invite intense depression, physical illness, or even suicide.

A person who chooses to, or is forced to, hold inside the feelings that accompany grieving, is "locked" into emotional, and often physical, suffering. If a person is given the **affection and support to face their emotions**, it is far better physically and emotionally for them. When a person is permitted to experience their feelings without heavy medication, they will be able to move through the pain to the pleasure on the other side of the suffering.

It is unfortunate when medication is prescribed to block feelings and is used to take the place of genuine caring in medical or psychological practice, or in families. Giving a pill is much quicker and seems more cost-effective than giving yourself. **Taking a pill—with its side effects—is far more costly in the long run than finding someone who is willing to take the time to give you their shoulder to cry on.**

The wife of a man in my congregation died. She and her husband were both in their seventies. I realized during the funeral that he was not facing her death. I emphasized to him that he could call me at any time, day or night. He didn't attend the church, but I kept contact with him, anticipating some future difficulty.

Three months later at 2:00 a.m., I got a call to go to his house. When I entered the kitchen, he pointed to a Bible on the table and said, "Convince me that I shouldn't commit suicide."

The tombstone for his wife's grave had arrived that day. That finally broke through his denial and cracked him open. He didn't know how to cope with the pain.

I spent about an hour with him. When I left his home to go back to bed, I thought he was okay, but there was still a question about what he would do. The next morning he called to let me know that he was dealing with the grief and to arrange to take me to dinner. Later we had a wonderful time together over a New England boiled dinner, his favorite meal, at his favorite restaurant.

If a person does not deal with their grief, they will have an emotional or physical breakdown at a later time. If they experience their emotions and move through them, they can return to a joyous life without their deceased loved one.

"Getting High"—The Best Way

People who cannot allow themselves to experience and express "negative" feelings usually cannot express the "positive" ones. The repression may get generalized to all feelings. These words are in quotation marks because I believe all feelings are positive when we know how to deal with them constructively, making them our friends.

There are people who attempt to find greater ecstasy by using drugs. In the long run, they never do. All they do is destroy themselves.

I believe emphatically that you don't need drugs to get high if you allow yourself to experience the full intensity of your feelings and, with loving support from friends and family, resolve them. You also don't crash afterward. The ecstasy thus achieved in your life is stable and lasting.

Pleasure is not an isolated feeling. I mentioned in the "Affection" chapter that affection and anger can exist together. Other emotions can accompany pleasure. You can have pleasure along with anger. For people who allow themselves to experience anger, there can be a tremendous sense of inner strength and self-confidence in choosing how to express anger. There can be pleasure in the accomplishments that were motivated by or achieved by venting anger into productive projects. There can be pleasure in releasing anger in constructive ways, either to build intimacy or to keep people away when you need to protect yourself from them.

Pain can lead to pleasure if you can cry the pain out and release it.

You can experience a lot of pleasure when someone shows you affection.

I have tried to show that feelings that are often considered "negative" can bring pleasure. The one feeling I have had the most difficulty connecting with pleasure is the feeling of helplessness. It is hard to see that there could be any pleasure derived from feeling helpless. However, I have discovered that there can be pleasure in feeling the satisfaction that you have made the best choice possible within the limitations of the available options. There is pleasure in knowing that you have done your best in a terrible situation. There is pleasure in the self-confidence you gain as you cope with apparently hopeless experiences. It is possible to have helplessness that results in joy.

Our culture discourages authentic joy, pleasure, and excitement. It appears as though a synthetic high from alcohol, prescribed medication, or street drugs is more acceptable than genuine joy.

Sometimes we are taught not to be exuberant. Everybody has had the experience of being excited and has had someone try to strip away their joy.

An example: You probably remember buying a holiday present, which you knew was exactly right for the recipient, and was just what you wanted to give to the person you love. While sharing your present with someone else, you heard "They won't like that," or "That's too expensive."

A personal example occurred when Matt was three. We went to the Ice Capades at Boston Garden. The performers were coming around the ice gathering children in the front row of the audience to take them for a ride in a sleigh. Matt started onto the ice to run to the sleigh. I told him to wait because I was afraid he would fall on the ice, and also because I thought the skaters would come to our seats to get him. Unfortunately, they stopped picking up the children just before reaching our seats.

I still feel sad when I think of the incident, because I prevented Matt from having an unusual experience. I used to feel guilty about it, because my fear had interfered with the initiative he had taken. Fortunately, there were many other opportunities to encourage and support him in his ambitions.

As an adult, Matt goes for it! When he was seventeen, he graduated with honors, but he didn't know what he wanted to study in college, so he registered his own business and established a very profitable and productive venture. The day before he graduated from high school, there was a picture and story about Matt's company in the business section of the newspaper.

Two years later he announced to me that he wanted to buy into my consulting and speaking business. Working with Matt tripled my fun. Two months after his twenty-first birthday, he bought a single-house-appearing duplex on a beautiful two and a half acre lot. (Parents, there is hope for our children even when we make mistakes.)

Matt goes for it!

Another way that we block joy from our life is by failing to allow ourselves to be the person we are.

You are being both yourself and human when you experience feelings. You are a beautiful person at the core of your being. To share your feelings and your inner beauty with trustworthy friends is sheer joy.

Putting walls around ourselves diminishes our pleasure. A wall around us keeps others out, locking us in isolation. Some of the clients whom I have seen in the most pain were those who felt isolated as children because it was unsafe for them to express their feelings without being punished or rejected. As adults, their fear of expressing feelings continued to inhibit them from releasing the pent-up feelings. Often the emotional pain is excruciating and many times there is intense physical pain as well.

Feelings are all a part of life. Joy is a natural emotion, just as pain, anger, affection, fear, and helplessness are all perfectly human. If we prohibit ourselves from experiencing any of the feelings, we separate ourselves from who we are.

Taking life too seriously obviously blocks having pleasure. Life can be a fun adventure, if we approach it that way.

It can be fun to be playful with the image we present to the world. Some people take their images very seriously. I take image seriously enough to play with it. I have "impress 'em" suits, which I reserve for wearing in special situations. I really enjoy "putting on the Ritz." At the same time, I can enjoy, when I'm dressed in my best, being loose as a goose.

One time, after dining in a Boston restaurant, I came out of the men's room with one pants leg purposely rolled up to my knee. My friend laughed and said, "I dare you to walk through the restaurant like that." I am not a person who takes a dare for the sake of taking a dare, but I thought it would be fun, so I agreed.

My friend and I had done a TV program earlier, and were dressed to project a glamorous and professional image. Picture a beautiful, well-dressed woman with her arm through the arm of a gray-haired man (prematurely gray, obviously!) in a vested pinstriped suit, walking through a restaurant with one pants leg rolled up to his knee. Some people had a chance to laugh and release some of their tension from a stressful day. We walked through the restaurant as though we were oblivious to what was happening, and later laughed as we enjoyed remembering our foolishness.

My father taught me how to walk with one leg bending at the knee with my foot on the curb and the other leg straight with my foot in the gutter. Only your legs move as your body goes forward without your head bobbing up and down. It is a maneuver both impressive and difficult, but can be mastered with some practice.

I sometimes assign curb-walking to clients who are concerned about appearing foolish. If you see a conservative businessman in Boston walking with one foot in the gutter and the other on the curb without moving his body up and down, you will know he is a client of mine.

Image can be fun if you know how to play at it, and don't get locked into taking image too seriously.

One of the most releasing and pleasurable things I know is laughing. Jeph, Matt and I went to a Disney movie with one of their friends. The movie was hilarious. I laughed robustly and Matt and Jeph laughed enthusiastically. The entire theater was roaring with laughter. It was fun.

A friend and I went to a movie. She was laughing so hard that the people sitting near us began to laugh. Then the laughter rippled through the theater in waves radiating from her as if from the center of a pool of water. It is fun when laughter is contagious and people join you.

Another time my parents, a psychologist friend, and I visited a restaurant in Boston. We enjoyed a wonderfully relaxing, fun evening. The waitress shared in our fun. When we left, she told us she found it hilarious that some of the other patrons thought we must have been drinking to enjoy ourselves so much. None of us had any alcoholic beverages, but we were having a great time.

If you allow anybody to inhibit your laughter and your excitement, then you are not going to have pleasure. I think anybody who tries to stifle your enthusiasm about life deserves to be flogged with a stick, an umbrella, or anything you can find to make them back off. There is nothing better in life than joy, fun, excitement, ecstasy, and pleasure. Laughter certainly is a great part of it.

Our culture often promotes excesses at celebrations as though they were pleasures, such as over-eating, over-drinking, or exhausting oneself at some activity. It is as though parties, sporting events, and holidays give license for self-destruction. I have considered writing an article on the topic, "Fun As Futility," because of the destructive way people approach leisure time.

It is a familiar story: The groom is miserable on his wedding day because of the antics at the previous night's bachelor party; a wedding party with guests who are so drunk that they can't drive home, or, at the least, are miserable for days; holiday gatherings—"celebrations"—that have so much food, sugar, and alcohol consumed—so much "fun"—that the resulting traffic accidents and/or fatalities, and affaires, not of the heart, at company parties, cause suffering for their families through the rest of the holidays, and beyond.

I feel pain for those people, including those who have to be carried out of a party. **What troubles me is the attitude about fun in our culture that supports excesses, especially those that encourage—even pressure—people to indulge in behavior that brings much unnecessary pain to themselves and to others.**

I can have consistent joy in my life by eating delicious foods that are healthy, and by having fun without alcohol or sugar. Sugar makes me drowsy, which makes it dangerous to have a lot of sugar and then drive. Alcohol contains a lot of sugar and can also be dangerous, so I avoid it. I have been accused of "sneak drinking" at parties because people could not believe I was having that much fun on just plain mineral water. Yes, I was!

Anything you do to abuse your body takes away from your pleasure. It is difficult to enjoy life when you do things that deplete your body so it will not function, or put stress on your body that drains your energy or even makes you sick. If you are to have joy, you must take care of your body, give it nutritious food, affectionate physical contact, sufficient rest, exercise, and abundant relaxation from the stresses of living.

Celebrate your body! Take good care of it. Be kind to it. The reward is that you will feel better and it will work better for you, so that you can have more pleasure in your life.

I have known people who can only relax and enjoy themselves when they get away. That doesn't make sense to me. I believe we need to build joy into our lives every day. That doesn't mean life is always going to be pleasurable, but it means that you can approach life from the perspective of joy. It means that you can make a decision to enjoy yourself to the best of your ability, whatever the setting or location.

I also know people who work all week long at jobs they hate, just so they can get away for the weekend. I once changed jobs so that I could do more of what I enjoy, even though I expected to earn about four thousand dollars a year less. Twenty years ago, that was a lot of money. Don't get the impression that I had so much money that it wouldn't matter. I didn't, and I don't, but I am rich beyond belief.

Roadblocks to Joy

Let me discuss more ways that people block themselves from

joy. One way is through an attitude that scarcity prevails in the universe. If you believe there is not enough love, joy, food, money, friends, jobs, time, and so on, then you approach the world from the perspective of fear. There is certainly no pleasure when you believe in and fear scarcity.

If you approach the world with the belief that it is a terrible place, or are approaching all people with distrust, you are going to be hurt, which will confirm your belief in scarcity, and life will continue to be miserable and full of suffering for you.

Many people experience a deficiency of their needs, and live in horrible conditions. It doesn't need to be that way.

The problem is not one of scarcity. The problem is priorities. Leaders in corporations and governments make decisions that affect great numbers of people. They have been making decisions that benefit a few people and increase suffering for others. It is a matter of choosing the wrong priorities, not a matter of inadequate resources. When our country's resources are used to create military weapons that are sold to warring countries to kill each other—and sold within our country with the result that we have war on our city streets—scarcity is not the problem. It is the wrong perspective and the wrong priorities.

Our country has the intellectual, material, and financial resources to feed, cloth, provide health care, build roads and bridges, provide sufficient housing, and educate all our citizens. If the people in power in our government and in our corporations made their choices with humanity in mind, things would change for the better.

That is not a "bleeding heart" approach. Historically, countries have decayed from within. When people in power use their power for the people, everyone benefits. There is plenty of wealth for the rich and enough for everyone else.

Anthony Robbins is a very wealthy man. He uses his money to help other people improve their lives. I have both observed and experienced him and have seen that he also gives a tremendous amount of caring to people. I don't know him personally, but from what I do know of him, I greatly respect his attitude and actions toward people.

If you approach life from the perspective of a belief in abundance for youself, and in the power of your choices, you will receive more of life's gifts and increase the joy in your life.

Another roadblock to joy is difficulty receiving. There are people who are quite able to give, but either cannot or will not let themselves receive. We miss the gratification of the gift—and the joy of giving someone else the pleasure of giving—if we do not allow ourselves to receive.

Some parents think their children will be happy if they give everything to them. What is often the case, though, is the children develop a sense that they don't have any worth. When a child wants to do something for you, or give something to you, perhaps something as simple as a flower, **take it.** The child will have an excellent sense of self-worth by having you receive their flower. You are receiving them as a person when you receive their gift. You are instilling self-confidence by approving of their choice of a gift.

There were very special times when my children gave me something. I received a beautiful letter from my son Jeph, which he had written for me at school for Father's Day. Matt bought me a picture of a sailboat with a spinnaker on the front. It was for no particular occasion—simply because he wanted to please me.

The spontaneous gifts from your children can be just as important to your friendship with them, and to their sense of self-worth, as anything you can buy for them.

A person who has difficulty receiving blocks others from the pleasure of giving.

The interesting thing about giving is that you can have a lot of pleasure if you give yourself and your possessions to others.

You have pleasure the first time when you give yourself, or something of yourself, and it is received. You have a second pleasure from the receiver's joy. The third pleasure is the vicarious thrill when you see the person use your gift.

When I was a teenager, my family moved to Kentucky. Even though I had some fine teachers, Kentucky public schools ranked forty-sixth in the country. I transferred to a private Methodist school my senior year of high school, and lived with my aunt, uncle, and cousins whose house was next to the Erie School.

Kentucky at the time had a rule that prohibited students from playing sports for a year after a transfer if their parents did not change residence and if they had played a sport in the previous school. Because of that rule, I was ineligible for all sports my senior year in high school, so I was the manager for the basketball team, and the coach asked me to assist him with coaching.

I felt like I was going to die on the night of the first game. When you have the ability to be in the starting lineup and you have to sit on the bench, it is agonizing.

The joy of giving, however, came to me through coaching. I noticed that my cousin, Jim, would get a foul called on him when he tried to block an opposing player's lay-up shot. He was trying to block the ball before the shooter got to the goal.

After the game, I suggested to him that he wait until the opponent brought the ball up toward the basket. Then he could put his hand on top of the ball as it came up, and block the shot cleanly, without fouling.

The next game . . . he did it!

I got a tremendous vicarious thrill from watching him block that shot. It was sheer joy!

It was, and it still is, exciting to recall (if the chills in my body are any indication). The pleasure of seeing someone receive and use what you give them is hard to beat.

I am not the only one who gets joy from seeing someone receive and use what they have been given. My friend, Bob, is a certified tennis instructor. He likes to win. His competitive juices flow, especially, he says, when he is on the opposite side of the net from me.

We were playing at a mixed doubles tennis party one night. I hit a drop shot to win the point. Bob got a big smile on his face, and said, "Great shot. Where'd you get that one?" Then he grinned some more.

Bob had shown me the proper stroke to make a drop shot two weeks earlier. He got a thrill from seeing me execute the shot he had taught me, even though his team lost the point.

It can even be pleasurable to see the recipient of your gift give it to someone else they love. It has been exciting for me to see clients, who have learned how to be caring from me, give caring to their friends. We enjoy talking together about the "ripple effect" of taking their therapy to others. One client during a session said, "We'll ripple them to death!" We both laughed.

Then I exclaimed, "We'll ripple them to *life*!" We both laughed some more. (Therapy sure can be fun.)

You can have pleasure the fourth time when what you give away comes back to you. It may not come back through the same person, but the universe flows with a giver, and it comes back to you.

I took a friend and her daughter to celebrate my friend's birthday at my favorite restaurant, Bishop's. Emily and Abe, the brother and sister who run the restaurant, are wonderful, friendly people, operating their family-owned business. They give a tremendous amount not only to their customers, but also to youth organizations and various charities in the area. The food at the birthday celebration was superb, the atmosphere was friendly, Emily and Abe were gracious, as usual. We had a marvelous time.

My friend called me later to thank me for a wonderful birthday together. I received her appreciation and exclaimed,

"That's right! It *was* your birthday. I had so much fun, I was beginning to think it was *my* birthday." I think I enjoyed her birthday as much as she did.

The pleasure can come from another's appreciation. This seems like such a simple story, but one freezing New England day I was all dressed up, on the way to a meeting, so I stopped at a gas station where an attendant would pump my gas. Usually I pump my own.

The attendant was courteous, even though it was unbearably cold. I gave him a tip and told him how much I appreciated his pumping my gas for me on such a cold day. His face opened in a great big smile as he expressed his gratitude, saying, "You made my day!"

It's hard to say who got more out of that transaction, the gas station attendant or me. I had a lot of pleasure rejoicing in his joy.

The Pleasure-Giving (and -Receiving) Attitude

How much joy you have in your life has to do with attitude. My attitude is to have as much joy and fun as possible.

Several years ago, when I was directing a clinic, I was asked to do some therapy at another center where a friend of mine was the director. I decided to accept the position because I enjoyed him, and it would be fun for us to work together.

The problem was that in order to have the time to work with him, I needed to drop something that I was doing, as I also had a private practice. Driving home from the clinic I directed, I pictured myself telling the people at The Institute for Life Learning, where I spent part of each week, that I intended to resign. It then dawned on me that I had more fun there than I did at the clinic I was directing.

As the director of the clinic, I had developed the record-keeping procedures, expanded the supervision, weathered some staffing difficulties, and brought the organization to be an efficient operation that served the broader community well; so it was in good shape. Part of my decision was influenced by the fact that I had been director of the clinic for a year, but I had been at the other facility part-time for eight years. That affiliation was meaningful to me. At that moment I decided to resign as the clinic's director. I gave myself a week to think about it, however, knowing I had already made my decision.

I called the administrative director of the organization to have lunch. We chatted a bit over our meal at the restaurant, then he asked why I had wanted to get together. I told him I had decided to leave the clinic.

He was shocked. When he recovered, he asked me why.

I responded, "I'm not having as much fun as I like to."

He looked confused, then burst into laughter. "You know," he said, "if anyone else said that, I would think they were crazy, but somehow, when you say it, it makes sense."

I told him that I take endings seriously, and would allow six weeks to finish the process of leaving.

He jokingly asked if I would take four years to leave. He wasn't happy about my resignation, but he and I always got along really well. He knew me, and understood. He knew that I could give the most to what I enjoy most.

I am not unique in that. **If we enjoy doing the service we provide, others will get joy from it. When we include joy in what we give, the gift is of immeasurable worth.**

What you give out comes back. I really enjoy people. I talk to clerks in stores, to people in elevators. Most people are friendly, if you are friendly to them.

I suppose I shouldn't tell stories about myself like the one that follows, but I will anyway. It emphasizes my point.

At a party one time, one of the other guests said to me, "It's great to have you here. Your smile must light up every room you enter."

At another party, the hostess expressed her appreciation for my presence by saying, "Thanks for coming, and bringing your enthusiasm."

The gift of yourself to others is the most precious present.

Joy and fun are gifts you give to yourself.

When I am anticipating an event, I visualize the circumstances of the event and put myself in the situation. If it feels good, I go. If it doesn't feel good, I don't go. Why should I waste my time and energy being some place that will be a drain, when the reason I'm going is to have fun and relax? That doesn't mean that I lie. People don't have to guess about my reasons.

My kids and I were invited to a cookout at the home of some acquaintances of mine, and I said I preferred not to go. When the woman in the family who had invited us asked why, I explained that I didn't want my kids to be exposed to, and I didn't want to be around, the hostility that went on between her and her husband. She understood, and agreed with, my decision, and thanked me for my honesty.

There are of course times when I get into places where I wish I weren't. Then I usually create some fun for myself, or I leave. People don't seem to mind or miss me if I leave, because it wasn't a fit anyway. **Just as I would not give money or a present when it would not be valued, so I try to avoid putting myself in settings where I would be discounted or unappreciated.**

Give of Yourself—Selectively

I discourage indiscriminate giving. There is no pleasure in giving when the gift is going to be used destructively. It is like throwing a diamond into a cesspool. There is no good that can come of it, and there is no pleasure in it.

It is important to know when to give, and when to withhold the gift. This is true for parents, and for therapists.

There is no benefit to giving to someone when the person needs to do something for themselves.

When my son was five years old, I found him sitting on the floor, totally frustrated with a clock he had taken apart. He was trying to put it back together, amidst fuming and fussing. I offered, "Jeph, would you like some help?"

He declared, "No, I want to do it myself."

Respecting his wishes, I replied, "If you want any help later, let me know."

He never did. He also did not get the clock repaired, but he sure had a great time fuming and fussing and giving it his best try.

I remember being asked to write a letter of reference for a woman who was entering a school to train as a social worker. I knew this woman to be a really mature, caring person, with a tremendous capacity to give.

I wrote a glowing letter of reference, which included a cautionary note that the woman needed to learn from her training when to give and when to hold back giving. One of her personal needs was to give, and it could interfere with the client's need to do for themselves. Sometimes people need to do it for themselves.

There are times when I have refused to see a person for therapy after the evaluation session, because the person's self-destructiveness and distrust of everyone would not allow them to receive the benefits that therapy can provide.

I have also stopped seeing a client when the person is not willing to give up a destructive behavior even though we have approached it from every therapeutic angle. The client's insistence on holding onto the behavior prevents further progress in the therapy. I do not want to take their time and money, and waste my energy, if they are not going to benefit from the therapy. I get uncomfortable making such Godlike decisions, but I feel a responsibility to do what I believe to be necessary.

Knowing when to give and when to withhold can be a difficult decision. It becomes even more difficult and puzzling when you are close to the person involved.

I received a call from a friend who really cared about another woman, who was sick. She was concerned about the medication her sick friend was taking.

My friend was pitting herself against the woman who was using the medication, the woman's family who supported her use of the medication, a doctor who was prescribing the medication, and the psychologist who had sent the woman to the doctor.

How can one person overcome all of this, particularly when the woman who was taking the medication did not want to give it up? She had been told by other physicians that the medication was harmful to her, but wouldn't hear it. I advised my friend to deal with her own feelings of frustration, and to stop putting her valuable energy into an unyielding mess.

In this type of predicament, you can either bang your head against the wall and give yourself a headache, or you can back off. When you care for someone who you perceive to be destroying themselves, you have a choice. You can attempt to control the situation; or you can let the situation go, and take control of yourself.

The only person you can realistically hope to control is yourself.

You will feel horrible when you believe that a loved one is harming themselves or refusing to take good care of themselves. You can't help anyone who won't help themselves, so you must let go and get on with your life.

You do not need poisonous people in your life. The way to discern when to give or act, and when not to, is to assess emotionally and intellectually what the circumstance calls for. If you feel uncomfortable about an option, your feelings are telling you something important. You need to check out the feelings. Perhaps you need more information about the situation. Then you need to look at the options, assess how accurate your emotional cues are, and compare them with the reality you perceive intellectually.

I want you to analyze both what you sense, and what you think, because there are times when your mind is the corrective for what your feelings tell you, and there are other times when your emotions are the corrective for what your mind tells you. Use both feelings and intellect to make your decisions.

Let us continue with the theme of giving. I am taking a major risk in saying that when you give, you get. The risk is that there are people who *give to get*. They give as a form of manipulation so the recipient will feel obligated when the giver wants something. Their attitude is: If I give something to somebody else, then I can "call in" my debts. What appears to be giving becomes an attempt at controlling.

This happens in families and in business. I have seen people in the business world who are afraid to receive from anybody, for fear they would be indebted and the other person could someday "call in their chips."

I think a person who gives to gain power in the form of control will eventually find that it backfires, unless the other person is playing the same game. Nobody wants to feel like an object. The manipulator may gain power, but they will also gain the distrust of others. They will probably feel isolated, unable to trust anyone, because they expect everyone else to act as manipulatively as they do.

If you always expect something in return for what you give, that expectation can take the joy out of giving. Giving is most enjoyable when it is done for the joy of giving.

After a dance, I invited six people to join me in another room. When the waiter delivered the beverages, I paid for the entire group.

The response was, "That's really nice. We will all have to take you out to dinner."

I replied, "Great. When?"

They laughed. Apparently most people reply, "Oh no, you don't have to do that!"

It occurred to me when they suggested the dinner that it would be an excellent excuse for us to get together again at a future time, which would be fun.

Some people believe that when you have been given something, you must immediately give something in return. I simply say, "Thank you, that is really wonderful."

I don't feel a compulsion to immediately return the favor. I assume the gift was given to me because the person wanted me to have it. If they gave it to me because they were looking for something for themselves, they will be disappointed.

Some people feel compelled to bring the host or hostess some sort of present when invited to dinner in their home. That can be really nice, but it is not necessary with me. Sometimes, when a person offers to bring something to add to the dinner, I will say, "Great," and suggest something suitable. Usually I say, "Bring yourself."

To bring yourself as an open, sharing, caring friend is a precious gift. The real joy is not because of what you bring, but because of who you are.

The Killjoy Attitude, and What to Do about It

The opposite is also true. If you don't have joy of your own, it is hard to find, and it's unlikely that you will let it in when you do find it.

I was at a wedding a few years ago, tap dancing with my partner to the wild and savage beat of a terrific drummer who was setting the fast-paced rhythm for the band, which was in turn supporting him. They were terrific.

An elderly couple later came over to my dance partner and me. The woman told us how much she had enjoyed watching us dance. Her husband said, "Tell him what *I* said." She would not, so he quoted himself. "I told her, 'I wish you would break your damned leg.'" I noticed that he had a crippled leg, which may have prevented him from dancing. It was, however, his *attitude*, crippled by bitterness, that prevented him from enjoying the party. I felt sorry that he had an injury, but it was frightening that someone would have that much venom toward me for having fun, and be so imprisoned by his bitterness.

When we are in a lot of pain ourselves and feel helpless to do anything about it, that pain spews out onto other people, like venom from a spitting cobra. We cannot have joy in our lives until we deal with our pain, anger, fear, and helplessness. Only then can we experience pleasure, and choose options better than being bitter.

I threw out my elbow hitting an overhead slam while playing tennis. My doctor told me not to play tennis for six weeks. I didn't—with that arm. I went to a left-handed teaching pro and took three lessons. That way I could play left-handed at the mixed doubles tennis parties I enjoy.

My confidence and competence are not the same left-handed as they are right, but my brain is the same. Hurting my arm did not take away my knowledge of doubles strategy. A hurt elbow is not as devastating as a crippled leg, but the strategy for having joy in your life isn't in either your elbow or your leg. The strategy for having joy is in your head.

W. Mitchell is a perfect example. The W is for Wonderful. His main source of mobility is a wheel chair and he has scars on his face and body, yet he is an inspiration to millions both as a speaker and as a human being. His voice exudes affection, strength and peace.

Bitterness blocks your options. Joy expands your fun. You can choose to be miserable, or you can chose to be happy!

Some people go to a place or function because they think the place itself will generate joy for them. It is sometimes true. Being around joyful people can be joyous. **I think it is far better, when you go someplace, to take your own joy with you.** There is a much better chance that you will enjoy yourself, because if it does not exist where you go, you can generate it yourself.

You can have pleasure in what you do, you can have pleasure in who you are, and you can have pleasure in others.

Sex can be an example of such joy. The more you like and accept yourself, the more comfortable you will feel sharing yourself with another person, first emotionally, and then physically. The more you give of yourself to another person, the more joyous your sexual experience with them will be. The pleasure comes from connecting with another person in a caring way. Sex done strictly for self-gratification is usually empty, at least for one of the people involved—usually for both of them.

Money provides another example of what I mean. Having a lot of money is NOT necessarily pleasurable. I knew a man who was making himself sick both physically and emotionally for a month, trying to decide whether to lease or to buy a piece of property for his business. I asked him for specific figures of what the differences between the two options would be, how much money he had, and how much he could spend in a year.

After I gathered the information, it was obvious he had a lot more money than he would ever be able to spend. I showed him how he had been making himself totally miserable for a month by trying to make a decision about some figures on paper that would in no way affect his quality of life. He made his decision instantly. He had more money than he could ever spend, but had lost perspective and was miserable.

Other people who have lots of money really enjoy their wealth. They know how to use it and share it.

For me money is freedom. It provides me the opportunity to do things for and with people whom I enjoy. I can get and do things for myself that give me joy. Money allows me to pay someone to do the things that I either do not have the talent for or don't want to do for myself. Money buys me the time to do the things that I do best. The more I have, the more I can give to other people to help them have more joy in their lives. Money allows me to contribute to causes that create constructive changes.

Money is like affection. If you don't have it for yourself, you will be under constant pressure and have limits to your freedom. If you don't have it for yourself, you don't have any to give to others. If you hang onto it for self-gratification, it becomes empty. If you use it to meet your needs, the needs of your loved ones, and share it with other people as an extension of yourself as a caring person who has humane values, then money can become an enormous source of joy.

The more you enjoy yourself, the more joy you will have in your life. The more affection you feel for yourself, the more you will allow yourself to receive pleasure from others.

The more pleasure you let yourself receive from others, the more joy you will have to give, and the more affection for yourself you will have.

The more pleasure you receive from others, the better they will feel, because they gave something to you.

The more others appreciate themselves, the more joy they have to give to you and to others—and on and on and on, as the ripple effect benefits more and more people, eventually coming back to you.

I wish for you every little particle of pleasure and every huge mountain of joy that you can attain in your life—all the fun, the enthusiasm, the ecstasy, the love, the laughter that you can experience. Give yourself *fully* to life.

Don't take yourself too seriously. Laugh at your foibles and dance at your follies. (Remember *Zorba, the Greek.*)

Enjoy yourself and the people around you—that is the ultimate joy in life.

MAKE LOVE!

And from time to time, have Sex.

Sexuality

Many people believe that having enjoyable sex is easy. The truth is: **Sex is learned.** That statement was confirmed for me when I was the chaplain at a state facility for adult mentally retarded men. A farm with animals was part of the hospital setting. I observed the farmers "teaching" horses how to breed.

They put a rope around the stud and led him to the mare. The first few times, the male became so excited that he ejaculated before he entered the female. It occurred to me that even wild horses have to learn how to mate. They learn by watching their parents, because horses running wild with the herd don't go off into the woods or some other secluded area. They have sex in the open. Wild horses learn about sex as they grow up watching other horses. It seems to be natural, but that is because it is learned as a part of nature.

Sex is as clumsy for inexperienced, insensitive, or unpracticed humans as it is for horses. If you haven't learned it somewhere, it is unlikely that you will be adept at it.

Most people have seen dogs have sex or, if they've been around a farm, have watched cattle have sex.

It seems obvious that animals and people have to learn—or have to be taught—how to have sex. It does not just come naturally, as we have often been led to believe.

Do *NOT* take this to mean that adults should teach children about having sex by having sex with them. As a therapist, I have suffered with clients through the painful devastation that occurs when an adult has had sex with a young person, especially their own child. This invasion affects a person's life for years, often forever.

I am NOT encouraging you, as parents, to allow your children to observe your sexual activity. Don't panic, however, if your child happens to walk in when you are sharing sex. Treat the incident as natural, and be kind to the intrusive child—but do NOT invite such situations.

I **do** strongly encourage you parents to allow your children to see you **making love,** as it is defined in the chapter on "Affection." To see you be affectionate with each other, to see you express your love by tender words and gestures, and to see you treat each other with kindness is essential for their development and essential for their future relationships. (See the chapters on "Affection" and "The Helpful, Fun Family.")

The Difference Between Making Love and Having Sex

Before we continue, I must clarify some terminology to make sure we are using the same language. People often use different terms for sex. This leads to confusion. Some people don't even like the word *sex*. People who have heard me give speaking presentations have told me that they don't like it when I use the word *sex*. They wish I would say "making love" or "sleeping together." Those phrases all convey different ideas, however.

Many people take sex and their sexuality too seriously. Sex is to be enjoyed. It can be playful. I hope you will read some of this with objectivity, and with a sense of humor.

Let's think about the phrase, "making love." That phrase is often used incorrectly, to mean sex. There is a lot of sex in our culture that has nothing to do with love. There may be no love at all in sex.

People can have sex without any consideration for the feelings, needs, or wishes of their sexual partner. Sex can occur without any intent on the part of the woman or man initiating sex to show affection. Sex can be a power play. Sex can be a way to make oneself feel better or feel loved, with no regard for the other person. Sex can be a way of attempting to confirm one's worth, one's manhood, or one's womanhood. Sex can be a way of expressing rebellion or anger toward the opposite gender, toward our parents, or toward society. Sex can be used as a way to try to control another person. Sex can be a lot of things that have nothing to do with love. In fact, having sex may be the opposite of making love.

Let me quickly add: To feel better or more worthwhile or loved, to soothe our dependency needs, to release tension, to express passion, to receive love can all happen when we make love by having sex with a willing, caring, involved mate.

The point is this: **Sexual activity as an action may have nothing to do with "making love"—or it may have everything to do with it.** It all depends on the motivation of each partner.

Making love, the way I use the phrase, **is giving and receiving caring.** You can **make love** by cooking together, shopping together, playing tennis, dancing, creating a budget, taking a walk, enjoying your kids, paying bills, being sick together, grieving for the loss of a loved one, praying, and on and on together—including sharing your sexuality.

I think it can be fantastic to **make love** by staying in bed for five or six hours in the morning with your beloved. You can talk, cry, laugh, stroke each other, have genital touching, eat breakfast in bed, share dreams, tell of your love for each other, talk, cry, kiss, share your ideas and feelings, have intercourse, laugh, play—in short, you can share affection with each other in a caring way. This is my idea of **making love.**

To me, the term **making love** means: *To be intimately connected, caring, and affectionate with each other.*

People use the term **sleeping together** when they mean **having sex**. That misuse can be really confusing—have you ever dreamed you were having sex, you awakened, and you were? It could be a pleasant surprise, but it's rather atypical.

I have slept with people I love tremendously, and have not had sex with them. At my grandmother's home, the only bed available meant I had to sleep with my father. He hadn't seen me with my beard. My father enjoys making people laugh. The next morning he told my grandmother that he was only frightened *three times* during the night when he awakened and saw me with a beard.

I have slept with my son, Jeph, and with my son, Matt.

Matt and I were flown to another state to stay with some people for a weekend to assist them with family problems. Matt and I slept together in the only bed available. I had previously explained to them my definition of the terms: making love, sex, and sleeping together. They were initially shocked when I said, "Last night I slept with one of the loves of my life." After they thought about it, we all laughed together.

We hear that a typical married couple has sex an average of three times a week. If it is true, there is a lot of literal **sleeping together** going on out there—a lot of married mates **sleeping together without having sex.**

Married couples can sleep together and **make love** without having sex. Single friends can sleep together and **make love**, by my definition, without having sex.

They may decide to sleep together without having sex BECAUSE they love each other. A woman friend and I, as the result of circumstances, slept together. We decided before we went to bed that we would not have sex. Neither of us was in a relationship, so betraying a partner was not a constraint. Our decision was based on one issue. Our friendship was important to us. We did not want to complicate it with sexual activity.

It was wonderful to be able to be close to a woman, to talk openly and warmly as friends, with the safety of giving each other a friendly goodnight kiss, and then go to sleep. We never had sex with each other during our years as friends.

Some of you may think this story is strange. I have found friendships with women from which sex is excluded to be very satisfying for me.

Unfortunately, for many people, sex has become a replacement for affection. I believe that affection is what most people really want.

You may wonder why I have been making such a big deal about terminology. I am challenging such phrases as "sleeping together" or "making love" to emphasize the importance of caring sex. I want to focus the issue so that we can choose to share our sexuality in ways that are emotionally fulfilling.

I believe that sex can be a wonderful and beautiful way to express love. It is impossible to underestimate the satisfaction which sex can bring as one way to make love. I want to highlight, though, that affection is the deepest need. Sex in our culture has become tragically distorted in comparison to its potential for giving lasting joy. Affection is the most important ingredient in sex, whether it is a first-time encounter or a relationship lasting fifty years.

So I want to give a big cheer for sex, and a cheer for affectionate caring that is twenty times louder and far more enthusiastic!

What Is Sex?

For the sake of clarity, let me explain what I mean by sex. When I use the word *sex*, I am not referring to sleeping together. I am not referring to making love. I am not referring to gender. I am not limiting it *only* to intercourse. I am talking specifically about **any form of genital contact**.

Stroking a woman's breasts or a man's chest can stimulate genital sensations. I consider that to be indirect genital contact.

Kissing can be hostile, it can be friendly, or it can be sexual; it all depends on the energy vibrations that are sent and received. A "French kiss" can be invasive or it can be sensuous. Kissing can be asexual or it can be an indirect form of genital contact.

You can be sexual without having sex. Sexual energy is a part of being human. Sexuality is a part of who you are. Expressing your sexuality can lead to sex.

To have sex is an action. To share your sexuality by having sex is blending sexuality and sex—blending sexual energy and action.

Our culture has many interpretations for this word *sex*. People have different definitions for the word. Some mean only intercourse; any other form of physical contact is not considered sex. Some people think sex is merely being aroused, and has nothing to do with the parts of the body that are touched. Some people say *sex* and mean male or female gender.

Let me emphasize that I am not judging how people talk. I am attempting to clarify terms so that you and I are clear about my meaning as you read this chapter, and to assist you to say what you mean when you talk with other people.

Accurately articulating our intentions and our actions is crucial for clear communication.

I would like to assert, just as I have regarding feelings, that sexual sensations are neither good nor bad. The ethical issue becomes important only when we consider what we do with our sexual sensations.

You may have noticed that I used the term "sexual sensations" instead of "sexual feelings." I make this distinction because, when I mention feelings, I am referring to anger, affection, fear, pain, helplessness, or joy, which are emotions. Our sexual sensations are experienced as bodily sensations that may coexist with any of the emotions. Feelings may cause sexual sensations, and feelings may be the result of sexual sensations.

When I discussed feelings with you, I mentioned that they are just energy. Feelings are not a moral issue. What you do with emotions may be a moral issue, but feelings merely exist. They are a part of being human.

Sensational Sexual Sensations

This is also true of sexual sensations. They are a part of being human. They exist at least from the time you are born, perhaps before, and I believe they endure until you die. It is important to acknowledge yourself as a sexual person, to allow yourself to have sexual sensations without judgment. It is just as important to make friends with our sexual sensations as it is to make friends with our feelings. Repressing sexual sensations only creates pressure. People are afraid that, if they allow themselves to experience sexual sensations, they will lose control and act out those sensations in destructive ways. The reality is that denying sexual sensations has much more to do with "losing control." To experience your sexual sensations allows you the opportunity to take control of yourself and to make choices.

I feel vulnerable to mention the two following situations as illustrations of what I mean. I will take the risk, however, because I asked you earlier to take risks as you read this book. Please be as kind to me when you read them as I have encouraged you to be to yourself, as you explore your own feelings.

There was a very attractive woman on the staff at a hospital where I was a consultant. She wanted me to see some of the work she was doing in her department. She was an art therapist who enjoyed making herself a beautiful work of art in the way she dressed and her use of makeup. As she escorted me to her section of the hospital, I was tremendously sexually attracted to her, and extremely uncomfortable with my sensations of attraction.

It was fortunate for me that shortly after I left the woman I had an opportunity to talk with a priest/therapist colleague about my discomfort. I mentioned my experience with this woman and my uneasiness about it. He assured me that of course I was having sexual thoughts in a situation with someone who was emotionally and physically attractive. That was natural and quite understandable—very human.

His "permission" allowed me to immediately feel comfortable with my sexual sensations and with myself. I had no further tension when I was with this magnetic woman. The approval to be sexually attracted to her alleviated my stress.

It is important to note that the woman no longer seemed irresistible. The intensity of the enormous pressure to have physical contact with her was due to the need to repress the idea of the sexual attraction. Once the urge was acceptable, there was absolutely no pressure to touch her. I could relax and simply appreciate her beauty.

Turning to the second incident: I was working very closely with a woman to provide couple and family therapy. We developed a great deal of affection, respect, and fondness for each other. I began to be sexually attracted to her. I had come to believe—from my previous experience and discussion with my priest colleague—that it was okay to have these sensations. I was concerned, however, that they would be misinterpreted by her and would get in the way of our working relationship, or place a barrier in it.

I confided to her that I found her sexually attractive, but it did not mean that I wanted to have sex with her. I did not. She said she was sexually attracted to me also, but neither did she want to have sex with me.

Because we could discuss our mutual sexual attraction openly, we were able to work together with comfort. We were safe to have affectionate feelings and sexual sensations, and know they would not lead to any complications. The discussion and ensuing understanding opened up the space for us to hug each other—as we often had done previously—and know that it would not be perceived by the other person as a sexual advance or invitation. By being open, clear, and direct with each other, our relationship continued to be relaxed and comfortable as it had been.

The first illustration demonstrates the discomfort that comes about when you attempt to repress sexual sensations, and exemplifies the relief of having permission to experience them. The second illustration shows the value, both for yourself and for your relationships, that comes from taking the risk to express the "unacceptable" in a safe friendship.

This is not to say that a discussion with the other person is appropriate in every situation. It may be totally unsafe to do so with the wrong person. To tell some people that you are attracted to them can be misinterpreted and frightening to them, causing more problems than it solves. When you are selective and can express yourself openly, it can alleviate and/or prevent many complications.

Denying your sexual sensations interferes with feeling good about yourself and believing that other people can like you. Acknowledging your sexuality as a part of being human is essential to believing in yourself as a wonderful person. It is essential to your well-being.

I want to dispel the myth that sexual sensations always lead to sexual actions. The fear is that experiencing your sexuality and being aware of your sexual sensations will lead to some immoral act over which you have no control. I believe the opposite is true. **Awareness leads to freedom of choice.**

Sexual Mythology

Let us consider other myths surrounding sex. There are some people who hold the myth that men are always ready for sex. There is also the mythical phrase, "An erect penis has no conscience."

Both are inaccurate. There are plenty of men who are very selective about when they have sex, and with whom they have it. Just because a woman approaches a man and presents him with the opportunity does not mean the man will respond to her advances.

There is also a myth that if a man has an erection, he is ready for intercourse. That is no more true than to say that a woman is emotionally ready for intercourse just because she has become lubricated. Erection for a man and lubrication for a woman are merely the first indications of arousal. Both men and women may be physically capable of intercourse because of their physical responses, but they often want to have a lot of emotional closeness, physical contact, and bodily pleasure before they engage in intimate sexual activity.

A man friend and I were talking recently. He said, "I like intercourse, but hugging and kissing and affection are what I really want. That's far more important to me than intercourse." His comments echo those made by many other men I have known.

Another common myth is that women desire sex less than men. I have seen more women in my practice as a therapist who expressed frustration because of their husband's unwillingness to have sex, than I have seen men who are frustrated because women don't want it.

The amount of sexual desire, and how a person expresses their sexuality, has little to do with being male or female. It has more to do with what they have learned about sexuality, their previous sexual experiences, feelings about the person they are with, whether or not they were molested as a child, the conscious or unconscious attitudes that cause or motivate their sexual sensations, and their attitude at a particular phase in their life. Emotions and attitudes have an enormous influence on our sexual actions.

Yet another myth involves age. There is a myth that men reach their peak of desire at age 19 and women at age 37. This is totally untrue. Men can be just as passionate in their 50s, 60s, and 70s as they were in their youth, and they can be just as potent in their 40s as they were in their teens. Women can be just as passionate in their teens as at age 37 or age 67.

Why does this myth exist? I think it is tied to an attitude that is less present now than it was in the past: Teenage males were *expected* to approach females, and teenage females were *expected* to resist. With the divorce rate as high as it is now, reaching approximately 50 percent of marriages, there are a lot more single people. These people are in their "second adolescence" at ages 40, 50, or 60. Their degree of sexual desire is just as intense as it was at 19, and they may be more sexually active now because they know more about sex, and because they have more freedom to express their sexuality.

The second reason for the sexual myth about age is a related myth about the elderly. The myth is: Sex is for the young, and old people can't have sex. I believe that healthy people can enjoy sex at any age. The belief that older people cannot have sex has developed because older people have not wanted to have sex. Their desire for sexual sharing diminished as resentment in their marriage increased. Resentment does not lead to an erect penis or a lubricated vagina.

Divorce was not an acceptable option several generations ago. People stayed in repressive marriages because of the social pressure. Sex was terminated because the mates had replaced passion and affection with anger. Because sexual activity had been reduced or eliminated, it was believed to be due to aging. The real cause was disinterest in their partner.

As is true of any activity, whether it be tennis or sex or whatever, if you do not practice your strokes, your muscles degenerate. Your capacity to "perform" is reduced. If a man or woman eliminates sexual activity, their sexual organs will not function as they do when they are used regularly.

The aging process is not the major problem. It is the relationship barriers that have ended use of the sexual organs and have led to the mistaken belief that smooth and pleasurable sex is impossible for the elderly.

I do not mean to imply that a person who is 90 has the same vitality as when they were young. Just as in other areas of life, there are physical differences between someone in their 80s and 90s and someone in their 20s or 30s.

There are, however, other ways to compensate for this change. Orgasms may not be as frequent, but there can be just as much lovemaking. It is possible to have an orgasm without ejaculation, because of the intensity of the sexual experience and the amount of emotion that has built up. There can be a heightening and a release, even if there is not the same seminal production.

This can happen for younger men, who have had several orgasms during a short period of sexual sharing. They can have another orgasm, even though little or no semen remains, because the passion is present. It is also possible for an older man to have an orgasm, because ejaculation of semen is not essential for an emotional release. Elderly people are more limited by their attitudes, by their relationships with their mates, and by their lack of energy or health than they are limited by the possibilities and options for sexual pleasure that are available to them.

Do not take these comments to overemphasize orgasms. What is most important is that people continue to **make love** at any age. If that includes exciting sexual sharing with orgasms, then great. If it includes sexual sharing without orgasms, great, too. The best sharing is the sharing of affection.

In the process of my training as a sex therapist, I have viewed many movies of sexual activity. The purpose was to prevent me from being shocked by anything I might be told by a client. The one movie that made the most powerful impression on me was a film of a couple—she was 63, he was 70—who brought a lifetime of caring to their sexual sharing. It was absolutely beautiful to observe them **making love**.

We are wise to remember that there are enormous differences between people of the same age. There are some people in their 70s who are more youthful and active than others in their 50s.

The significance of appreciating your sexual potency at any age is to avail yourself of the excitement and vitality that come from mutual sexual expression. Blocking sexual energy can reduce the joy of life and lead to physical illness. The flow of sexual energy is healthy. The flow of sexual energy enhances our life. For an older person to exclude themselves from sex because of inaccurate information and myths is sadly unfortunate.

Sexuality Education for Children

Let me shift the focus from the elderly to the importance of educating children about their sexuality. It is very important for parents to inform their children about sex in a positive way, instead of having them hear about it from somebody else, who may give them misinformation or impart harmful attitudes.

From the time my children were young, I tried to provide information and attitudes as they were ready to receive them. When something came on television that had to do with sex, I would ask them if they understood what it meant. Sometimes the answer was "yes," sometimes "no." If they didn't understand, then we would talk about it after the program. I would get out books or pictures that I could use to explain how the body works, or I would explain different facets of the sexual experience. I had an advantage over most parents because of my training as a sex therapist.

Parents sometimes try to explain things their children are not ready for or not curious about. The children become puzzled, because they don't understand what is being said.

More often in our culture, children have more information about the subject than their parents do. Parents, to be responsible, might have to learn a lot more than they already know in order to teach their children to feel comfortable with their sexuality and with their sexual sensations.

Children are going to do something with their sexuality. Sexual energy is a powerful drive. If parents provide positive attitudes about sex for their children and validate their children's sexuality, the children will make decisions about their sexual activities with greater wisdom.

When asked to speak on the topic of sexuality for a community-wide youth program, I chose the title "Lead Us Into Temptation." The talk emphasized understanding your sexuality, and making decisions about how you will express it or not express it, **before** you get into a sexual situation. That was in 1962. I believe such an approach is just as relevant today—perhaps more so in this age of AIDS.

I also think children need to be taught what is today called "safer" sex. At the point of this writing there is no such thing as "safe sex" when it comes to AIDS. However, children need to be taught ways of avoiding sexually transmitted diseases of ALL kinds. They need to be taught preventive methods and behavior options, as well as the ill effects of various diseases.

The denial about AIDS is a major concern. People hold to the belief, "I will not get AIDS." Thinking in terms of "high risk groups" rather than "high risk activities" encourages this denial. I hope people are taking heed, realizing that AIDS is not limited to being a homosexual or an intravenous drug user. The heterosexual person is at great risk.

Unfortunately, some self-destructive sexual actions are rebellion against the rigid prohibitions of religious leaders, against uninformed and/or frightened repression by parents, and against distortions which remain from the Victorian era.

Many people are taking the warnings seriously and are either abstaining or limiting sex to one partner, or at the very least, are always using "safer sex" AIDS prevention measures. **There is a big difference between being a prude and being prudent.**

One positive value that may come from the AIDS epidemic, which makes sex a life-and-death matter, is that people will assess what sex really means. Becoming more cautious and selective about sexual partners may result in more emotional intimacy in sexual sharing.

Enticing, harmless-appearing sex is presented constantly in commercials. Sex has taken its place in the commercial world with other objects as a way of making money, thus detracting from sexual intimacy as a significant form of human caring. Perhaps being forced by AIDS to step back and reconsider sexual activity will lead people to gain a perspective that gives sex its rightful place—one of expressing affection and human warmth between people.

I would encourage you to be selective about your choice of a partner so you can meet your deepest need, which is your need to be loved. When you are indiscriminate about your partner, there is the strong possibility that you will feel angry, guilty, or empty inside, and so the sexual experience will leave you unsatisfied. When you choose a kind, caring partner, you will feel loved and your life will be enriched by the sexual sharing.

About twenty years ago, a friend told me about a training conference on sexuality that he had attended. The program opened by having three screens with X-rated movies projected on them. He told me that, for the first 20 minutes, the visual impact of the sexual activity in the movies was really exciting. (Remember, back then there were not many movies of a sexually explicit nature as openly available as they are today.) There was a lot of stimulation in the audience at first. Then it became boring. This continued for about three hours with three movie screens showing people having sex. My colleague said people were bored and falling asleep until, at the end of the three hours, on one screen there appeared a movie showing a couple *making love.* The place came alive. Everyone was energized by the tenderness shown by the caring couple.

It has been consistently conspicuous to me that caring and sharing are the most important parts of a sexual relationship. I mentioned earlier the sex therapy training movie with the elderly couple. I learned, after watching the film, that the older couple had met for the first time for the sole purpose of making the sex education film. These two people were able to share their sexuality in such a beautiful, expressive way because they had both spent a lifetime of lovingly caring for people in their professions. The woman was a physical therapist and the man was a psychologist. They had spent their lives giving to others. This knowledge highlighted for me the significance of personal caring qualities, and their benefit for sexual expression. Joyful giving and receiving will endure well beyond the time-limited physical, sexual contact, as an emotionally satisfying experience.

There has been a lot of emphasis recently on focusing on yourself and your own sexuality. I agree that to know yourself, to know what is pleasing to you, and to know what you experience as your sexual excitement escalates can be gratifyingly.

However, this kind of thinking has been overemphasized. To focus on yourself can be important, but it does not create the most satisfying shared sex. Nor does focusing totally on your partner. Too much thinking can even detract.

Sexual sharing is most fulfilling when you intricately blend an awareness of your own sensations and emotions with an awareness of your partner's. Our excitement is heightened by the escalating ecstasy of our partner. It becomes an emotional flow of energy back and forth between us, building to sensual bliss. This getting under each other's skin, so to speak, leads to the utmost sense of sexual excitement and sharing.

Beyond the Barriers to Sexual Intimacy

So far in this chapter, I have presented my perspective on sexuality. As I have done in the other chapters, I will present ways to deal with difficulties and ways to enhance your life at the end. Now I would like to explore with you the things that interfere with sexual intimacy. My intent is to emphasize the connection between sexual sensations, emotions, and the relationship aspect of sexual sharing.

Pleasurable sexual sharing is often disrupted by a deficiency in communication skills and relationship skills more than by poor technique. The most pleasurable sex does not result from technique. It results from the way partners share their wishes, their feelings—their energy.

Sexual difficulties can occur because a person is uninformed or unaware. People lack accurate information because they either have no good source or because they are hesitant to get the facts. That is not the same as being unaware. The woman of a client-couple felt pain during intercourse. I suggested to the man that he change his angle of entry. They were unaware that to have his penis enter her vagina at a different angle could eliminate her pain.

I will only deal with techniques or physiological aspects of sexuality in this chapter to the extent that they relate to a particular issue. Other authorities have written extensively on those subjects. I want especially to express my enormous respect and appreciation to Drs. William H. Masters and Virginia E. Johnson for the courageous and meticulous work they have done in the field of human sexuality.

Sexual difficulties usually have little to do with physical sexual capacity. One common example of misinformation is the belief that impotence is caused by sugar diabetes. Many people who have sugar diebetes have been assisted to have full erections during sexual sharing.

The major barrier to sexual intimacy is the fear of intimacy itself. There is the fear of being close, for fear of being hurt. There is the fear of commitment, the fear of being controlled, the fear of losing control, the fear that dependency will result in abuse or neglect. All of these contribute to keeping distance—remaining detached.

Men have told me that one of the quickest ways to get "picked up at singles' bars is to wear a wedding ring." This is because there are so many people who do not want a commitment, yet *do* want physical contact and sexual expression. They have a need to be with somebody to assuage their feelings of loneliness or emptiness. Because of the fear of getting hurt, they avoid close and committed relationships, and invest their emotional energy in work or some other activity.

People who had experiences in their families of learning that promote fear and pain avoid closeness. Those same persons, through either education or a mentor, have learned to achieve, to be productive, and to receive gratification in their work. It is not surprising that people can feel more comfortable investing emotionally in work settings than in committed relationships.

There can be positive personal reasons to avoid a commitment or a marriage; however, to do so from fear leaves a person very empty and unsatisfied. "Pick-up" sexual activity may temporarily soothe some surface need, but it fails to meet the deeper need for a supportive relationship. Such activity, therefore, often leads to frustration, and sometimes to despair.

Let me remind you: **The fear of being hurt does not mean you will be hurt. Fear does not predict the future; it only tells you that you are afraid.** A fear of being hurt does not necessarily mean that the person you are with will hurt you.

I encourage you to take the risk of giving other persons the benefit of the doubt. Attribute to the other person positive motivation, rather than believing in your fears from the past. Trust and take the risk of revealing yourself to the other person. If the response assures you they are safe, move closer, one step at a time. If they match each risky step by a kind, safe response, whatever appropriate sexual expression follows will be based on the mutual trust and affection that meets your deepest needs. You can continue to build a fulfilling relationship, as you freely express your caring, and receive caring—physically, emotionally, and sexually.

Up to this point I have been addressing the fear of being close because of painful emotional experiences. There can also be fear that stems from sexual abuse. A person can be best friends with their mate, feel safe in the friendship, and yet have difficulty with their own sexuality and with sexual sharing with the one they love. This is not something to feel helpless about or on which to give up. It can be changed. I have helped people to find sexual fulfillment with their mate.

Let me help you to understand the suffering that has led to such complications. Incestuous experiences when a person was young create tremendous conflicts of fear, rage, and guilt that, if unresolved, surface in present sexual contact with a mate, no matter how fond the sexually abused person is of the beloved. This causes confusion, because often our unconscious mind has used amnesia to protect us from experiencing the memory of the physical and emotional trauma associated with childhood sexual abuse. It can seem "easier" to avoid sex with someone you love than it is to face the upsetting feelings from previous horrible sexual experiences. People who as children have been sexually abused by a family member may find it difficult to have sex with their family-member-mate because of the familial similarity.

In my years of working with adults who have had childhood sexual contact with a parent or relative, I have found that, once the abusive experience is uncovered, they feel guilty that their need to be noticed was met by the incestuous experience. Do not in any way interpret this to indicate that the child needed the incest. What everyone needs is some form of recognition as a person. For many such children, their only source of positive attention was from the person who was also an incestuous family member.

Children feel ashamed for any small gratification they received from the sexual contact imposed on them by the adult. They experience self-blame for any pleasure they might have received while asleep, even though they had no awareness that the sensations were stimulated by a parent.

They blame themselves for failing to stop nocturnal advances, even though they abhorred such events. The adult who was a molested child feels guilty, and takes responsibility for the sexual trauma they endured as a child.

The adult who was a molested child may suppress their rage because the incestuous parent or relative was the only source of attention or affection they had during those childhood years. Receiving even minuscule attention was something the child needed. The child therefore had a fear that, if they alienated the incestuous parent or relative, they would get no affection or attention *at all*.

This ambivalence of needing attention/affection and the ensuing rage growing out of the incest—even though deeply buried in the unconscious—make for ambivalent feelings toward the child-molested adult's mate, and serves as a barrier to sexual expression with their mate.

The incest victim can be unconsciously motivated to avoid sex with their mate. Sex with their mate brings back memories of their sexual activity with the earlier family member. Even when their mate is their best friend, it is not surprising that the adult who was an incest victim as a child goes outside their committed relationship to have sexual contact with a partner where that superimposing does not exist. (See "Superimposing" in the "Affection" chapter.)

Sometimes the extramarital sexual partner is a buffer to the anticipated abandonment by a mate. If you believe that you do not deserve the genuine love of a kind mate because of your guilt about incest—or if you believe that you do not deserve the pleasure of sexual sharing with your beloved—it will be difficult to have sex with that person. If your shame-filled expectation is that your mate will eventually leave you because you are "bad," you will protect yourself from being totally alone by having another person in your life.

When you believe to the core of your being that the only way you can get any attention from anyone is by your sexuality, it is not surprising that you would send out sexual vibrations to gain attention. It is not surprising that you would seek sex as a substitute for affection, if you don't believe you can have or keep the real thing.

The problem is that, even though it is not surprising that the person I've described finds sexual sharing difficult, or seeks sex for the reasons I've just outlined, it is also common for that person to suffer unbearably for their actions, while also causing a lot of pain to others.

I am not suggesting that the circumstances that I have described are the only reasons why someone would avoid commitment or seek an extramarital sex partner, but I *am* suggesting that people who are caught in the kind of trap I've described, rather than being judged, need understanding, comfort, and professional help instead of judgment. They are suffering from the consequences of childhood trauma.

This is sad, and unnecessary, suffering. If a person is willing to face their guilt, pain, and rage in therapy, they can become free of this burden from the past. One of the unconscious barriers to getting help with these difficulties is the traumatizing fear that the threats made by the incestuous abuser will come true if the adult abused child tells anyone of their experiences. Children are often threatened by the abuser with horrible consequences—including death—if they tell anyone what happened to them. Yet those who take the risk to tell me the secrets of their abuse achieve self-acceptance and freedom that they never believed possible.

Few events are more devastating to an adult's inner harmony than to have been sexually abused as a child. When a child's family, religious community or culture judges all sex and sexuality as bad, it multiplies the child's belief that they are bad. Belief in their own badness permeates their total being and the child carries it into and through adulthood. It is a tragedy for a person to have their self-perception destroyed by sexual activity that was imposed on them. No one should add to that travesty by arbitrarily condemning sex and sexuality.

Let me call attention to one other source of sexual inhibition between partners. Some people have had the "fear of God" put into them about sexuality and sex either from parents, teachers, friends, or organized religious institutions. An indictment of our sexuality during our developmental years causes a conflict between our natural human sensations and our fear of having those sensations. Attempts to resolve this confusion can lead to the extremes of a flurry of sexual activity, sexual dysfunction, or avoidance of sexual sharing with a loved one. Any of these extremes can lead to personal and/or marital distress.

Religious organizations would do well to evaluate many of their positions about sexuality. It would be a virtue to encourage a healthy respect for human nature, including sexuality. If God created us, as is claimed, it is anti-worshipful toward God and God's creation to treat sexuality as a curse from the devil.

The present posture of judgment by some religious leaders only leads to a disbelief in its proclaimers, and to ridicule of them and their faith. It also leads to self-hate, when a person of faith judges their own sexuality harshly. The issue is not simply to praise or repress sexuality. The moral judgment must be based upon whether the sex is manipulative, abusive, and dehumanizing or is it a way to share affection, caring, and kindness and does it contribute to the well-being of each partner. To value human sexuality, and to respect caring expressions of it, could offset the pornographic distortions that prevail on TV, in advertising, movies, and books. This is a responsibility of religious institutions.

The universal truth is that sexuality is a part of being human. The place of religion, as I see it, is to encourage attitudes of self-worth, self-appreciation, and self-acceptance. A realistic, positive approach to sexuality by religious leaders would give more credibility to the teachings about God's love, and about human beings as the people of God who were created in God's image.

Up to this point, I have been focusing on the fear that comes from family experiences or from early teachings outside the family. There is one more fear that may be painful to face, but which will ruin your life if you don't. *That is the fear you experience because the person you are with abuses you.* If you are afraid of sex with a person who has frequently hurt you, your fear is a message not only to avoid sex with that person—but also to get away from them, **now**.

I have seen clients who have stayed in sexually abusive relationships for the sake of their children or from fear of losing their children. Others have remained in sexually abusive settings because they had experienced sexual abuse since the time they were young and it was familiar. Still others remain in abusive settings because they were frightened by the threats of the abusing partner, or by the fear that they could not make it on their own. Those who remained in an abusive situation only extended the torture, because they always left the abusive person sooner or later. Better to end it sooner—like **now!**

Difficulties with erection, lubrication, untimely ejaculation, or orgasmic inhibition can have many causes. One possible cause is your present relationship. If it is not caring and safe or is demeaning and abusive, it can be the cause of your dysfunction. At times these difficulties are due to one partner. Usually they are a couple issue.

Let me conclude this segment on fear and sexual inhibition by restating: The fear you feel can be the fear of being close because you have been hurt emotionally in the past. It can come from sexual abuse as a child. It can come from a lack of of accurate information or lack of awareness. It can come from your family of learning or religious teachings attributed to God. In any of these instances, the fear needs to be seriously assessed.

When your fear rests on earlier life experiences, and you are with a person who is kind and caring, then move closer to them in spite of your fear. It will be worth it. Accept the presence of your fear. Share your fear and your sexuality with your partner. **You have a choice. You can focus on your fear, which will *interfere*, or you can focus on the joy of giving pleasure to your partner and to yourself.** Sexual sensations are NOT to be feared. Sexual sensations are to be **enjoyed**. We were not created, with our sexual sensations and passion, by any sinister or vicious force in the universe, with the purpose of complicating our lives by prohibiting sex. **Our sexuality exists for us to share and enjoy within the context of a caring relationship.**

My comments about fear are partly to help you to understand how fears influence sexual sharing, but they are also efforts to dispel the idea that sexual pleasure can only occur when you are feeling affection.

I believe it is possible to have a broad range of feelings during sexual sharing, which range from joy to helplessness. This is contrary to the misinformation that affection is the only feeling that should be present.

If two people are in an argument and angry at each other, it can benefit both to take time out from the controversy to have sex. Anger is only a feeling. A couple can choose a variety of ways of expressing that feeling, including to share their sexuality aggressively. I am not encouraging harm or pain. I am encouraging sex as a safe and pleasurable way to release mutual anger. Releasing the anger can make space for affection. The suggestion to have sex instead of continuing the fight might in itself remind the combatants of their affection for each other. A blunt invitation to have sex in the middle of a conflict can even be humorous or playful, and break the tension. Whatever the effect, a sex break in the middle of a conflict can lead to the desire to seek a creative solution to the dispute.

Few disagreements are of such importance that to have sex in the middle of them would not be an improvement!

Most people cannot even imagine that this could happen, so let me elaborate. When people are angry at each other, their usual approach is either to attack or to withdraw. People, have difficulty grasping the concept of constructive verbal sharing, let alone the idea of sharing sex when they are angry.

In the chapter on "Anger," I have given two reasons to express anger. One is to get it out of your system. The second is to build intimacy in a relationship. The idea of sharing your sexuality when you are angry accomplishes both goals. I suggest it in the same context that I encourage expressing your anger verbally in a constructive way. It is in no way abusive.

Anger is not the opposite of affection and caring. It is simply an emotion about which you can make a choice. I am suggesting one choice you can make when you are angry is to share your sexuality. This sharing can lead to greater emotional intimacy. Many marriages and families would be less painful, and much more fun, if they selected this option.

Unfortunately, most people are better fighters than they are lovers. I say, "Hooray for the lovers!"

I mentioned earlier that people may appear angry or combative when their true feeling is helplessness, pain, or fear. To share caring by means of a sex break can reduce the feeling of helplessness, pain, or fear, especially since one common reason for a fight is that the fight is an attempt to cope with feelings of helplessness or fear related to getting your needs met. Another common reason for fighting is that you are feeling the pain of isolation from your mate and a fight is an attempt to connect. In any case, connecting sexually can alleviate the motive behind the combat.

I pointed out earlier that anger is a barrier to affection. Releasing anger in this way allows space for re-experiencing affection. It can create the intimacy and safety to move the disagreement to a mutually caring solution.

Allow me to summarize: **Many feelings from both the past and the present can arise in the process of sexual sharing. These feelings can include** *affection, pleasure and* *joy, pain (which may include shame), anger, fear, and helplessness.*

You need not be upset, distracted, or deterred by this. Talking about your emotions with your partner and having your feelings graciously received create safety and closeness. Your feelings are, then, just a part of the continuous process of making love.

Sometimes, the appropriate tactic for dealing with a feeling is simply to notice it, accept it, and shift the focus away from the feeling. Instead, focus on sharing sexual pleasure with your partner.

When people have difficulty with either erection for the male or lubrication for the female, it is often because they have lost the focus of the sexual sharing. When you are emotionally upset, when your feelings are blocked, when you have disconnected from yourself or from your partner, sexual gratification becomes an effort. Pain or anger can become the focus of your attention if you are feeling hurt by something your partner has said. In this state, arousal or lubrication is unlikely. When you are afraid of your partner, you lose your erection or lubrication because fear of your partner is not arousing. When you are consumed with anger toward your partner, it can be difficult to be aroused. (Unfortunately, rape, marital or otherwise, is an exception to the previous sentence.)

It is difficult to be aroused when your partner is disconnected from you emotionally. Men have told me they are concerned when they cannot get an erection, or keep an erection, with a partner, when they never had any such problem before. When a man describes the situation to me, it is obvious that the loss of his erection is due to the detachment of his partner. She is not connecting emotionally with him. There is no intimacy or interactive energy flow between the two people. The kindling clearly lacks spark.

In spite of what some people think: **Physical friction without emotional warmth leaves a person cold.**

When feelings—or lack of them—block you from being aroused, you must face the feelings to resolve the sexual difficulty. A way to face the feelings, and also to connect with your partner, is to share your feelings so that you can more freely share your body and soul—your sexuality.

Share Your Passion

Sex is most pleasurable when it involves emotion—when there is passion. *Webster's Dictionary* defines passion as "ardent, adoring love." Pain is not passion. Anger is not passion. Guilt is not passion. When the focus is on an emotion that prevents passion, it is *not* arousing. You cannot expect yourself to be stimulated. When passionate sexual sharing is blocked by a feeling, it can be an indication that you need to talk about the feeling. Expressing the feeling to an understanding mate can clear it and make way for passion.

Also, when you experience a block to passionate sexual sharing, it can be an indication that you need to shift your focus to sexual sensations and feelings of pleasure, so that you can have a satisfying experience.

While we are considering emotions and sex, let me expand a bit. After a person has an orgasm, they sometimes cry. This is especially true of women. Do not be concerned if this occurs. In order to release pain by crying or to release sexual tension that has built up, a person must relax and **let go**. When we relax sufficiently to let go to have an orgasm, we may also let go of other feelings at the same time, and cry.

If you are with a man or woman who cries after (or before) an orgasm, don't be concerned about it. Instead, be pleased that your partner feels safe enough to let go and expose their feelings to you. Instead of being upset, be appreciative. Comfort your partner who is crying. Just keep on hugging and crying and snuggling together, and the affection will deepen. That is MAKING LOVE!

The most gratifying experiences of sex occur with a person who is safe and caring, and where the two partners respect each other.

The loss of an erection is a concern a man may have about himself, or that a woman may have about a man. It is common for a man, through extended lovemaking (as I have defined it—with caressing, talking, and sharing) to lose his erection. If a man becomes frightened at losing his erection and fears that he will not be able to regain it, he can't, because fear is not arousing. He has created a self-fulfilling fear. The fear then continues to build, which creates panic. Panic isn't particularly arousing, either, which can lead to real problems such as an aversion to sexual contact.

Remember: Fear does not predict the future; it only tells you that you are afraid.

If you turn your attention to expressing your affection to your partner and to sexual sharing, you will shift your focus from the fear to passion, and your erection will return.

You, my diligent reader, may wonder why sex in a marriage may seem to lack luster. Let's explore why.

Marital sex may not seem nearly as exciting as it was as a teenager in a car, or sneaking off somewhere to "do it," or having clandestine sex with your family nearby, or indulging in a "quickie" at a chance moment, or having extramarital sex. The reason is that marital sex is different from all of these.

When you have sex in a car as a teenager, that may involve a whole combination of feelings. There can be fear of being caught. There can be the excitement leading up to the first time. (Speaking realistically, the first time can be more painful and frightening than exciting.) Perhaps affection is an additional emotion involved. There may also be feelings of guilt.

The point I want to make is this: Sex can seem to be better or more intense at different times, but marital sex does not necessarily have fewer sexual sensations; rather, marital sex lacks the multiplicity of feelings that are involved in premarital or extramarital sex. There may be several emotions combined with the sexual sensations in the case of the teenager or the person involved in an extramarital affair. This heightens the intensity of the experience.

Also, an extramarital relationship may be less difficult and take less effort, due to the lack of responsibilities such as finances, children, schedules. The sexual sharing is uncomplicated by responsibilities and decisions that a committed relationship require.

Usually, however, there are other complications that are subtle; therefore, they are less noticeable to the person who is caught up in the affair. An extramarital relationship may be very painful to one or both members of the affair, but the multiplicity of emotions that focus on the sexual sharing gives it a disproportionate perspective that is glue to the relationship. For some, the pain of the extramarital relationship is less painful than the isolation of being single and alone or lonely in a marriage.

The committed couple need not despair because they are not adolescents or because they have chosen to share responsibilities as people who love each other. It can be very exciting to anticipate making love sexually to a person with whom you have invested your life energy and experiences. To **make time** to make love a priority in your friendship with your mate can add joy to every other part of your life.

My parents, who have been married for over fifty years, hug and kiss each other when they are alone or when other people are with them. They tell each other of their love several times a day. When we moved to Kentucky, they went to the courthouse together to get their driver's licenses. Noting their obvious affection for each other, the county clerk pulled out the forms for a marriage license. They had only been married for **fifteen** years!

One approach to improving your sexual lovemaking is to resolve personal or relational barriers so that sexual sharing and the intimacy of physical caring with your mate become stimulating events in your life together.

Express Your Likes—Kindly

Intimate sexual sharing does not come naturally. It must be learned through experiencing another person. That means expressing to the other *what you like and what you don't like.* If you have the attitude that you should *know* how to please your partner and that your partner should also *know* what is pleasing to you, you are placing an unrealistic expectation on your relationship.

What may please one person may not please another. What is pleasing at one moment may lose its pleasure, or even become painful. To be stroked on one part of your body can be very satisfying and stimulating, and then become irritating. To be touched with a certain amount of pressure may feel good at one moment, and be too hard or too gentle the next. How will your partner know what feels pleasurable and what does not? The only way is to let them know.

Nonverbal messages, such as gently moving your partner's hand, or shifting position, can be done with tenderness and can lead to more intimacy. Nonverbal symbols may also come into play to send a message to your partner, but both of you must understand their meaning clearly.

It causes misunderstandings when you fail to clarify the meaning of the symbolic gestures. Even opportunities for sexual sharing may be missed! A wonderful woman named Sylvia Cohen, who supervised my sex therapy certification process, gave me an example. During a therapy session, she asked a couple how they conveyed a desire to have sex.

He replied, "Oh, I go take a shower."

The woman responded, "You what?"

He said again, "Yeah, I take a shower!"

She then informed him, "I didn't know that when you took a shower, you wanted sex!"

This is an example of one person being very clear about the message being sent—without the partner even knowing there is a message. They must have had sex often enough after his shower that, if they did not, he simply assumed she was not interested.

Many people have learned during their childhood that they should not talk about sex. They may have been told this directly. They may have learned it indirectly. Everyone knows that sex is a conspicuous part of being human. With anything as much a part of life from birth to death as sexual sensations, a lack of discussion about sexuality leads to the implication that sex must be "bad." People therefore are afraid to talk about "it."

It is essential during sex therapy to ask specific questions about sexual activity. People often respond by saying "That's too personal," or "I can't talk about *that*." It can be difficult to reduce the person's hesitancy, because the fear of being punished for talking about sex prevails. The fear is learned as a child. To allow the fear to inhibit discussion of sex as an adult can block pleasurable sexual sharing.

Perk up your ears for this one. It is astounding how many people express themselves in a negative way and then wonder why their partner is offended. You may have noticed that I mentioned earlier "gently moving your partner's hand." I also suggested, "Express what you like and don't like."

Let me accentuate GENTLY, and LIKE. Since we are discussing the birds and the bees, remember, "You catch more bees with honey than you do with vinegar." This is very true during sexual sharing.

I want to emphasize the enormous difference between disclosing to your partner what you would like, and telling them what you don't like. It is wonderful to hear your partner say, "I would like you to...." Or, "I enjoy it when you...." It is equally wonderful to have your partner move your hand to where they like it to be. The tenderness intensifies the warmth and closeness between you.

Contrast this image with saying, "I don't like that!" Or, "Stop that, it feels awful!" There is also the apparent rejection of pushing your partner away. Such actions and expressions cause more friction than fusion.

If your partner does not respond to information kindly given, you need to make more emphatic pronouncements. However, most people err on the side of gruffness, not gentleness.

If there is something you just don't like, never have liked, and can't imagine liking, then tell your partner about your distaste in a considerate manner. Discussing likes and dislikes in greater detail at a time other than during sex—when there is more objectivity and less vulnerability—allows you to clarify your wishes and avoid discomfort in the future. A kind, thoughtful discussion may even lead to intimacy that builds to passion as an outgrowth of your conversation.

You may get the impression, while you are reflecting on this chapter, that sex is a very serious business. The purpose of this chapter, and its detailed explanations, is to help you appreciate your own sexuality, and to provide information about sex so that you may experience the fullness of joy in sexual sharing. As in music, sports, work, or art, after you know the basics, you have a foundation that allows you to be spontaneous, free, and creative. Seldom are we taught the basics of sexuality and sexual sharing. I am attempting to fill that unfortunate deficit.

When I was counseling a couple before their marriage (back in the days when people did not have sex before marriage, if that time ever really existed), I instructed them not to take sex too seriously on their wedding night. I told them to approach sex with a sense of humor, and have fun.

After they returned from their honeymoon they told me that, of all the suggestions, recommendations, instructions, and suggestions they had been given before their wedding, the one that was the most valuable was the encouragement to have a sense of humor about their first night, and to have fun!

You couples who have been married for years can increase your fun and pleasure when you increase your efforts to please each other. Using massage and scented oils can give you pleasure. Incense and candles can enhance the mood. Mirrors can add variety and excitement to sex.

Variety is the spice of life—and spice is nice. Seasoning is sensuous.

Romance can provide perpetual rejuvenation. When your partner knows that you care enough to devise new ways of **making love** by creating exciting experiences using new, premeditated ideas, activities, and places, your enchantment with each other will blossom perennially. Be creative and have fun.

I hope this chapter has helped you to relax and enjoy your sexual sensations. They go with being human, and go with being you. To enjoy your sexuality and express yourself sexually can be one of the greatest joys in life when you do it with zestful affection and focused caring for your partner—with passion.

My wish for you is this: **Make love to everyone you meet, and to yourself. Seek the satisfaction of making love to all of life. It can be beautiful.**

AND YOU ARE BEAUTIFUL.

Rejoice in your sexuality. Enjoy the excitement and pleasure of being human.

When you have sex, MAKE LOVE. Affectionately share your sexuality with the person you believe is worthy of your love. Be thoughtfully romantic as you caringly create passionate, intimate sexual sharing with an equally loving partner....

...And as you experience fulfillment, be thankful.

*It is helpful to understand
where we are.*

*It builds hope to know
what we can become.*

The Helpful, Fun Family

Welcome to a dream, a vision, an anticipation of what can be.

This model of The Helpful, Fun Family, when I created it in 1971, was only a model of what could be. However, the exciting thing about visions and dreams is that they lay a foundation for us to become what we dream, what we envision. Our imagination is the farm where we grow the crops that we harvest in real life.

In my younger days as a minister in the parish, before we had children, my wife and I would take car rides in the evening to relax. On some of those rides we would talk about my vision of being in private practice as a psychologist. Three years later, I had a part-time private practice, and then moved into independent practice full time.

When I anticipate a speaking engagement, a workshop, or serving as master of ceremonies for an event, I not only plan the material, but I also envision the particular mood or atmosphere that I want to create. I picture myself in front of the audience, go through the presentation in my mind as I envision the emotional tone, and watch the group dynamics unfold. Then, when I am in the situation, I enjoy the results of my daydream.

I had a celebration of my birthday, which was also the anniversary of my ordination as a minister. I had for two years envisioned "a laughing, loving evening" (as the invitation read) as my gift to the special people who had been a part of my life over the years. When people left the celebration of my life and theirs, they were walking three feet off the ground. The most popular comment afterward was, "I felt so loved." One couple canceled plans and spent the next day together sharing their love as an extension of the love they had experienced the night before. What I envisioned had come true.

I have been doing this type of mental preparation in my mind for years. It came to my attention that someone has given a name to it. It has been labeled "visualization."

One of the intents of this chapter is to encourage you to visualize the family you would like to create. I am giving you my concept of The Helpful, Fun Family as a model to plant the seed and fertilize your dream life. Have fun creating your own fantasy family!

One of my responsibilities as a consultant at a Massachusetts state hospital was to train psychologists, social workers, and psychiatrists in the Medical Education Program. During that time I gave a theoretical construct within the framework of traditional psychological terminology, presenting the dynamics of three types of families: the Neurotic, the Schizophrenic, and the Character Disorder as classifications for families. I renamed them in lay terms as the Dysfunctional, the Fragmented, and the Fractured Family.

One of the precocious psychologists in the program approached me after a seminar session and asked, "Jay, what is a healthy family like?" So I formulated the model of a Functional Family. I now call it "The Helpful, Fun Family."

What a gift that young psychologist gave to us. I have found when I give presentations on the various types of families that the concept of The Helpful, Fun Family attracts the most interest. **It is helpful to understand where you are. It builds hope to know what you can become.**

Let me emphasize that this is **a model.** This family does not exist. My intent is to assist you in your attempts to achieve the best family of which you are capable. I want to help you to create your own model, your own mental picture, your own vision for the kind of family you want.

Let's not stop there, though. It is worth enlarging our vision to include the world family.

Once, when I presented the model of The Helpful, Fun Family to a group of laypeople, a woman in the audience became enraged at me because she took the presentation to be a judgment of her.

I have attempted to emphasize throughout this book: Be kind to yourself as you read it. I would encourage the same attitude as you read this particular chapter. I am not here to judge. My intent is to expand your awareness and your options, to enlarge your hope and your joy.

This vision of an ideal family has helped me in the midst of being involved with the members of my own family. I have looked to this model in my attempts to be a good parent and friend, so I am doubly grateful to the bright man in my course who asked the question, "What is a *healthy* family?" The following ideas are for you to consider as you develop your dream family.

The parents set the tone in the family. This does not just apply to the family that resides together. The parents may be elderly and continue to set the tone for several generations that follow them. Whatever that tone, it can be changed or shifted by purposeful self-awareness and the intentional choices of generations that follow.

In The Helpful, Fun Family, the tone that the parents establish is one of **safety**. Each person feels safe to be himself or herself—to be **Uniquely Human.**

The atmosphere of safety is set by the way the parents perceive themselves. In The Helpful, Fun Family, they like themselves. They are positive about themselves. They celebrate life itself, and they celebrate themselves as a part of life. The parents care about themselves, which sets a positive, praising tone for the interactions with other family members.

Whatever your position in your family, this is crucial for you to recognize: *To be taught your beauty, to be valued for the unique person you are, and to be encouraged to be all that you can be—that is the major role of the family.* In a safe family, you can feel joy about being who you are. When you receive the affection and caring and support from your family for being yourself, affection and caring and support flow through all your relationships, especially the relationship you have with yourself. You win the war within. You have patience with yourself, which brings you peace.

This inner peace and self-patience carry over to others. They experience safety when they are with you. Your inner peace and patience influence the family you create, influence your work environment, and affect the people around you, no matter what the setting. The relaxed, friendly response of the people who feel safe with you returns in the form of peaceful surroundings for you.

Sound good? It is. I have experienced it.

How do messages get sent within The Helpful, Fun Family? They are open and direct. A question is asked not to control or restrict, but is instead a request for information. If someone inquires, "What time are you going to be home for supper?", the response is, "I'll be home at 6 o'clock." If a person asks, "Where are you going?", the other person replies, "I am going out to the store." At other times, people volunteer information without being asked. For example: "I am going to the bathroom." "I have to run an errand. I'll be back shortly." "I will be in the garage if you need me." Such information, freely given, helps you to feel safe, because you know where to locate other members of your family, and you know what to expect.

Explaining is different from defending. The words may be the same, but **defending is attached to fear. Explaining comes from caring,** which is the primary motive in The Helpful, Fun Family. There is a wish to prevent other family members from worrying about you or being fearful of your whereabouts, so you freely and often give them information about yourself, and your location, as a way to allay their fears about you. There is a desire to stay emotionally connected, even though you are apart.

There is a sense of security in The Helpful, Fun Family. You trust other family members even when you don't know where they are. You know that they will respect your needs and they will return.

There is no need to panic if you do not know where a family member is at a particular moment. You are not isolated when you are alone, because you have a bond of affection which extends for miles. You may miss a family member, but you feel secure in their love.

Messages are sent clearly and directly, because no one needs to hide anything or has anything to hide. Each family member is safe. Whatever is said in The Helpful, Fun Family is believed and responded to in a kind, considerate, and affirming way. All this contributes to safety.

When a family member does something "wrong," it is reviewed with an attempt to understand. There is an awareness of the feelings involved. There is open discussion, with the attitude that life's events and mistakes are opportunities to learn to master the future.

Conflicts lead to constructive solutions in The Helpful, Fun Family. Conflict exists to resolve differences or disagreements. Being different can be interesting and exciting. It does not mean that discord cannot be resolved. Because each member of The Helpful, Fun Family feels safe, each can express their thoughts about their wants and needs, confident that the response will be kind, even if the points of view are different.

When people who disagree approach a conflict with the spirit of uniting to find a satisfactory answer, they have the possibility of finding a conclusion that benefits them all. The key is for each to state their thoughts and their needs as clearly as possible. When they do this, there is no need for guessing. It is much easier. Direct statements can lead to constructive conclusions.

Each person is expected to state their opinions, to say what they think, in The Helpful, Fun Family. Children are to be both **seen and heard**. You develop confidence for yourself and for the process of resolving conflict. The parents have explored, and come to understand, their families of learning and the effects those families had on them in their present interactions. The parents have put energy into learning the skills necessary to have intimacy and caring for all the members of the family.

My sons and I were planning to go to my parents' home in Kentucky for Easter Sunday. I had not been to church with my parents on Easter for years. It meant a lot to my Mother, and to me, to share that. The plan was that I would get my children in New Jersey on Friday, and arrive in Kentucky late Saturday afternoon.

Jeph, who was twelve at the time, called on the preceding Monday to say that his team had a lacrosse game on Saturday morning, and he wanted to play.

I said, "Jeph, we have a problem. Mamaw and I have been looking forward to going to church as a family." I suggested, "You think about it, and I'll think about it, and we can talk later in the week."

That was fine with Jeph. As I remember how easily he agreed, it strikes me that he totally trusted that his needs would be met.

He called back on Wednesday, saying, "Dad, I have a plan. We can pack a lunch and leave immediately after my game is over. When you have been driving a long time and it gets dark, I'll stay awake and talk to you so you won't get sleepy while you drive. That way I can play my game and we can go to church with Mamaw."

Our commitment to each other's needs, and the outcome of our creativity, brought us a wonderful time. We were able to spend Friday night with friends of both my sons, who piled into my car after lacrosse practice. We all went to a restaurant where we had a lot of fun together.

Saturday night, Matt slept in the back seat of the car while Jeph and I had a great time talking as we rode through the mountains and the blackness of West Virginia. Since I was alert and awake, we contacted the Holiday Inn, which aided us in our flexible plan to stop there or to continue to Kentucky. The desk clerk had helped earlier by providing information that would make either option easy, and was just as gracious in hearing that we planned to go on without stopping.

We made the trip from New Jersey to Kentucky in twelve and a half hours, with Matt rested, my parents delighted to see us, and Jeph and me excited about the wonderful time we had together. We had resolved a conflict with everyone's needs being met.

In The Helpful, Fun Family there is give and take, and safety. The Helpful, Fun Family resolves conflicts in a positive way, so people feel affection toward each other and themselves afterward. Ideas, needs, and opinions are expressed in a clear, kind, considerate, respectful manner. This allows each family member to express their thoughts, put suggestions into the creative process of seeking solutions, and provides the opportunity to establish priorities of needs, leading to beneficial conclusions.

In resolving a conflict, it may mean one person will not get their needs met. They will concede to the other person's needs, because they are the more urgent needs at the moment. With a belief that their needs will be met in the future, they will be considerate and patient. In this approach to getting along, **fear and deprivation are replaced by giving and receiving.**

There are also times when people's needs are so different that they must go in separate directions, each feeling safe and secure that they will soon return to the other. Affection, caring, and commitment are the springboards that permit them to go their own ways, knowing that on their return the bond of intimacy remains intact.

This type of connection between family members can put a bounce in your walk, keep joy in your heart, and give you security in the broader world—wherever you go. Appreciation for that kind of freedom adds to the affection trust and closeness that you share as a family when you are together.

How do feelings get expressed in The Helpful, Fun Family? Affection is given and received—often. There is a lot of: "I love you!" "I am proud of you!" "I really appreciate the way you did that!" "You are great!" "You look magnificent!" "You are so beautiful!" Verbal affection is expressed freely.

Physical warmth is shared. Hugging, kissing, tender touching, even playful wrestling, convey in a variety of ways to each member how much they are appreciated.

Comfort is given and received by emotional support and/or physical holding or hugging when a family member is hurt or upset. These expressions of affection are abundant.

I mention hurt or upset because pain is a part of the world we live in, even in The Helpful, Fun Family. We can fantasize the world as one big Helpful, Fun Family, but it obviously does not exist that way yet. Even if it were possible to have no pain in The Helpful, Fun Family, a person interacting with the hurtful, frightening world will experience pain.

Here is an example: I was standing in a grocery store checkout line. I had never seen the clerk before, but she and I were chatting and laughing and just plain having fun, while she efficiently totalled the cost of my food. Shockingly, I got hit by a grocery cart from behind. I was totally confused and hurt. If I had been wearing low cut shoes, rather than leather boots, my skin would have been cut and bruised from the force of the cart.

I looked back to see a hostile stranger.

I asked him why he did that. He just looked angrily back at me without saying a word.

I think the clerk was afraid I would jump over the cart and strangle him, which had crossed my mind, because she said, "He didn't mean to do it."

All I could do was guess about his angry actions. Apparently he was miserable inside and couldn't tolerate seeing someone have so much fun. He didn't seem to be in any hurry, just angry.

A painful experience came out of nowhere. This is minor, compared to the cruelty many people experience. It is a pain-filled world. Your family cannot possibly protect you from it. They can only comfort you in it.

Safety in The Helpful, Fun Family does not prevent pain. Any time you care for someone, there will be pain. You may bring it from your Hurtful, Frightening Family of learning into the relationship with your present family members. It may result from unintentional comments. Pain will occur when you see your loved ones in pain.

The difference between The Hurtful, Frightening Family and The Helpful, Fun Family is not absence of pain. It is in the way that pain is handled. In the former, isolation adds to the pain. In The Helpful, Fun Family pain can be expressed. The Helpful, Fun Family responds to pain with comfort, affection, and support to release the pain.

In The Helpful, Fun Family, there is no need on the part of the members to believe that they are responsible for another person's pain. When you take responsibility for someone's pain, you may believe that you should alleviate their pain. This belief will make you feel helpless. If someone is hurt, there is not much you can do to take their pain away. You can provide the safety and comfort for them to express their pain, which encourages your loved one to release it, purging the pain from their body. If they cannot cry, at least they can have the comfort of your caring, instead of the added pain of isolation.

In The Helpful, Fun Family, the pain can be safely expressed. The Helpful, Fun Family responds to it with comfort. Crying is encouraged as a way to release the hurt, and the tears are a way of washing out the pain.

How does anger get expressed in The Helpful, Fun Family? Anger is verbalized directly. If a family member is angry, they say, "I am really angry because...." Or they may say, "I am angry and I don't know why. Will you help me to understand it?" Anger is expressed with the assurance that the family member to whom you express your anger will not retaliate, but will respond in a caring way.

The advantage to expressing anger directly is that, when it is expressed, the other person has an opportunity to respond to it. This may nullify the reason for your anger. This does not mean that you should not have the feeling. You do, and that's *perfectly human*. There may have been a distorted perception of what happened. It is astonishing how often misperceptions occur with others because of our experiences in our family of learning, or because of incidents in other previous settings.

It is important to be aware of the multiple influences from your past as you seek to understand yourself, and attempt to create your own family.

As an example: Carol brought home a cream-filled dessert to her husband, Bill. She thought it would make him happy. His response was, "What are you trying to do, kill me? I am trying to lose weight." He was upset, not perceiving this as a caring gesture, when in fact it was.

If Bill expresses his frustration directly, saying, "I am really upset about you giving that cream puff to me. Why did you bring me something that will add to my weight?" Carol then has the opportunity to explain—non-defensively, "Oh my. You're right. I wasn't thinking about your weight. I was thinking about how much you enjoy cream puffs. I love you, and I like to please you."

He has the opportunity to hold a grudge or to receive the affection without eating the cream puff. If he takes the affection, he probably won't need the cream puff. You can guess that in The Helpful, Fun Family that I am envisioning, they would laugh and hug each other—and who knows what else! In The Helpful, Fun Family, anger is expressed, which makes space for affection.

Another feeling that is perfectly human and acceptable in The Helpful, Fun Family is the natural emotion of fear. You cannot live in this country, perhaps on this planet, without having fear.

You cannot avoid frightening situations. There are many such occasions in everyday living. Driving in Massachusetts is frightening. I mentioned before about getting hit by a grocery cart while standing in the checkout line. It is frightening that there are people like that man who will attack someone with no apparent reason.

Since I have been mugged, do I scrutinize my surroundings when I'm in potentially unpredictable settings? You better believe I do. Why? Because I'm afraid.

Fear may not predict the future, but "just because you're paranoid doesn't mean they're not out to get you!"

You are going to have fear if you have had painful experiences. If you watch the news on TV, you are going to see every horrendous event imaginable. These add to the fear we experience personally.

I watched a panel of television producers and newspaper editors expressing to an antagonistic moderator why they did not present some pictures and tapes of a news event, even though they had access to them. The producers and editors believed the images added nothing but pointless gore, and also believed it was improper to expose the public to such brutality. I was tremendously impressed by their integrity.

When I was in college, I enjoyed waking up to music. Now I can't stomach beginning my day hearing the gory details of murders, rapes, and other disasters in the news that come on with the music. That can get your day off to a fearful start.

There are enough reasons to be frightened, without watching or listening to unnecessary stomach-turning details from the media, which contribute to our conscious or unconscious fears.

Avoiding reality? No. Controlling my life? Yes.

You are going to be afraid. It is a part of being human. In The Helpful, Fun Family, it is acceptable to express your fear. It is safe to allow yourself to be vulnerable. You are given the comfort you need. By sharing your fears, you alleviate the pain and additional fear that comes with isolation. You know you are not alone: You are cared for. It is obvious by the actions of your family members that you are cared for.

In The Helpful, Fun Family, your feelings of helplessness are voiced to other members of your family. They respond by accepting those feelings, by assisting you to discover all of your options, and by serving as a sounding board as you consider the best choice.

Sexuality is considered natural in The Helpful, Fun Family. It is discussed openly with family members, depending on their age and readiness to receive information about sexuality and sex. Children are not reprimanded for having sexual sensations or visible signs of arousal. They are taught what is appropriate and what is not. Sexual sensations are seen as a part of being human.

Once, when I was speaking about family dynamics in a church, a man asked the question, "My 16-year-old daughter likes to wrestle with me. Is that okay, or should I stop doing it?"

I responded, "I assume that you are concerned that sexual sensations are a part of the wrestling. If no sexual actions follow the wrestling, and if there is no genital contact or no attempt to arouse each other, but the sexual sensations just naturally occur as a result of two people who care for each other having physical contact, then I believe that it can actually be beneficial for your daughter. It is advantageous for her to know that there is nothing wrong with having sexual sensations toward someone whom she loves. It is also good for her to know that just because a man has sexual sensations does not mean that he will act on them."

The key to the issue is that his daughter wants to wrestle and that she feels safe with whatever feelings or sensations occur.

I have seen many women in therapy who have been terribly hurt by their fathers, who stopped hugging or holding them when they reached puberty. Losing your father's affection in the form of physical contact is a major loss and a young woman can easily take it as a rejection of her emerging sexuality.

It would be wise on the part of the father who asked the question about wrestling with his daughter—and it is wise for every parent—to have discussions about sex with their children of both genders. Parents need to caution their children about members of the opposite sex (or of their own sex) who may try to get them into compromising and upsetting situations. It is imperative to convey to young people the importance of being selective with whom, and under what circumstances, they share their sexuality. It is advantageous to discuss sex and sexuality in an accepting way, so that there will be open channels to share future issues and complications as they arise for your children.

Children benefit from knowing that one of the ways their parents express affection for each other is by sharing their sexuality. It helps the child to know that when their parents are together with the door closed, it is not to reject the child. It is a time of privacy together for the parents to **make love**, which includes sharing their sexuality.

In the Helpful, Fun Family, the parents consider sexuality to be beautiful. Because they set the tone for the family, the Helpful, Fun Family members consider sexuality to be as natural as any other aspect of being human. The children learn sexual manners as openly as they are taught other forms of etiquette.

Also, The Helpful Fun Family members encourage and appreciate creativity. The parents like themselves and feel good about themselves. They are not threatened by other members of the family, their mates, or their children. They are not afraid of free speech, differences, or accomplishments.

Because the parents like themselves, their own image isn't dependent on their children. They can feel comfortable if their children are different. They realize it is not a reflection on themselves as parents. They encourage their children to be who they are, and all that they can be. They enjoy the variety, the uniqueness.

One of the many days I have been proud of my son, Jeph, was when he asked me for an old sweatshirt. I got one for him. He went to my bedroom where the sewing machine given to me by my grandmother was located. A few minutes later he came downstairs with a shirt tailored to fit him. He had learned to sew in school and was putting it to good use. He then went outside to compete in a sporting event with his friends, wearing the shirt he had tailored.

The Helpful, Fun Family encourages its members to pursue their individual interests, regardless of the member's gender. For example, woodworking, working on cars, enjoying art, washing and ironing, gardening, dressing according to individual styles, plumbing, sports are all accepted—whether the person doing them is male or female.

Gender is not the deciding factor as to how a person uses their talents. Their interests and actions are supported because they are an expression of themselves. They are valued for the person they are.

The Helpful, Fun Family supports leadership. Making decisions is encouraged here. Parents trust the child. One positive way to encourage this leadership is for each member to take turns deciding in what restaurant the family will eat.

Different people have different tastes. Children know what they want to eat. To take turns making decisions in the family of learning teaches them how to assert themselves and how to feel comfortable in a leadership role. If a child learns how to be a decisive leader, *and* learns how to graciously follow others, they have a distinct advantage in their adult life.

Adults think children want what they want when they want it. I know lots of adults just like that. I must confess: I am one of them. Children are not that way any more than adults.

If children know that they will get their needs met at another time, they can sacrifice what they want now. Children can wait to get what they want. I can, too.

When my children and I traveled, I would let Matt and Jeph "roughhouse" as much as they wanted, with chaos reigning in the backseat of the car. We had an understanding that if something occurred along the highway that called for quiet so that I could give it my full attention, or if the noise distracted me so that I could not concentrate on driving, they would stop their play and the noise. When I asked them to be quiet, they would be quiet. Always!

They appreciated the flexibility they had in being able to play and, because they were given freedom, they could understand when I expressed my need for freedom from distraction. The mutual respect made our trips really fun.

The Helpful, Fun Family encourages and validates shifting the leadership to each member.

Roles are discussed, decided on, and clarified in The Helpful, Fun Family. My wife and I agreed on roles that influenced how decisions were made in our family. We used each other's expertise to pick options. Her role and expertise were related to our home, and mine were related to cars and vocation. That arrangement influenced the authority we gave to each other and received from each other.

When we bought furniture and there was a piece that I hated, we wouldn't get it. When we saw a car that she didn't like, we wouldn't get it. We would search to find something we both liked, rather than have one person impose their wishes on the other.

However, each of us made the final judgment for the purchase based on the guidelines we had established about areas of responsibility and authority developed from our individual expertise and our roles.

Said another way: If one of us did not like something, we didn't get it. If it was okay for one of us, even though not great, the person with the most expertise, or the person who would use it most, was granted the decision. I supported choices based on her decorative abilities, and she agreed with my judgment about durability in furniture.

It is wise for each family to decide who is the expert in any given area and who has responsibility in that area—before conflicts arise.

It was probably much easier to establish roles for family members in earlier years, because the husband was the one who earned the money and the wife was the one who cooked and took care of the house and the children. Their roles were clear.

The suggestion that roles be clear does not intend for those roles to be established the way previous generations defined them. Your family may decide that the woman earns the money and the man takes care of the children, the house, and the cooking, because each of you prefers it that way, or because necessity demands it. Alternatively, you may both work and both share the household responsibilities.

The important issue is NOT what roles each person has. The important issue is whether or not the roles are discussed so that everyone clearly understands what their roles are. The result of such clarity is a sense of comfort and fairness about tasks, as each fulfills their part of living cooperatively in a family.

Children need to have a say in what their roles are, and a clear understanding of their roles. Children are more comfortable with and more willing to take responsibility for tasks that are explained to them. They can appreciate the value of fulfilling their role when they understand that other family members have roles that result in the child getting their own needs met. That knowledge helps them to realize that other people rely on them to meet the needs of other family members. They can see that everyone benefits from the contribution of every other. It is to everyone's advantage when responsibilities are shared, when there is caring flexibility, and when roles are clearly defined.

None of this is intended to mean that either a child OR an adult has the right to make a decision that would make everybody else in the family miserable. These ideas intend to show ways in which family members can work together.

Within The Helpful, Fun Family, there is a time, at some point, for the children to leave. Separations are painful, but can be constructive. Parents release their children to take whatever roles, responsibilities, or tasks in life that the children choose for themselves. The children feel safe to leave the family, knowing that they take support and affection with them wherever they go.

One day in Kentucky, before my parents took me to the airport to get my plane back to Boston, my Dad prayed before the meal, "Help Jay to remember, when he is back in Boston, that there is a lot of love here for him."

The Helpful, Fun Family provides positive separations because the parents are emotionally sufficient without their children. The parents like themselves, and value themselves. They do not have to live through their children.

The separation or transition may be a child going to college, going into the military, getting married, or moving to another locale. All of these situations require grieving. Because it is safe to have emotions within The Helpful, Fun Family, the children and parents discuss together their feelings of sadness and loss about their anticipated separation, and they cry together. They talk about any frustrations they have related to the leaving. They enjoy together their excitement about the opportunities that the future will bring. They voice whatever guilt exists. (Guilt is a part of separation.)

They articulate their fears about being apart, and about the future. They share all these emotions openly, and discuss them candidly. All thoughts and feelings are safe to express in The Helpful, Fun Family.

The shared separation process becomes a secure springboard for the child to move on to be themselves, living their life as they choose. Because the child has felt safe and cared for in The Helpful, Fun Family, they feel secure to leave.

I have provided a model for The Helpful, Fun Family. I hope it is obvious that in this type of family every attempt is made to meet the needs of its members. Each person is able to express their ideas, knowing that they will be thoughtfully received. Each member can say clearly and directly, "I need a ride," or "I need a hug," or "Will you help me with...?" Needs are expressed directly in The Helpful, Fun Family. and are responded to respectfully .

In The Helpful, Fun Family each member's enthusiasm and excitement are shared. SUCCESSES ARE CHEERED! Accomplishments are **praised**.

Such a family is fun. Being together is play. There is a lot of laughter. Jokes are home-grown. Humor is free-flowing.

Even upsetting events in The Helpful, Fun Family can turn into joy. Family members do not dread disaster. They know that the distress will pass and that they are surrounded by love. They know that they will never walk alone. There are people in their family who care for them. Affection and support are always available.

This, then, is my model of The Helpful, Fun Family. It is not easy to live up to. I don't. I do know that I am a better person because I try.

I thank the psychologist in my seminar who asked the question, "Jay, what is a healthy family like?" Perhaps some day you will thank me for asking you to visualize your model of the family you would like to create.

Have fun visualizing it.

Who knows? Perhaps someday you will *live* in it.

*Tell yourself of your love,
until you believe it.*

*Then, because you have love,
you will LIVE it.*

THANK YOU

Thank you for taking this journey with me. It has been quite a quest; at times, more like a maze. I have enjoyed and appreciated being your guide.

I hope you have made friends with your feelings.

I hope you can see your inner beauty, your beauty at the core, and let it shine through to others.

I hope you are excited about who you are.

I hope you appreciate yourself as a human being.

I hope you value every thought, emotion, idea, and talent that you have.

I hope you **make love**—to yourself and to others.

Let me leave you with a few **YOU-hlerisms**:

Fear does not predict the future.

Unexpressed anger is a barrier to affection.

It is helpful to understand where we are, but it builds hope to know what we can become.

Love is an emotion. Caring is a decision.

When there is a knowledge vacuum, fantasy fills it—and the fantasy is usually frightening and seldom accurate.

Most people are better fighters than lovers. Hooray for the lovers!

Making love is giving and receiving affection.

Don't let anyone else define you.

Love yourself and you will have more confident children.

Two cooperative heads are better than a million antagonists.

When you express anger constructively, you make room for affection.

Crying is not breaking down, it is letting go.

People need to act toward each other as though they are making up after a fight—without having the fight first.

Tears can be beautiful. Shared tears can be *exceptionally beautiful!*

Making love is learned, person to person, moment to moment.

There is a difference between being a prude and being prudent.

Helplessness is not terminal.

Joy is a decision. Take it with you everywhere.

Shower yourself with affection and caring. Then invite others to share the shower with you.

The last YOU-hlerism is the most important of all. It is worth writing on your refrigerator door, on your bathroom mirror, on the inside of your eyeglass lenses:

Caring is Contagious.

You are unique in all the universe. I hope you have come to cherish your uniqueness.

You are beautiful!

Enjoy being You!

And have fun!

*L*ife Enhancing Resources

Awaken the Giant Within: How to take immediate control of your mental, emotional, physical and financial destiny! (A Fireside Book, Simon & Schuster) and audio tapes *Unlimited Power* (Nightingale-Conant Corp.) and *Living Health* (Guthy-Renker Corp.) are about transforming the quality of your life. Anthony Robbins is a master at presenting practical methods and motivation to change. His workshops are enlightening, inspiring, and empowering. There are not enough positive words to describe "Date with Destiny."

Gifts From Eykis by Wayne Dyer (Pocket Books, Simon & Schuster) describes the adventure of a man who discovers a wonderfully loving woman from another world. He brings her here to earth. This is no mere fantasy. The woman Eykis provides a brilliant analysis of and set of suggestions for our world. The section "Eykis Gifts" was thrilling to read as she provides practical models for a loving planet Earth.

Insight, a tape by Leo Buscaglia (Nightingale-Conant Corp.) is my favorite tape ever. Leo talks about feelings and it is filled with humorous stories which are typically Buscaglian. Every now and then when I have felt down, I played the tape and laughed myself into joy.

Romance 101: Lessons in Love, 1001 Ways To Be Romantic, and *1001 More Ways To Be Romantic* by Gregory J.P. Godek (Casablanca Press, Inc.). These books have playful and sometimes serious suggestions. They help adults to release their inner fun-loving child and help the inner child to **make love** as a sensuous adult.

Legacy of the Heart: The Spiritual Advantages of a Painful Childhood by Wayne Muller (A Fireside Book, Simon & Schuster) is a very special book. It shows how to change our perspective about our painful experiences and the negative training we received in our lives into a positive focus on the strengths which flow from those early years.

Your Money or Your Life: Transforming Your Relationship with Money and Achieving Financial Independence by Joe Dominguez and Vicki Robin (Penguin Books) is an excellent book with practical steps for achieving financial independence. The focus is on the **unique needs** of each individual or couple rather than on budgets and rules. I like the emphasis on personal and global integrity.

INDEX

This index is intended to be a quick reference to help you with your life. I do not want to overwhelm you with page numbers. As you read you will find words on pages without that number listed in the index. They are omitted to save you time. Some numbers are bold to emphasize their importance.

Neither the index nor the book is intended to take the place of therapy when that is called for. Specialized physical, emotional or spiritual assistance may be to your advantage. Please seek professional help when you need it.

About the Author

Jay Uhler's mission in life is *"to assist individuals, families, companies, and nations to cherish their unique beauty, to improve their quality of life, and to find peace."* He pursues this mission with a passion.

Minister

Born in Pennsylvania and raised in Kentucky, Jay worked in a brickyard and a steel mill before entering the parish ministry. Still a minister in the United Methodist Church, he is appointed by the bishop to "Ministry in the Secular World."

Psychologist

Jay is an industrial and clinical psychologist, licensed in Massachusetts. His private practice is unique in that he is often referred cases where traditional treatment programs have failed.

His approach to therapy has been referred to by colleagues as "creative" therapy, because he develops the therapeutic process to meet the specific needs of each client. He humorously refers to his method as "YOU-hlerian." It is the natural expression of his profound and unshakable conviction in the ability of people, with the proper guidance, to heal themselves.

Consultant

As President of Catalyst World-Wide, Jay applies his training in industrial psychology locally and internationally to help companies. He works with company owners and directors to maximize their organization's potential. CEO's, and managers are coached to build an efficient work environment. They are guided through conflict resolution. Seminars, workshops, and individual contact are utilized to develop and motivate employees.

Catalyst World-Wide works with companies to improve the working atmosphere in the organization. They have expertise in how to create constructive communication, how to master change, and how to reduce stress—all directed toward increased productivity. When it is appropriate, they assist in restructuring corporate human systems to reduce cost-consuming employee distress.

Family-owned businesses call on Catalyst World-Wide to evaluate and design appropriate interventions that resolve family issues when those issues detract from the realization of the company's potential.

Speaker

Jay is a popular keynote speaker. He impacts thousands of people through his innovative, enthusiastic, and engaging presentation style.

Media Experience

Jay has had a call-in radio program called "Let's Talk Life" and a newspaper series entitled "Jay's Jottings." He is a guest on radio and television talk shows. He is quoted in newspapers and radio news clips on psychological and industrial issues. He has consulted on educational videos, as well as been the host for some of the productions. For several years, Jay was the Consultant on Public Information for the Massachusetts Psychological Association.

Professional Affiliations

Jay is listed in the National Register of Health Service Providers in Psychology, is a Fellow of the Massachusetts Psychological Association, and is a charter member of the American Family Therapy Academy. He is a member of both the National Speakers Association and the New England Speakers Association, of which he was on the board of directors for four years.

Jay Uhler can be reached through:

Catalyst World-Wide
2 Andrew Circle
North Andover, MA 01845 USA
Phone: (508)-685-8550

Share with your friends

Now that you have experienced this caring and inspiring message from Jay Uhler, you know the positive impact it can have on a person's life. Share that wonderful message with other members of your family and with your friends. For your convenience, an order form is on the back of this page.

Call 1-800-Book-Jay
(266-5529) for
Master Card or VISA orders

ORDER FORM

To order books for yourself or your friends, please mail to:

Ambassador Press International
PO Box 1661
Andover, MA 01810-0028 USA

_____Copies of *How to Make Friends With*
Your Feelings @ $12.95 (U.S. Currency) $_____

Shipping: $2.00 for the first book and 50 cents
for each additional book . . . . $_____

Sales tax: (Add where applicable) . . . . $_____

Total . . . .$_____

Thank You.

Name: _____

Address: _____

City: _____ State: _____

Country: _____ Zip Code_____

ORDER FORM

To order books for yourself or your friends, please mail to:

Ambassador Press International
PO Box 1661
Andover, MA 01810-0028 USA

_____Copies of *How to Make Friends With
Your Feelings* @ $12.95 (U.S. Currency) $_____

Shipping: $2.00 for the first book and 50 cents
for each additional book . . . . $_____

Sales tax: (Add where applicable) . . . . $_____

Total . . . .$_____

Thank You.

Name: _____

Address: _____

City: _____ State: _____

Country: _____ Zip Code_____

Call 1-800-Book-Jay
(266-5529) for
Master Card or VISA orders

Share with your friends

Now that you have experienced this caring and inspiring message from Jay Uhler, you know the positive impact it can have on a person's life. Share that wonderful message with other members of your family and with your friends. For your convenience, an order form is on the back of this page.